Public Policy and Politics

Series Editors: Colin Fudge and Robin Hambleton

Important shifts in the nature of public policy-making are taking place, particularly at the local level. Increasing financial pressures on local government, the struggle to maintain public services, the emergence of new areas of concern, such as employment and economic development, and increasing partisanship in local politics, are all creating new strains but at the same time opening up new possibilities.

The series is designed to provide up-to-date, comprehensive and authoritative analyses of public policy and politics in practice. Public policy involves the expression of explicit or implicit intentions by government which result in specific consequences for different groups within society. It is used by power-holders to control, regulate, influence or change our lives and therefore has to be located within a political context. Two key themes are stressed throughout the series. First, the books link discussion of the substance of policy to the politics of the policy-making process. Second, each volume aims to bridge theory and practice. The books capture the dynamics of public-policy-making but, equally important, aim to increase understanding of practice by locating these discussions within differing theoretical perspectives. Given the complexity of the processes and the issues involved, there is a strong emphasis on interdisciplinary approaches.

The series is focused on public policy and politics in contemporary Britain. It embraces not only local and central government activity, but also central–local relations, public-sector/private-sector relations and the role of non-governmental agencies. Comparisons with other advanced societies will form an integral part of appropriate volumes. Each book presents and evaluates practice by drawing on relevant theories and applying them to both the *substance* of policy (for example, housing, employment, local government finance) and to the *process* of policy development and implementation (for example, planning, management, organisational and political bargaining).

Every effort has been made to make the books in the series as readable and usable as possible. Our hope is that it will be of value to all those interested in public policy and politics – whether as students, practitioners or academics. We shall be satisfied if the series helps in a modest way to improve understanding and debate about public policy and politics in Britain in the 1990s.

Public Policy and Politics
Series Editors: Colin Fudge and Robin Hambleton

PUBLISHED

Kate Ascher, *The Politics of Privatisation: Contracting Out Public Services*

Gideon Ben-Tovim, John Gabriel, Ian Law and Kathleen Stredder *The Local Politics of Race*

Christopher C. Hood, *The Tools of Government*

Martin Laffin, *Managing under Pressure: Industrial Relations in Local Government*

Stewart Lansley, Sue Goss and Christian Wolmar, *Councils in Conflict: The Rise and Fall of the Municipal Left*

Peter Malpass and Alan Murie, *Housing Policy and Practice*

K. Newton and T. J. Karran, *The Politics of Local Expenditure*

Gerry Stoker, *The Politics of Local Government*

Ken Young and Charlie Mason (eds), *Urban Economic Development*

FORTHCOMING

Jacqueline Barron, Gerald Crawley and Tony Wood, *The Private Face of Politics*

Danny Burns, Robin Hambleton and Paul Hoggett, *The Politics of Decentralisation*

Tony Eddison and Eugene Ring, *Management and Human Behaviour*

Aram Eisenschitz and Jamie Gough, *Local Economic Initiatives*

Robin Hambleton, *An Introduction to Local Policy-Making*

Clive Harris, Michael Keith and John Solomos, *Racial Inequality and Public Policy*

Patsy Healey, *Places We Could Make: The Future of Environmental Planning*

Ian Henry, *The Politics of Leisure Policy*

Councils in Conflict

The Rise and Fall of the Municipal Left

Stewart Lansley
Sue Goss
and
Christian Wolmar

MACMILLAN

First published 1989

Published by
MACMILLAN EDUCATION LTD
Houndmills, Basingstoke, Hampshire RG21 2XS
and London
Companies and representatives
throughout the world

Typeset by Footnote Graphics,
Warminster, Wilts

Printed in Hong Kong

British Library Cataloguing in Publication Data
Lansley, Stewart
Councils in conflict: the rise and fall of
the municipal left
1. Great Britain. Local government. Role of
Labour Party (Great Britain), 1978–1988
Great Britain. Political parties. Labour
Party (Great Britain). Role in local
government, 1978–1988
I. Title II. Goss, Sue
III. Wolmar, Christian
352.041
ISBN 0–333–45412–X (hardcover)
ISBN 0–333–45413–8 (paperback)

Contents

Acknowledgements

The authors saw and spoke to so many people in compiling this book that it is impossible to acknowledge them all. However, we would like to thank them all and express our particular appreciation to Toby Harris, Margaret Hodge, Ken Hulme, Chris King, Brenda Kirsch, Martin Pilgrim, Mary Rogers, John Stewart, Graham Stringer, Richard Twining, John Tilley and Michael Ward. The views in the book are, or course, entirely those of the authors.

STEWART LANSLEY
SUE GOSS
CHRISTIAN WOLMAR

Preface

'We are well on the way to making Britain a country safe from socialism' (Mrs Thatcher, *Sunday Express*, 17 May 1987).

For most of the post-war period, local government took a back seat in national politics. Yet, during the last decade, it has rarely been out of the headlines. The roots of this new-found fame lay in the simultaneous arrival of Mrs Thatcher at 'Number 10' and the 'new Left' in Labour town halls.

The new Left's vision of the role of the town hall contrasted so sharply with Mrs Thatcher's that conflict was inevitable. The new councillors wanted to increase spending, to extend the role of local councils, and to use local authorities as a weapon to campaign for a variety of political causes. Mrs Thatcher wanted an imprint of a very different kind. She believed that excessive state intervention lay at the root of Britain's 'malaise', and was committed to resurrecting the role of free enterprise and market forces. At first only concerned with cutting spending, she has moved to shed long-held responsibilities, to encourage the privatisation of key services, and to weaken the role of collectivism in public services.

These contrasting attempts to change the role of councils have led to a decade-long political confrontation that shows no sign of abatement. The ensuing upheavals have transformed both the nature of local government and the face of local politics. More-over, the clashes have not only been between Whitehall and Labour town halls. Mrs Thatcher's policies have angered many Conservative councils, and more importantly, have been accompanied by major conflicts within the Labour Left over how to respond, and about the role of the Left in local government.

This book examines these clashes. Chapter 2 looks at the roots

of the new Left who came to power in order to engineer the new
municipal socialism. Chapter 3 charts the battles over spending
and shows how Labour's early, successful attempts to resist Mrs
Thatcher's plans led to more and more draconian steps from
Whitehall. As spending continued to rise, Mrs Thatcher, through
the introduction of ratecapping, decided to remove the long-held
right to determine rate levels. Chapter 4 looks at the bitter
divisions in the Labour party over how to resist ratecapping that
led to the surcharge and disqualification of 80 councillors in
London and Liverpool and eventually forced the increasing isolation of the hard Left.

Chapter 5 considers the record of the GLC, the flagship of local
socialism, and the events that led to its abolition and that of the six
metropolitan county councils. Chapter 6 examines the new Left's
wider attempts to transform the politics of the town halls. Chapter
7 looks at the reality behind the rhetoric on spending on traditional
services such as housing and welfare. Chapters 8, 9 and 10 review
the pioneering measures to promote equal opportunities for
blacks, women and gays and lesbians.

To date these clashes have had profound repercussions for both
the Labour party and national politics. But the story is far from
over. As we see in Chapter 11, Mrs Thatcher's third successive
election victory has forced Labour onto the defensive and led to
the launch of an even more draconian assault on the role of the
local state. The first year of the new parliament saw no less than
four major Acts aimed at weakening the power of local councils.
These have scrapped the rates in favour of a flat-rate poll tax,
abolished the Inner London Education Authority, opened the way
for state schools to opt out of local authority control, paved the
way for the dismantling of public housing, and imposed compulsory tendering for a number of local services with the aim of
encouraging widespread privatisation.

How councils respond in the next few years to this latest
legislative battering ram will have an even more decisive impact on
the future of local government. In Chapter 12, we examine the
options facing Labour in this even more hostile climate and the
chances of thwarting Mrs Thatcher's aim to make Britain 'safe
from socialism'.

1 The Beginnings

'Local government was regarded by the Left as nothing more
than the rest home for the geriatric Right' (Seyd, 1987).

During the 1960s and 1970s, no one paid much attention to the
politics of local government. It was a political backwater, an
administrative arm of central government without an independent
'politics' of its own. Local councils were assumed by many academics and policy makers to be concerned with making practical,
non-political decisions, guided by the judgement of professional
officers.

In the late 1970s, there was a marked transformation and local
government was to be at the centre of the political stage for a
decade. The reasons can be traced to a number of processes of
change in inner city communities, and to the growth of what has
been called 'the new urban Left' in the 1970s. New ideas were
emerging within the Labour party, and local government was seen
as a 'testing ground'. These events coincided with the election of
three successive Tory governments that had an ideological commitment to centralisation and to reductions in the power and
resources of local councils.

Origins

Labour councils have had a complex and diverse past. From 1919,
the Labour councillors who won control in a large number of cities
and London boroughs saw themselves as 'municipal socialists'
determined to use their new power to apply collective solutions to
problems of bad housing, poor health and insecurity. Labour local

1

government built much of the early welfare state from the bottom. Labour Boards of Guardians provided higher levels of poor relief to the unemployed, and councils used municipal construction of baths, housing and clinics to provide work. There were periods of socialist fervour and conflict with central government considerably more dramatic than during the past decade. The struggles of the Poplar Board of Guardians in 1921 to pay adequate poor relief, and their refusal in 1926 to cut their workers' pay, brought prison, surcharge and a place in the history books. West Ham, Chester-le-Street and Bedwelty were also surcharged. In 1929 control over poor relief was lost because the Tory government argued that Labour councils were irresponsibly extravagant. Councils developed sophisticated public health services, including clinics, TB treatment, dentistry and chiropody – and social services provision, including assistance to pregnant mothers, and holiday homes for convalescents. From the early days of West Ham, Poplar and Bermondsey many Labour councils have been big spenders. John Gyford says that:

> By the late 1930s it was already clear that Labour-controlled councils were providing more generous public assistance benefits, more extensive maternity and child welfare services and more spending per child on education. In the decades after 1945 Labour control became widely associated with higher standards of service provision and more generous spending, especially in the case of redistributive and ameliorative services such as education, housing and welfare (Gyford, 1985, p. 5).

Although powers were progressively shifted from local to central government during the post-war years, local councils continued to have considerable resources with which to develop local schemes. They lacked imagination as much as they lacked power. By the 1950s, the attention of Labour councils was concentrated on planning and, above all, housing. The high spending policies of both Conservative and Labour governments allowed Labour councils in inner city areas to carry out major redevelopment plans.

But housing was seen as a technical problem, with technological solutions. The ambitions of Labour councils to clear slums, combined, in the 1960s, with the determination of the planning profession to build monuments and of the construction companies to cut costs, led to a sometimes disastrous process of wholesale redevelopment, forcing people into high-rise flats and leaving whole areas derelict. The close-knit inner city communities were broken up irrevocably, which in turn weakened the relationship between local Labour parties and the people living in these communities.

Local councils became increasingly paternalistic in their approach. Tenants were rarely consulted and it was considered inappropriate to ask local people what they wanted – the job of deciding what they needed was left to politicians and experts.

Local government lost its radical edge. Labour councillors began to see themselves as pragmatic rather than as class warriors. They were predominantly old, as Richard Crossman put it, describing Jim Mathews, the Labour boss of Southampton in 1966: 'now he is seventy-four, and his chair of housing, Mrs Coulter, is seventy-eight, the usual age, I am afraid, in Labour local authorities' (Crossman, 1975). According to Widdicombe (1986), while the proportion of councillors under 45 was the same in 1976 and 1986 (26 per cent), there was a marked increase in younger councillors over that period in London and the metropolitan areas, precisely where the Left was to score most of its successes.

The reorganisation of local government in London in 1964, and ten years later elsewhere, marked an important change in the relationship between local councils and their communities. The small councils who had often related closely to their constituents were swallowed up into larger, more impersonal, authorities. Their creation coincided with a bias towards centralised service provision, bigger departments and more 'professional' council administrations with new management structures headed by 'chief executives' rather than town clerks.

The reforms also later abolished aldermen, an additional tier of councillors who were co-opted by the controlling group in each council. While this had little immediate political effect, in the longer term the abolition of aldermen meant that Labour groups were much more susceptible to rapid changes in political complexion. Elected councillors have always been reselected by the ward and constituency parties at each election and the absence of aldermen meant that co-optees could not be brought in to shore up a weak administration.

None of these changes was to have an immediate effect. The

politics enshrined within the bureaucracies of many Labour councils were often the politics of an old fashioned, insular Labour
Party – the sort that said it was 'full up' to enthusiastic newcomers.
Labour councils mostly conducted their business on the basis of a
benevolent paternalism. Decisions were taken behind closed
doors, by a handful of senior councillors. Backbenchers were
expected to act as lobby fodder – and newcomers were advised
not to rock the boat. Councils were run with pomp and ceremony,
and offices allocated according to Buggins' turn and masonry. The
absence of both any innovative spirit and any search for radical
solutions was a lost opportunity. As David Blunkett, describing his
early days as a councillor, put it to a press briefing at the 1987
Labour local government conference: 'We used to argue for
months about whether to put a penny or tuppence on the rates. If
we had known then what we know now about local government
finance and how to get the most out of our money, we could have
done a lot more.'

While this picture was not universal, it was the norm and for
good reason. In many ways the old-style Labour councils did
represent their communities, and the prejudices of many local
working people. Their hostility to community groups, to squatters,
indeed to any minority, was often shared by the traditional white
working-class communities. But the old working-class heartlands
were changing. Inner city areas were facing economic collapse, as
skilled workers moved out, often taking the jobs with them. The
population was ageing, and fewer people were in full-time work.
Black and Asian communities were establishing themselves in
London and many major cities and, initially, they were excluded
from council housing and other services due to strict residence
qualifications and a failure to recognise their needs. Longstanding
family and community ties were broken by slum clearance and by
increasing social mobility. The experience of redevelopment had,
for many people, been a bitter one, and led to the rebirth of
community organisations and tenant associations. Voluntary
organisations were beginning to spread both to fill gaps in council
services, such as advice centres or social activities, and to act as
pressure groups. One vital result of these developments was the
arrival into the inner city of a new wave of younger, educated,
often socially committed professional people to fill jobs with both
local authorities and voluntary organisations.

The origins of the new Left

The roots of the new urban Left, as it came to be known, are complex but can, in part, be traced back to the 'spirit of 1968'. The year of the big Vietnam demonstrations in London and the student revolution on the streets of Paris provided the inspiration for a generation of Left activists. Not that there was an immediate influx of the Left into the Labour party in 1968. Far from it. The Labour party in the Wilson years was seen as 'Establishment' and shunned by young left-wingers. Ken Livingstone was very unusual in joining the Labour party in that year. Indeed as the first recruit for two years the chair of his first meeting told everyone to 'make sure he doesn't get away'! (Livingstone, 1987, p. 13).

The majority of these 1960s activists did not immediately join the Labour party. It was only in the late 1970s after they had exhausted their energy in single issue campaigns that they turned to the Labour party and began to exert an influence. Some of the new Left developed their political skills through the student movement, or in the tiny Trotskyist groups that formed, split and reformed throughout the 1970s.

It was not until the late 1970s that organised Trotskyist groups showed any interest in joining the Labour party. The Socialist Labour League (later the Workers Revolutionary Party) and the International Socialists (later the Socialist Workers Party) had both rejected entryism into the Labour party in the 1960s, choosing instead to build their own mass parties based on a revolutionary strategy and concentrating their energies on industrial action. The only organised Trotskyist group within the Labour party was Militant, which outside a few strongholds such as Liverpool, has never exerted any significant influence. In any case Militant was uneasy with many of the concerns of the new Left, such as equal opportunities and community politics – and often found itself at odds with the majority of the 'new Left'.

As early as 1968 a small grouping of activists called Socialist Charter or Chartists was formed to put pressure from the constituencies on the Parliamentary Labour Party, and to form a non-parliamentary Left within the Labour party. However, as the Trotskyist influence within the group increased, some members became disillusioned and departed. Some individuals moved into the Labour party after breaking from established Trotskyist groups. Ted Knight, a former member of the Socialist Labour League, the Trotskyist forerunner of the Workers Revolutionary Party, had been expelled in the 1950s for active membership of a proscribed organisation, but was readmitted in 1971 when Labour softened its attitude towards former militants.

Only the International Marxist Group, later called Socialist Action, decided on entryist strategy and, after much internal disagreement in 1978 instructed its membership – 600 at its peak – to join the Labour party. The IMG had always been less sectarian than other Trotskyist groups and this made it possible for its members to work closely with unaligned left-wingers. The importance of the Trotskyist presence was less to do with numbers, and more to do with the confidence of their analysis combined with their organisational ability at a time when many of the non-aligned activists were very unclear about the precise direction and focus of their politics.

Indeed, the vast majority of the new activists did not come from a revolutionary Marxist tradition, but emerged from the trade unions, particularly the growing white-collar unions, or from single issue campaigns such as the anti-apartheid movement, the Anti-Nazi League, Chile Solidarity and CND. For others, political consciousness was developed through the emerging women's, black and gay movements. Many women gained the experience and the confidence to move into 'established' politics through consciousness-raising groups and women's conferences.

By the late 1970s, many of these activists began to join the Labour party, disillusioned with single issue politics and encouraged by the leftwards shift within constituency parties and the ideas of politicians such as Tony Benn. They soon became equally disillusioned with the slow 'non-political' proceedings of moribund local Labour parties, realising that to inject vigour back into the party, they would have to recruit like minded new members, take over party offices from the pensioners who had held them for decades and raise wider political issues.

It is easy to overestimate the homogeneity of these people who were to form the municipal Left. Contrary to the thesis of many commentators, the prevailing *modus operandi* was not of a tightly knit group with a carefully worked out programme but an assortment of individuals prepared to unite on certain issues. These newcomers formed the nucleus of a wide group on the Left of the

Labour party dissatisfied with what they saw as the stuffy conservatism of national Labour politics and with the powerlessness of constituency parties to make changes. They were determined to move the party leftwards, and to force it to take on issues such as women's rights, and racism. A precondition was the democratisation of the party to ensure that constituencies could influence policy. The Left began to form loose alliances and caucuses. In 1973 the Campaign for Labour Party Democracy had been formed to campaign for a series of reforms including the mandatory reselection of MPs. Many of the leading members of CLPD had been part of Socialist Charter but had been opposed to the growing Trotskyist influence within the group. In 1978 the Labour Co-ordinating Committee was formed, a wide alliance of socialists with a commitment to extra-parliamentary activity. A broad alliance emerged on the Left, which included a spectrum from Socialist Organiser, an overtly Trotskyist group, through to the LCC and many non-aligned socialists, organised around the campaigns for constitutional reform and for the election of Tony Benn as deputy leader of the Labour party.

As Chris King, one of the organisers of the Islington Left caucus in the 1970s, put it

> Our caucus was a great big mob of several hundred angry people, an aggregate grouping tied by what they didn't want. Each individual ward was a battleground. Each was organised by the central 'Left caucus' as it was known. There were Trotskyists who joined later, as well as squatters, but they were not the guiding lights. Initially, it was dominated by the middle class Labour party members who had come from other parts of the country where the Labour parties were not organised in the way that Islington was, where you couldn't even transfer into the party without great efforts. We were linked by knowing what we didn't want – O'Halloran [the sitting MP for Islington North] and Tammany Hall politics. We wanted a politics that was much more outgoing, which involved people more effectively and with some worked out policies. It was not an infiltrating left (interview).

Many of the issues that brought people into politics were local or community campaigns. The concept of 'community action' had emerged in the 1960s as a response to paternalistic councils and 'evangelistic bureaucrats'. Campaigns were launched around opposition to office building, redevelopment plans, poor housing conditions, and new motorways, and for the improvement of local amenities. A growing number of community activists, paid voluntary sector workers and advice workers shared a suspicion of the councils which employed or funded their groups, and aligned themselves with the campaigns of local tenants and residents. Highly committed, they were determined to get a better deal for their clients. Thus a number of local residents and professionals keenly interested in housing and planning policies and better service delivery, were drawn into politics through frustration with the local council. In Southwark, for example, the issue that created a Left alliance was opposition to plans to demolish a large chunk of Peckham to build a new town hall. Elsewhere it was issues relating to squatters and homeless families, local voluntary organisations, and racial and sexual discrimination.

Focusing on local government

The attention of the Left in the Labour party turned to local government for a number of reasons. First, a critique had been developed by the Left of the way that councils interfered with people's lives yet offered no share in decision-making or proper consultation or a share in decision making. Marxist ideas about the role of the state were translated into local government terms through books like *The Local State* (Cockburn, 1977) and *In and Against the State* (London Edinburgh Weekend Return Group, 1979). They portrayed traditional Labour councils as part of the capitalist state apparatus and called for radical campaigns with trade unionists and service users to challenge the relationship between the council and its customers, the methods of providing services and the lack of resources.

A number of activists had been involved in campaigns on behalf of homeless people and squatters, against the old style Labour councils. Peter Hain and Simon Hebditch argued that the Left should encompass the needs of 'the homeless, disabled, gypsies . . . the inner city poor and low paid non-unionised workers' and 'minority groups – such as gays and blacks' (Hain and Hebditch, 1978). The fragmentation of communities meant that there were new interests to be represented outside of the traditional white working class such as single parents, women and ethnic minorities. This new Left politics, which attempted to take on board issues of racism, sexism and discrimination led to attempts to create a 'rainbow alliance' of people who were seen as being 'left out' of Labour party politics and local government provision.

Secondly, there was a growing commitment to the idea of local power and local government, as a way of reversing the centralisation of power and increasing the influence of local people and local Labour parties. As we see in Chapter 6, decentralisation of power was a key idea for the new Left, and was part of a commitment to more open government and more participatory structures which were only possible at a local government level. Local councils were also seen as the testing ground for new ideas about economic intervention and planning, transport and housing. The Left identified the cause of the decline in Labour's support as the cautious politics espoused by Labour's right wing. Old style councils were seen as 'paternalistic, authoritarian or plain inefficient' (Blunkett and Green, 1983, p. 2) and by promoting new policies at a local level, Left wing politicians could demonstrate the success of new approaches, distancing themselves from what they saw as the reactionary Labour leadership. The Left of the Labour party had been in the forefront of the campaign against the cuts in capital spending imposed by the Callaghan government, and broadened the focus of the campaign to encompass the defence of local services and opposition to traditional Labour councils willing to make the cuts.

After 1979, local government became an obvious base for campaigning against the new Tory government. Perhaps equally important, local councils were the only remaining site of power for Labour politicians. Changes could not be effected at a national level until Labour won a general election. But in local councils, especially the large inner city authorities, policies could be pursued which demonstrated the difference between Tory and Labour policies, and which posed a direct challenge to the new Tory government.

The beginnings of change

The process of change in local government began, ironically, when Labour suffered its worst post-war electoral performance at the local elections in 1968. The previous year Labour had lost control of the Greater London Council, 10 county councils and a number of provincial towns, including Coventry, Liverpool, Manchester and Newcastle. In 1968 Labour did even worse, retaining just 4 out of the 20 London boroughs it had previously controlled. The effect was to clear out hundreds of Labour councillors, many of whom had served since the war, and to make way for the selection of younger and more radical candidates when Labour regained control in many of these areas in the early 1970s.

By the mid-1970s, several councils had younger, middle class and more innovative councillors in key positions and some authorities began to experiment with new ideas. The 1973 Labour administration at the GLC was elected on a radical programme, committed to an ambitious housebuilding programme and service expansion. However, the hopes of its left-wing minority soon foundered on a financial crisis caused by inflation, a massive wage rise to London Transport workers and the costs of its housing programme. It was the first administration to consider rate rises which, even given the prevailing high level of inflation, seemed like misprints on a council agenda. The GLC faced a choice between the promised housebuilding programme or huge fare increases which would embarrass councillors who had once proposed free travel. In 1975 the GLC rate rise was 80 per cent, and despite this, within three weeks, the council found itself forced to agree to housing cuts in order to limit future rate rises. Nine councillors formed a group called Labour Against the Housing Cuts to campaign against the decision. The creation of this small group indicated the growing influence of a few activists such as Ken Livingstone, Ted Knight and Tony Banks (later to be MP for Newham North West). The group made no pretence of forming a mass campaign, but instead concentrated on organising a network within the London Labour Party.

In Islington, rapid gentrification brought in several new professional middle-class councillors. In 1974 the Left gained control of the Council – not with a coherently-worked-out ideology, but linked by opposition to the old right wing and the desire to spend more money to improve services, especially housing. The emphasis of its housing policy was on municipalisation rather than redevelopment. Until 1976 it bought up large numbers of old Victorian and Georgian houses owned by private landlords, modernised them and relet them as council housing, at the same time as beginning to modernise older council estates and creating a new housebuilding programme.

The Right was highly organised, however, with Michael O'Halloran, a mysterious Irishman who was MP for Islington North, as its figurehead. Between 1974 and 1978 the constituency parties in Islington became a battleground between Left and Right. Annual ward meetings were sometimes packed with several hundred people and often lasted into the early hours of the morning. The parties and wards frequently changed hands between factions. Power depended in part on the local unions – while the Right controlled the Holloway bus garage, the Left dominated NUPE and the white collar ASTMS. In the run-up to the 1978 elections the Left lost the selection battles for councillors. Labour had its usual massive majority but the Right regained power, with 27 seats to the Left's 20. The Left had been out-organised but defeat galvanised it into a coherent force which successfully organised to take control in 1982 on a very radical manifesto.

In Wandsworth, the Left found itself in control of the council almost by accident. The council leader, Sidney Sporle, was jailed in 1971 for his role in influencing the allocation of contracts on the Doddington Estate in Battersea. Out of a dozen or so Labour councillors who survived the 1968 Tory landslide, most, known as 'Sporle's nodders', were probably glad to disappear from politics without suffering the same fate as Sporle. In 1971, Labour again won control of Wandsworth. The old guard were swept out of power as the leadership was taken by Ian Megarry and a group of 'new style councillors'. As in Islington, the new leadership was united more by its opposition to the old guard than by a precise notion of what it wanted. The new councillors' immediate target, according to John Tilley, first elected in 1971 and later to become leader, 'was to do better than Harold Wilson. There was certainly no overall strategy' (interview).

The new Wandsworth councillors were keen to break the old guard's mould. One of their first moves was to scrap the residency qualification for the council waiting list. At the time, as in other London Boroughs, people had to wait five years to be considered for housing, a rule which discriminated against local black people.

The new administration's most radical feature was the way it took up the sort of local community politics through which many of its members had first become active. For example, the Left won a fight to preserve the old Battersea Town Hall, after a major internal struggle and a strong grassroots campaign. The old administration had wanted to demolish it but the Left turned it into an arts centre. The new administration tried to cultivate a very different relationship with community groups, seeing them as allies in the fight against the council's entrenched bureaucracy. A new community development team was created, reporting directly to councillors and therefore able to put pressure on other departments and formulate policy initiatives. Part of its brief was to 'encourage and stimulate the development of voluntary participation in community projects'. The Left administration was so intent on supporting community activity that it even produced a pamphlet on how to influence the Town Hall.

Wandsworth also took one of the first initiatives in creating a local economic strategy. Led by Mike Ward, later to be the architect of a similar strategy at the GLC, the council developed both an analysis of the local economy and a set of radical proposals for council intervention. The administration's determination to increase the level of spending was to be its undoing. Two successive rate rises of 25 per cent in 1977 and 1978 contributed heavily to Labour's defeat at the 1978 local elections.

Hillingdon, another high-spending Labour administration and led by John Bartlett, attracted attention in the press because of a huge overspend on a new Town Hall built in Swiss chalet style (a project inherited from the Tories but always blamed on Labour), and a ski slope that was the butt of endless jokes. Hillingdon also succumbed to the Tories in 1978, although this was probably due as much to social and economic changes in the borough and national political trends, as to local factors.

Camden had a reputation as a progressive and efficient borough in the 1970s. The Labour administration prided itself on its high-spending, large municipalisation programmes in which 5000 homes were acquired in the first two years of the 1974 administration and its comprehensive housing service, including progressive allocation policies, private sector initiatives and the creation of a Housing Advice Centre. Lewisham another progressive administration under Andy Hawkins, began to improve links with the local community and to fund a wide range of community organisations. As early as 1979, Lewisham established a women's rights working party, and began to try to tackle racial discrimination within the borough. Lewisham also began to liberalise housing allocation policies, making provision for single people, and agreeing to house both partners when a relationship broke down.

Outside London, in what had become called the Socialist Republic of South Yorkshire, radical policies were pursued with real success. The new council elected in 1974 began with the unprecedented step of issuing a copy of the full Labour manifesto to every newly appointed member of staff. The new councillors battled, against officers' advice, and an unhelpful Labour government, to set up a fully integrated public transport system, standardising fares, and, despite rising costs, freezing fares in 1975. By 1977 the limited local rail transport network had been brought into the scheme, a flat 2p fare introduced for children and a free city centre bus service introduced in Sheffield.

Sheffield, the biggest authority in South Yorkshire, was developing a reputation for high spending and efficiency. Once left-winger David Blunkett took over the leadership in 1980, Sheffield was seen as the vanguard of a new municipal socialism. Unlike in London and Manchester, however, there were none of the struggles and battles which had characterised other Left takeovers. The election of Blunkett did not represent the same kind of sea change as the Left victories in other authorities. It was a more gradual change as Sheffield never faced a heavily polarised power struggle between Left and Right. Union links remained strong and Labour maintained its popular support in this industrial city throughout. Blunkett himself describes it as 'a much more gradual shift towards democracy'. The Labour party had controlled Sheffield, with the exception of 1968/9, for fifty years and the party, strongly rooted in the local heavy industries, remained the focus of political activity throughout the move leftwards. As Wainwright (1987, p. 108) put it, 'there was no lost generation of the 1960s and 1970s, repelled by the Labour Party of Harold Wilson'. Perhaps because of this, and the continued trade union domination of the local party, there was less of the 'rainbow coalition' politics in Sheffield and more concentration on the local economy and job creation.

In Manchester, there was very much a missing generation and a fierce battle within the Labour group before the Left gained control. The Left in Manchester, along with their counterparts in

Bristol, formed the most vociferous opposition to the 1980 spending cuts forced on their authorities by Michael Heseltine's changes
to the rate support grant system (see Chapter 3). A group of
thirteen Manchester rebels had the whip removed for their opposition to cuts in that year but it was restored by the Labour party's
National Executive Committee. The following year the same
rebels, joined by four more councillors, suffered the same fate and
although the NEC reinstated them, they had to suffer the indignity of
being an opposition group on the council since the NEC was not prepared to enforce its decision. This struggle added momentum to the
Left's progress and by 1982 it had 29 of the party's 69 seats and two
years later it gained control, installing Graham Stringer as leader.

The Manchester Left was much more like its London counter-
part in terms of its political interests and priorities. The repeated
expulsions of councillors from the group forced them to link with
campaigns outside the party. As Graham Stringer put it: 'During
our three or four years in opposition, we made alliances at all sorts
of levels with all sorts of people who put feminist politics and the
politics of the gay movement on to the agendas in Manchester. If
we had not been fighting the cuts with them, these issues would
have dropped from most agendas' (interview).

Lothian council in Scotland was also developing a reputation for
high spending and progressive policies. Labour came to power in
May 1978 and the hold of the Left was strengthened in February
1980 by a couple of by-election victories. The 26-member Labour
group was split into three, with 'soft' and 'hard' groups on the
Left, and a Right and centre group. The Left managed to gain
control, and as we see in Chapter 3, was to lead the council into
confrontation with the Government.

The situation in Liverpool was very different. The city had been
one of the Militant Tendency's few centres of operation since the
1950s. The Left took control in 1972, when the Labour group split
over the vote on the Housing Finance Act. Originally the group
had voted to defy the Act, but once it became law, Bill Sefton, the
leader, changed his position. A group of 21 left-wingers voted against
Sefton and formed a separate group on the council. By 1979, Militant
had become a powerful force on the Council, with a block of seven
members. John Hamilton, an unassuming left-winger, had become
leader in 1973, leading a coalition on the Left which included,
although was not dominated by, Militant.

Other councils which were moving to the left – though more slowly – during this period, included Merseyside, Manchester, Walsall and Edinburgh. But it was Lambeth that hit the headlines in the late 1970s, putting the Left firmly on the local government map.

In 1974 Lambeth was taken over by David Stimpson, who in contrast to previous right-wing leaderships, ran a relatively open and progressive council. Lambeth inherited a 'streamlined' management system designed on private sector lines, but the new administration set out to develop better links with the local community. A network of Neighbourhood Councils was set up, and the council became more open. Services were improved, although a number of conflicts developed between the council and community groups. Ted Knight and Ken Livingstone worked together to build a Left base within the local Labour parties. The Left saw the demarcation line as the attitude towards the Housing Finance Act 1972, when only 18 of the 51 councillors voted in defiance of the Act. By 1974 Norwood, the most radical of the constituency parties, had organised a Left caucus which ensured that any councillor who refused to defy the Act was deselected.

In May 1974, therefore, a larger group of left-wingers were elected to the council. A caucus of about a dozen councillors 'functioned as a disciplined group' according to Livingstone (1987, p. 36), and acted as an opposition within the ruling group. Their bid for power was helped by a series of blunders by Stimpson. In 1977 squatters were evicted by the police from a row of terraced houses in St Agnes Place, and the properties vandalised by the council's workforce. This provoked a huge row which made headlines in the national press. That year, Knight challenged Stimpson for the leadership and lost by only five votes. In 1978, Stimpson withdrew and Knight defeated a centre candidate, Peter Lane, by 23 votes to 19. Knight saw as his first task the implementation of the 1978 manifesto's commitment to expansion. He said: 'We will demand extra money and powers from the government to create employment, ensure good housing for all and to provide properly for the under-fives, the old and the needy.'

The council was by no means dominated by the hard Left but the Left and centre outnumbered the supporters of the old leadership and wanted a change in style. They were also committed to high spending and it was this which characterised the early period of Knight's regime. The increases in spending and the resulting conflict with the new Conservative government are explored in the next chapter.

1979 – the build up of the Left

By the late 1970s, the pace of change had accelerated. While Labour had lost control of several of its innovative councils such as Wandsworth in 1978, in others Labour groups were engaged in protracted warfare between Left and Right, most notably in Islington and Southwark. The election of the Tory government in 1979 made the attempts to innovate and to expand provision more urgent.

The Tory government itself promised to make local government a battleground. The widely disparate elements of the Left organised into an alliance despite its jumble of objectives. In July 1978 Ted Knight chaired the inaugural meeting of the Socialist Campaign for a Labour Victory, which was an amalgam of various party groupings, including the Chartists, but not Militant and an obscure group called Workers Action, whose newspaper was called *Socialist Organiser*.

Almost immediately, serious splits emerged within SCLV, principally over tactics during the cuts battles of 1979 and 1980. As a result, many of those who could not follow the hard-line SCLV policy, including Livingstone and Knight, departed and joined with the Chartists to set up what was to become the principal organising engine of the Left in the capital, London Labour Briefing. The new grouping and the paper it quickly began producing were much less rigid. Indeed, Briefing's early strength lay in its openness and looseness which enabled it to encompass a wide range of Left opinion from liberals to Trotskyists. *Briefing* was launched in February 1980 with a core editorial team of Ted Knight, Jeremy Corbyn and two Chartists, Chris Knight and Graham Bash. *Briefing* allowed contributions from a wider range of Labour party members, including, in February 1981, the soon to be deposed leader of the GLC Labour Group Andrew McIntosh. This pluralism was outlined in a statement in the inaugural issue, which set out editorial policy: 'In this issue, we have succeeded in printing every article or letter submitted to us without cuts or alterations. . . . The aim is to provide information which cannot be obtained elsewhere, not to harangue readers with an artificially concocted ideological line.'

This policy survived for only a couple of years and from the beginning *Briefing* was a means of identifying supporters and constructing slates. The first issue promised, 'We will systematically cover each borough's record, what its Labour councillors have done and the issues locally that affect the labour movement. We will also follow the new reselection procedures for parliamentary candidates and sitting MPs, which we strongly support as a means of making our elected representatives more accountable.'

Briefing in London soon became monthly and later spawned sister publications in a number of provincial towns. Gradually it began to take an increasingly hard line, and both Knight and Livingstone who were faced with the chilly reality of running large authorities that were always short of money found themselves on the receiving end of sharp attacks.

Eighteen months after the launch of *Briefing*, Knight and Livingstone launched yet another paper, *Labour Herald*. It was unlike any other Left publication as it was an expensively produced full colour weekly newspaper. Despite the gloss, its sales remained tiny. *Labour Herald* was printed at the Workers Revolutionary Party works in Runcorn and its finance was the subject of widespread speculation. *Private Eye* was forced into a substantial out of court settlement for alleging that the paper had been funded by payments from Colonel Gadafy of Libya into a Swiss bank account in the names of Knight and Livingstone. Ironically, it was the *Private Eye* cash that, according to Livingstone, was to finance the paper for several years.

Briefing's initial *raison d'être* was the campaign to win the GLC for the Left. Until *Briefing*'s creation, Livingstone had single-handedly been traipsing round the London Labour Party trying to generate interest and support for his campaign to take over the GLC. Livingstone wrote an article in the first edition of *Briefing* entitled 'Taking over the GLC: Labour must win in 1981'. As he described it in his biography, 'I remember going round the Labour Party Conference in October 1979 to just about everyone who lived in London and was on the Left saying: you really have got to think about standing for the GLC . . . I did the work on my own. Nobody paid much attention to the GLC' (Carvel, 1984, p. 71).

The Left had by now taken control of the London region of the Labour Party and introduced new rules which ensured that each GLC candidate would have to undergo a full reselection procedure, and that the manifesto would have to be agreed by the London party rather than merely a sub-committee of the GLC Labour group. In the event, only three sitting Labour members of the GLC were deselected. Instead, the Left's success was due to the tactic suggested by Livingstone of ensuring that left-wing candidates were standing in three-quarters of the marginal seats which were necessary to ensure a Labour majority on the GLC. Labour won the 1981 GLC election with 50 seats to 41 for the Tories and one for the Liberals. The following day all the hard work by the Left paid off, when Ken Livingstone beat Andrew McIntosh by 30 to 20 for the leadership, having persuaded the centre to support him.

The GLC victory became a source of inspiration for the Left. Across London, and elsewhere, left-wingers began to plan a takeover of local councils, and to draw up manifestos which promised a renewal of municipal socialism. In December 1980, Jeremy Corbyn launched the 'Target 82' campaign in *Briefing*. He focused, not on local issues and initiatives which the councils could undertake, but on their role as an oppositional force to the government. He wrote: 'The 1982 elections must be fought on the strategy of opposition to, not administration of, Tory policies. To achieve left control of a council means that work must begin now on nominating people to the council panel who accept that they have a political role in fighting the government. The record of London's councils in this respect has not been inspiring.'

Local Labour parties prepared manifestos in the way that the GLC had drawn up its programme, with working groups and a borough conference of activists to approve the policies. The new manifestos promised open government, community participation and a new campaigning style, as well as significant increases in service provision. Target 82 became adept at targeting seats where left-wingers should stand to gain control of councils. Council candidates were to be held accountable to the local parties for the implementation of the manifesto. These arguments were greatly strengthened by the defections of rightwingers to the SDP.

The new approach to London local government was summed up in the objectives set out by Tony Banks in *Briefing* (September 1980):

The Labour GLC must give a political lead in London to Party, unions and Labour boroughs in total opposition to Thatcher. The financial and organisational power of County Hall must be used as never before to defend working-class interests and support those Labour boroughs involved in the same struggle.

Second the entire Labour movement inside and outside County Hall must pledge its strength to implement the manifesto.

Third the Labour GLC must not be allowed once again to distance itself from the Party. The leader of the Labour group must be elected by the annual meeting. The primacy of annual meeting policies must be accepted and the role of the regional executive as custodians of those policies accepted.

Fourth, individual GLC members must be held accountable for their actions by their respective GCs.

There was one major omission from all this fine talk. The key issue of how these manifestos with their large expansionary programmes were to be funded during a time when local councils were under attack was fudged. This was inevitable. The Left groupings in most constituency parties were loose caucuses involving a wide cross-section of Left activists, often organised around *Briefing*. The common determination to create open, campaigning and democratic local councils which could spearhead the fightback against the government hid major differences in position.

First, for the Trotskyist Left, and many unaligned sympathisers, the objective was to commit Labour councils to building opposition to the Government's policies. This would lead, if necessary, to an all-out confrontation with the government provoking a showdown which would demonstrate the damage caused by Thatcher's policies. Such a showdown was seen as inevitable, since it was unthinkable that clear socialist policies could be pursued under a Tory government. And it was to be built through an alliance of town hall trade unions, local working people and the Labour party. Taking control of local councils gave the Left a vehicle from which to mobilise these alliances. They rejected the idea of using Labour administrations to mitigate the effects of the Tory government and to improve services, since they argued that under a Tory government this would prove impossible and would merely suck left-wingers into implementing cuts and therefore losing political support. At the same time they were deeply suspicious of expansion plans based on rate increases, since they merely placed 'an intolerable burden on working people'. Frank Hansen, later a Brent councillor, writing in *Briefing* in October 1980 argued that 'Only political action backed by concerted industrial muscle, plus the mobilisation of entire working class communities can confront and turn back Thatcher's onslaught', and called for a commitment from all Labour groups that 'they will not implement cuts under any circumstances', and the recognition that 'if we want to win we must be prepared for the possibility of a general strike if necessary and the removal of the Thatcher government'.

A second group used the rhetoric of confrontation, without necessarily agreeing with such an apocalyptic strategy. Livingstone in 1981 argued in *Briefing* that the Tory cuts in GLC programmes constituted 'a massive attack which will demand industrial action by the trade union movement and disruption of Parliament by the Parliamentary Labour Party if it is to be defeated'.

But other sections of the Left were enthusiastically supporting the idea of taking control of councils in order to improve and expand services, introduce progressive policies and change the relationship between the council and the people. The LCC, which by now had started to soften its line, argued in a pamphlet in 1984 that changing the way services were delivered was more important under a Tory government. The group argued that past failures meant that 'council services were literally indefensible' and left the way clear for the Tories to introduce privatisation, penalties and rate-capping. 'It is this horrifying prospect that the people won't defend their services that makes decentralisation essential. Unless the services are delivered more locally so that people can use them more easily then they will be dismantled or diminished ... changing local government is therefore a precondition for defending it effectively' (LCC, 1984, p. 6).

Confrontation was not ruled out, but improving services and changing the power relations in local government had to happen first. The problem was that the conflict between these two strategies was not resolved, and little attention was paid to time scales or priorities. Should councils spend their energies on improving services, or on campaigning? Was it possible or practical to do both? The issues were never resolved.

For other local activists, the task at hand was much more down to earth. They merely felt that they could do better than the councillors they replaced. A 'Southwark rebel' writing in *Briefing* in July 1981 said

> May 82 is likely to see the departure of nearly all the deadbeats and most of the younger reactionaries . . . the newcomers replacing them will, after election, be facing almost intractable problems. They will probably disagree – sometimes bitterly – about the best ways of coping with inadequate finance from central government and increasingly restrictive legislation . . . but in Southwark we will have people who are prepared to grapple with the day-to-day difficulties of dealing with a government which is acting with unparalleled fanaticism.

And, of course, there was always the hope that Labour councils could hold the line against cuts until a Left Labour government came to the rescue. The strategies agreed in the manifesto formulated for the elections in the early 1980s manifestos were often fudged to ensure unity – for example opposing 'massive' rate rises without defining the word. But it was this tentative unity that created a Left alliance capable of taking power from old Right or progressive but technocratic administrations. Socialism was on the local government agenda. Perhaps the inevitable collision of different approaches could have been anticipated, but the new Labour party activists were inexperienced and overworked, buoyed up by the prospect of victory, and too busy working for the success of the Left to think beyond the next leaflet. In any case, the fundamental nature of the differences was not, initially, so obvious and few activists saw clearly the divide that was to open up between them in the next few years, or could have predicted with confidence on which side of it they would find themselves.

Takeover

In the 1982 local elections, Labour did relatively poorly in London, failing to regain any of the three boroughs it had lost in 1978 – Ealing, Wandsworth and Hillingdon – and losing control, for a time, of Lambeth. But the Left within the party was much more successful, thanks in part to Jeremy Corbyn's Target 82 campaign. The Left's arguments for greater accountability of members to their parties had been greatly strengthened by the defections to the SDP. The Left took over, or made sizeable inroads, in Camden, Greenwich, Hackney, Lewisham and Southwark. The increase in the number of Left councillors was enormously helped by the departure of older longstanding councillors. In Greenwich, 15 Labour councillors with a combined council experience of 170 years retired. In Hackney, 21 stood down, in Lewisham 17, Lambeth 16, Camden 12, Haringey 10 and 9 each in Brent, Tower Hamlets and Waltham Forest. Some of these had been deselected while others had defected to the newly formed SDP. For the most part those who replaced them were younger radical members of the new 'urban Left'.

The history of Labour in local government since 1982 is complex, and no Left council can be treated as either a model or an exception. All over the country, Labour councils were beginning to change their approach and tactics. In this book we concentrate on the adventures and policies of those councils that saw themselves most clearly as representing the new Left. Many of them were in London – the GLC, Lambeth, Southwark, Lewisham, Hackney, Greenwich, Islington, Camden – and later Haringey, Brent, Hammersmith, Ealing and even Waltham Forest. Outside London the councils most affected by the politics of the new urban Left were Sheffield, several metropolitan counties and Scottish authorities and later Manchester. This is not a comprehensive list. The experience of other councils, with interesting histories or which made exciting initiatives or tried radical approaches, such as Basildon, Bradford, Bristol, Leicester, Norwich, St Helens and Southampton, is often omitted. The group we concentrate on are those authorities which identified themselves most clearly as being in the forefront of changing the face of local government and developing a clear campaigning style.

2 'The Black Queen versus the Red Knight'

'We have to face the facts of the present position. . . . It is tempting to say to hell with them and continue all our programmes as if nothing had happened with continued growth and unabated recruitment. This would be political suicide' (Ted Knight, June 1979).

When Mrs Thatcher won the 1979 general election, a power struggle with town halls was inevitable. Like other Prime Ministers, her instincts were essentially centralist. She had a longstanding distrust of Labour local government stemming from her days as Education Secretary in the 1970–4 Heath government. This was reinforced in the late 1970s when she saw the potential of urban councils to grow into power bases of municipal socialism, determined to thwart the assumed supremacy of the Westminster mandate.

The attacks on spending

Mrs Thatcher also had a broader commitment. The 1979 Conservative manifesto had pledged to reduce public spending. Since it had also promised to increase spending on defence and protect social security and health, the brunt of this new attack would have to be borne by programmes such as housing, education and social services which are provided by local government.

Since the war, local spending had risen steadily under both Labour and Conservative governments – the product of the

23

post-war 'Butskellite' consensus embracing both the major parties that there were substantial social and economic benefits from publicly provided and controlled services. Political differences were more a matter of degree than principle.

Ironically, it was the Callaghan government of 1976–9 which first attempted to apply a brake to this rising tide of local spending. Previously, governments had shown little interest in controlling local government spending, and had only limited powers to do so. Labour's new attempt stemmed from the severe economic problems of the time, and the strong pressure from the International Monetary Fund to cut public spending. The Treasury under Labour attempted to introduce new controls over local spending by cutting both central government grant and capital spending, with the brunt falling on capital. Capital spending, particularly on housing, fell sharply while current spending levelled off.

When Mrs Thatcher came to power she was determined to reduce current spending. A committed monetarist, she believed that controlling the money supply by cutting public borrowing would reduce interest rates and inflation, and promote private activity. She was also opposed to high rate levels which she saw as damaging to industry and commerce. Whatever the validity of monetarist theories, however, the monetarist case for control of local authority spending *per se* is very weak. The money supply and interest rates are largely independent of the level of local revenue spending since spending not financed by central government grant is met by local rates, not by borrowing. There is a stronger economic case for controlling capital spending over which Whitehall already exercised strong control. The real economic issue concerning local government spending is not one of the management of demand, but of the overall level of taxation, and, in fact, the evidence on the effect of high rates on private activity is ambiguous.

Mrs Thatcher's motives were not merely economic. The attacks on town hall spending served her wider political objectives – to weaken the power of local councils and reduce the grip of collectivism. They delighted the party faithful who year after year had condemned 'socialist profligacy' and high rates at Conservative party conferences. The subsequent cuts can therefore be seen alongside other initiatives – the forced sale of council houses, restrictions on direct labour organisations, privatisation and the

introduction of enterprise zones and urban development corporation – as part of a political strategy to weaken the role of the local
state and, as she later put it, 'to roll back the frontiers of
socialism'.

Mrs Thatcher's first move in her campaign to bring Labour
councils to heel was to appoint the flamboyant Michael Heseltine
as Secretary of State for the Environment. He still faced the
problem of how to control spending and rate levels. Local government spending was not subject to direct control and town halls had
the power to fix both budgets and rates dating back to Elizabethan
times.

This problem was to plague the Tories in their attempts to tame
Labour town halls. The only weapons initially available to the
government were exhortation and the level of central government
grant – the Rate Support Grant (RSG). Heseltine used both. He
asked councils to cut spending a third of the way into the 1979/80
financial year – a very difficult task. And, by way of encouragement, he cut the RSG with immediate effect by £310m. He called
for further cuts in spending the following year and announced
another cut in the RSG.

The block grant

To a government committed to lower rates as well as lower
spending, this was not an ideal solution. Councils retained the
option of maintaining spending by increasing the rates and many
did so. Another problem for Heseltine was that the existing grant
system did not discriminate between high (usually Labour) and
low (usually Tory) spending councils. It gave grant in proportion
to the amount spent and thus benefited the high spenders. Cuts in
the level of central grant would, in turn, hit all councils. In order to
resolve this political problem, Heseltine instructed his civil servants to come up with a new grant system to give him power to
'reward thrift' and 'penalise profligacy'. In response, his senior
officials dusted off an old 'block grant' scheme rejected by the
previous Labour Environment Secretary.

The civil servants made a convincing case for their pet scheme.
They promised an improved system of assessing need, a way of
encouraging restraint by high spenders through a system of

progressive grant withdrawal and, above all, better control over local authority spending. Seeing the chance to bring high spending councils to heel without hurting 'thrifty' Tory councils, Heseltine was quickly persuaded. Block grant was incorporated into a huge measure – the Local Government, Planning and Land Bill, and after a stormy Parliamentary ride, eventually became law in November 1980 for implementation in 1981/2.

Block grant became the government's central weapon in the early days of its war against Labour councils. Under the new system, for the first time the government made detailed estimates, based on local social and economic characteristics, of how much each council should spend to provide a common level of service. This is known as the grant related expenditure assessment (or GREA). As councils spend above their GREA, grant tapers off proportionately until a point at which it begins to fall. In this way higher spending requires disproportionately higher rate levels.

Heseltine hoped that the new block grant system, combined with annual reductions in the share of spending met by central grant, would force local councils to moderate both their spending and their rate increases. Councils, however, were not so obliging. In the first year of its use – 1981/2 – local spending rose. While some councils cut spending, most increased it, including some Tory authorities who found that they were spending below their new GREAs. Rather than cut spending to meet lower levels of grant, many increased the rates. The net effect was higher total spending and sharp rate increases.

With his plans coming unstuck, an irate Heseltine took steps to tighten the system with the introduction of 'targets and penalties'. On top of their GREAs, councils were given individual spending targets related to actual spending and were penalised by pro-gressively larger withdrawals of grant if they exceeded them. These penalties were introduced in 1981/2, and then gradually tightened. Even then, the changes failed to achieve the desired result. Most of the high spending councils losing grant were Labour-controlled, and with the increasing influence of the new Left, there was a growing determination to thwart the govern-ment's plans even at the price of much higher rates. On top of this, the uncertainty of the new system led many councils to build up their reserves through fuelling rate increases.

The block grant system became increasingly discredited as a way of meeting the government's objectives, not least because these aims were confused. Initially, the government wanted to cut spending overall. It then switched to singling out a large group of 'overspenders'. It also wanted to limit rate rises in order to win over ratepayers. Block grant failed in each of these aims. Without overall control over spending, favoured by Treasury ministers, the objectives were contradictory. Such control was ruled out because the government still wanted to maintain a rhetoric about councils retaining freedom over spending levels and patterns. However, without such control, grant reductions were bound to lead to soaring rates. In addition, several of the government's chief targets – the ILEA, the GLC and the London Borough of Camden – were so heavily penalised for high spending that they received no grant, leaving the government no powers to control them.

Block grant also proved to be a technical nightmare. It was formidably complex – even more so than the previous system which was allegedly understood by only a handful of officials – and was incomprehensible to the bulk of councillors, officials and MPs, let alone the general public. It has led to some bizarre and irrational shifts in the distribution of grant. As a result, rate changes often bore little resemblance to changes in local spending. Unpredictable and large shifts in grant have also led to instability and uncertainty playing havoc with long-term planning.

Criticism of the new proposals was widespread. They were bitterly attacked as unworkable by leading Tories such as Sir Geoffrey Rippon, a former Environment Secretary, and by the Tory-controlled local authority associations who were concerned that the proposals would inhibit local authority freedom. The associations' fears were well founded. By forcing councils to spend more closely to government determined spending levels, block grant shifted the delicate balance of power firmly from town hall to Whitehall.

Labour's response

When Heseltine set out in May 1979 to curb local spending, resistance was inevitable. Although Labour councils were then mainly run by traditional councillors of the Centre and Right, they were mostly committed to high spending. But it was the gradual

Left takeover of town halls which turned the skirmishes into a full-
blooded battle.

Lambeth, committed by its new left-wing leadership to growth,
was at the centre of this struggle. To meet manifesto plans for
expansion, the council raised its rates by a massive 40 per cent
in April 1979, the third highest in Britain after Hackney and
Kirklees.

After Labour's general election defeat in May 1979, Heseltine
imposed cuts in RSG on Lambeth of £3m. Ted Knight's response
was swift and unexpected. In a paper to the Labour group in June
1979, he warned,

> It would be easy to ignore the realities and carry on regardless.
> But we have to face the facts of the present position. . . . It is
> tempting to say 'to hell with them' and continue all our pro-
> grammes as if nothing had happened with continued growth and
> unabated recruitment. This would be political suicide. The
> result would be cuts, a massive rate increase on top of this year's
> 40 per cent or a combination of the two.

Dismissing continued high spending as unrealistic, Knight
argued that the council had only two real choices, a supplementary
rate to meet the grant reduction or spending cuts. Unenthusiastic
about a supplementary rate on top of the 40 per cent, he got
overwhelming backing from the Labour group for cuts of 4.5 per
cent.

This move was greeted with dismay by the growing ranks of the
Labour Left who had been looking to Lambeth for determined
opposition. As the Trotskyite *Workers Action* put it, 'Thus the
Black Queen has taken the Red Knight in Lambeth without a
struggle, a fight or even a whimper. Lambeth has given in'. The
decision eased the way for other councils, under more moderate
leadership, to make similar decisions. Ken Livingstone, Knight's
former colleague in Lambeth and since 1978 on Camden council
where he was arguing for defiance, was angry. 'After all the
posturing at Marxist Lambeth, already the right-wing councillors
here say we'll do no more than Lambeth. The real tragedy is that
Ted has given a cover for every rightwinger to put through the
cuts.'

Knight had also reckoned without the local Labour party which, partly through his own influence, had been moving to the Left. In a stormy conference of the four constituencies, Knight was accused of 'capitulation'. Both the cuts and the supplementary rate were overwhelmingly rejected. Bowing to the pressure, Knight and the Labour group made a big public show of lifting the 4.5 per cent cuts, but by discreetly slowing recruitment and under spending, Lambeth was able to end the year in healthy surplus.

With deft footwork, Ted Knight emerged as the national champion of the anti-cuts campaign. In Lambeth, there were marches, festivals, door to door leafleting, and public meetings – mostly poorly attended – aimed at mobilising public opinion against the government's cuts. Knight used platforms across the country including Labour party conferences to persuade councils to adopt a 'no cuts' stance in an attempt to 'build a united wall of defiance against the government'. In the process, Knight alienated the national leadership and many other councils who did not like being dictated to.

As already pointed out by Knight, Lambeth and the other councils committed to 'no cuts' could not hold out indefinitely. In January 1981, after two hefty rate increases, Lambeth was forced to levy a 20p supplementary rate – £50 per household per year – following further mid-year penalty cuts by Heseltine. Hopes that the council would be able to pin the blame on the Government backfired. The local Tories and ratepayer associations combined to muster unprecedented opposition. Thousands were attracted to meetings and rallies against the rate rise. Even in solid Labour areas, stickers demanded an 'End to the Knightmare'.

This opposition was not a response to the supplementary rate alone. Lambeth and its leader had become increasingly unpopular as Knight's high profile and high spending policies had earned him early recognition in Fleet Street as 'Red Ted' and the 'Marxist Menace'. In May 1981, Ted Knight stood as the GLC candidate for Norwood and lost badly. Labour had been expected to hold the seat but did much worse in the three Lambeth constituencies than elsewhere in London. Some other councils were pursuing similar policies but because they did so with less bravado, the public's response was less hostile.

Eventually, Lambeth was forced to cave in as the council became more and more unpopular. The supplementary rate was the last straw. In April 1981, the council admitted defeat and agreed a 10 per cent cuts package. Yet it was still forced to levy a 37 per cent rate increase. Rates had risen threefold in just three years. The following year, the council suffered the political consequences of its four years in power, losing 10 seats in the council elections and its overall majority. Again, Labour did much worse in Lambeth than elsewhere in London, losing 14 percentage points over 1978 compared with a London average of 8 points.

The split over tactics

Knight's personal campaign against the cuts coincided with the intense bloodletting by Labour in the aftermath of its 1979 election defeat. The Left was growing in influence and Knight was able to gain considerable support among party activists and backbench councillors.

The hard Left, however, was far from united in its tactics for resisting the cuts. During the cuts battles of 1979 and 1980, a serious split emerged within the Socialist Campaign for a Labour Victory, the Left group launched in 1978 by Knight, Livingstone and other left-wingers. The Campaign's position at first was to use the rates to prevent cuts. Both Knight and Livingstone argued that since in most areas over half the rates were met by commerce and industry, they were a powerful redistributive weapon. This view also gained the backing of *News Line*, the newspaper of the Workers' Revolutionary Party.

Support for this tactic was not shared by all groups on the sectarian Left. Gradually, SCLV and its newspaper, *Socialist Organiser*, both originally controlled by Knight and Livingstone, developed a much harder line. A new dominant faction led by John O'Mahony argued that rate increases were as much a cut in living standards as cuts in services. It wanted a much more confrontational strategy through the tactic of the 'three nos' – no rate increase, no rent increase and no cuts. Freezing rates and rents while increasing spending would have led to insolvency, the sacking of staff and the collapse of services. This, it was argued, would provoke a confrontation between the local government unions and Whitehall and would force the government to retreat, or even bring it down.

Knight and his supporters consistently rejected this option as naive. In turn he was taunted by his Left opponents. As John O'Mahony put it in *Socialist Organiser*,

> There is a major contradiction between your projection of yourself as a man of the revolutionary left and the actual political role you now play. You now occupy a position not too far from what we used to call the 'fake left'. Your talk is a great deal more left than your actions. . . . Instead of preparing for confrontation you have turned the local council into a major school of reformist class collaboration.

To his opponents on the Left, Knight appeared to want it both ways. He maintained close links with the revolutionary Left and constantly used the rhetoric of class struggle. Sympathetic to their fundamental ideology, he subsequently advocated a similar 'confrontational' strategy in the battle over ratecapping. But he was also a pragmatist. He knew the limits of what could be achieved and enjoyed running Lambeth council even with the daily compromises that it entailed.

Knight, Livingstone and others who backed the 'no cuts, high rates' stance did, however, flirt with confrontation. With councils flouting the Government's policies by jacking up the rates, in mid-1981, Heseltine and the Treasury suggested a Bill to force councils to call a full local election before they could levy a rate beyond a centrally determined limit. This was opposed by the Cabinet which preferred a Bill to force a referendum.

Faced with the threat of such draconian legislation, a debate took place within Labour councils over the issue of risking bankruptcy and consequent loss of office and personal surcharge. In *London Labour Briefing* (November 1981), Livingstone argued that councils should refuse to vote for 'cuts in services or rent and fare increases, and rate increases under the Tories' new system. There is no way Labour councils can balance the books under the proposals.' A similar line was argued by Knight in the same issue.

These views, however, were not universally shared. The leader of Sheffield, David Blunkett, with Left credentials at least as strong as those of Livingstone and Knight, wrote in a paper to his Labour group, 'Many of us would be delighted actually to be sent to gaol for our principles, but not ignominiously forgotten after disqualification and lingering surcharge if we failed. . . . The clever complexity of the Government's proposals make simple stands extremely difficult.' Instead he suggested a package of measures to strengthen the council's hand and leave its critics with minimum ammunition. These included 'A continual review of Sheffield's budget to eliminate waste or under-used resources' and 'Scrutiny of any job vacancies arising to assess their priority'. In the event, confrontational strategies of the type being floated by Livingstone and Knight were not necessary. In the face of powerful opposition from Tory backbenchers, the government's initial proposals were dropped and supplementary rates were abolished instead.

Elsewhere, most Labour leaders were taking a pragmatic view of the situation, with a much lower level of rhetoric. Up to 1982, most Labour councils were still in the hands of the Centre or the Right rather than the new Left. Neighbouring Southwark, in sharp contrast to Lambeth, had always prided itself on keeping the rates down and was not going for expansion. It had much less difficulty in coping with reductions in grant.

Other councils like Camden, Lewisham and Newcastle were committed to high spending, but although they too resented the Government's attacks, they engaged in much less tub thumping. More willing to accept the 'realities' initially pointed out by Ted Knight, they responded to grant cuts with a mixture of high rate increases and some spending cuts. They took the view that rate increases hit living standards as much as spending cuts and saw the political limits to the size of rate increases.

The 'pragmatists' were also prepared to accept, along with David Blunkett, that services were often far from efficient and that a similar level of service could be delivered with less spending through reorganisation. This view cut little ice with the Labour Left. Their watchword was 'no cuts', and they responded to talk of value for money with derision. Moreover, high spending itself had taken on a new meaning, becoming a symbol of Left commitment and of defiance against the government.

Outside of Lambeth and Sheffield, the main source of resistance to these early cuts came in Scotland where the arrangements for local government finance were very different. Local spending was the responsibility of the Secretary of State for Scotland, George Younger. Like Heseltine, he cut grants in an attempt to reduce spending. Most councils, Labour-controlled and elected on a programme of expansion, refused to make the cuts and rates rose sharply as in England.

The noisiest opposition came from Lothian Regional Council which includes Edinburgh. Its rates rose by 41 per cent in 1980 amidst much anti-government rhetoric. In response, Lothian was attacked by one Scottish Minister as a 'caucus of militant Marxists', a little far from the truth. Along with other councils including Dundee and Stirling, Lothian sought a much higher political profile, and relations with the Scottish office, backed by ratepayers and small business groups became increasingly sour.

While in England, a similar resistance to spending cuts was met by the introduction of the block grant, in Scotland, the Government introduced new and draconian selective powers to penalise individual councils directly for their spending decisions. A highly provocative act, it led to greater determination to resist. Initially, seven councils were selected for action under the new powers. These enabled the Scottish Secretary to cut grant even after a rate had been levied. Since supplementary rates had been outlawed, councils were left with a choice of cutting spending or breaking the law by going into deficit. One by one the councils accepted defeat with compromise cuts. Lothian spurred on by local party activists and trade unions and by support in London, stuck out the longest. The streets of Edinburgh saw some of the biggest demonstrations ever in the city. Despite the rhetoric, however, Lothian like Lambeth was eventually forced to give in and adopt a package of cuts. After 1982, the Left strengthened its grip on Labour town halls. With their commitments to expansion, the battles with Whitehall intensified. Despite tougher penalties, spending soared in the very areas singled out for the sharpest cuts by Mrs Thatcher. In her first term, local spending on staff and other revenue costs rose by 3 per cent in real terms. But the Government's chief targets – the Labour-controlled metropolitan county councils and the inner London boroughs increased their spending by 18 per cent and 10 per cent respectively.

This not only played havoc with the Treasury's public spending plans, it made Mrs Thatcher more and more irritated. Determined to impose her will, she turned to a weapon – ratecapping – that was to prove the major test for the Labour Left.

3 The Ratecapping Struggle

'The grotesque chaos of a Labour council hiring taxis to scuttle round the city handing out redundancy notices to its own workers!' (Neil Kinnock on Liverpool Council, Labour Party Conference, 1985).

When, as expected, the Tories won the 1983 general election, it was inevitable that the skirmishes with local councils turned rapidly into all out war. As the increasingly tough penalties had failed to curb spending, the Tory manifesto had committed the Tories to a new power to control rate levels – 'ratecapping', as it soon became known.

In the past, the idea of ratecapping had been considered by the Cabinet but despite Treasury support, two successive Environment Secretaries, Michael Heseltine and Tom King, had vetoed it. Following the election, Tom King was moved and Patrick Jenkin, a colourless yes man who did not share these qualms, was installed as Secretary of State. The subsequent Bill gave the Environment Secretary formidable powers, both to control rates in a few councils and, more generally, to impose a limit over all authorities. It was a fundamental constitutional change, taking away for the first time since 1601 the right of local authorities to set their own rates.

The change was based on the view that strong local government posed too much threat to the authority of Parliament. Yet strong local democracy has always been viewed as a powerful block on the potential abuse of central power. With ratecapping, even where the local electorate chooses a council committed to high spending, that choice can be overturned by central government. The introduction of ratecapping confirmed the centralising trend of Mrs Thatcher's previous administration.

34

The government's expressed reason for the change was that high local government spending and rates were damaging national economic regeneration. Yet, as we saw in Chapter 2, the macro-economic case for controlling revenue spending is very weak. Indeed, the government undermined its own case by stressing that it would only resort to its general ratecapping power in very exceptional circumstances, in effect admitting that the measure would only have a tiny impact on overall local government expenditure. In essence, ratecapping was little more than a shabby vendetta against the political challenge presented by Left Labour councils.

Opposition to the Bill included constitutional academics and pro-Tory newspapers such as the *Financial Times* and *The Times*. Twenty-six Tory MPs voted against or abstained on the second reading of the Bill and there was hostility from the leadership of the Conservative controlled local authority associations. Nevertheless, the Bill passed unscathed.

Faced with this draconian power, scheduled for implementation in April 1985, Labour councillors and activists met in Sheffield to discuss tactics just two weeks before Jenkin was due to announce his first ratecapping hit list in July 1984. This gathering was to prove a watershed for the municipal Left.

The choice before Labour councils was presented starkly – defiance or compliance. Several options for defiance were aired, including mass resignation, majority opposition, deficit budgeting (setting a legal rate but with a higher 'no cuts' budget) or refusing to set a rate. The latter was put forward forcefully, having already been worked out by a group of London leaders headed by Ted Knight of Lambeth.

The mood of determination at Sheffield, which contrasted with previous meetings, stemmed from a sense of outrage shared by most sections of the Labour Party. More important, the timing of the conference coincided with Liverpool's recent claimed victory in allegedly forcing the government into retreat over financial support, following a similar tactic of refusing to set a rate.

Liverpool

For ten years the failure of any party to gain control of Liverpool City Council had contributed to the city's decline and the growing

crisis in its public services. When Labour came to power in May
1983, it was committed to higher spending but had inherited a
sabotage budget from the outgoing Liberals who had deliberately
set a rate that necessitated sharp but unspecified spending cuts.
Far from making these cuts, Labour expanded spending and
approached the budget for 1984/5 needing a huge rate increase or,
as the activists inevitably put it, 'massive' cuts to bridge the
growing financial gap. Unwilling to do either, the council refused
to make a rate, hoping to press the government into financial
concessions. Liverpool held out for over three months, forcing a
nervous Patrick Jenkin into negotiations.

When the council set a rate on July 11, over three months into
the financial year, the politicians claimed that Whitehall had been
forced into substantial concessions. In fact, the government had
allowed a bit of tinkering about with the RSG which saved the
council £5 million, and which it was able to claim was worth much
more to the people of Liverpool because grant penalties were
reduced as a consequence. In reality, the biggest concessions had
come from the council which said it would cut spending and reduce
reserves. Nevertheless, Liverpool's 'victory' entered Left mytho-
logy, and its impact was to be enormous because it was interpreted
as a sign of government weakness and suggested an ambiguity over
the legality of not making a rate. While it made the Left more
determined to stand firm, it also strengthened the government's
resolve not to wilt in the face of pressure from local councils.

Defiance

Two weeks after the Sheffield conference, Jenkin announced his
hit list of 18 'overspending' councils singled out for ratecapping.
Sixteen were Labour controlled: three metropolitan counties, the
GLC, South Yorkshire and Merseyside; the London Boroughs of
Camden, Greenwich, Hackney, Haringey, Islington, Lambeth,
Lewisham and Southwark; and Basildon, Leicester, Sheffield and
Thamesdown (Swindon). The other two were Tory-controlled
Portsmouth and Brent, ruled by a Tory–Liberal coalition. The
councils were given spending limits which implied cuts of around 5
per cent. They were given until October 1 to appeal against the
spending limit.

At a series of meetings over the summer and autumn of 1984, the leaders of the hit list authorities thrashed out tactics. The political climate favoured those arguing for defiance adding to the mood of determination from the Sheffield conference: the miners' strike was at its peak, the government was on the defensive over the abolition of the GLC, having just conceded direct elections for ILEA, and Jenkin had mishandled the fight with Liverpool. Ted Knight, leading the argument for defiance, found allies in Derek Hatton and John McDonnell, the deputy leaders of Liverpool and the GLC. The soft Left went along with the argument, partly because they were swept along by the tide but principally because they were forced into a political corner. They had not worked out an alternative strategy and the mood within the party would not allow them to suggest any policy which entailed cuts. Some of the soft Left leaders were aware that defiance was based on two fallacies – that immediate widespread cuts would be necessary and that victory against the Government was possible. Yet they held their fire in the hope of getting Jenkin to the negotiating table and retreating honourably. In the meantime they went along with the fight and the slogans. As a first sign of unity and defiance, the leaders unanimously rejected using the appeal procedure against the spending limit as it gave enormous power to the Environment Secretary to examine budgets.

There were only two realistic options for defiance: deficit budgeting, which involved setting a rate but agreeing to spend more than the amount implied by that rate level, and the tactic adopted by Liverpool the previous year of refusing to set a rate. The soft Left vainly argued for deficit budgeting because it bought time without immediately breaking the law. To the hardliners, intent on a confrontation, it was seen as a fudge. They knew that it was a recipe for hidden cuts, and it did not offer a united campaigning tactic as councils varied widely in their ability to avoid cuts.

Instead, Knight and his allies argued successfully for the 'no rate' option. They said that if enough councils stood firm, the ensuing crisis would force the government to back down and grant concessions. Boosted by the misreading of Liverpool's experience and by arguments that cuts would be much greater than the 5 per cent implied by the spending limits, they created an unstoppable momentum. March 7 1985 was chosen as the date at which all the councils would hold a meeting and simultaneously refuse to set a date, aiming to alert the public to the anti-democratic nature of ratecapping.

The tactic was intrinsically flawed because the unity on which it depended, both within and between Labour groups, could never be sustained. Not only were the councillors and councils who were expected to back the tactic remarkably different in political hue, the issue of breaking the law was always going to be the key dividing line. The law itself was unclear, depending on a judge's interpretation of the words 'wilful misconduct' in the Local Government Finance Act 1982. If it could be demonstrated that the delay causing the losses were a result of deliberate action, councillors could be surcharged for the losses and be disqualified from office. Liverpool had escaped legal challenge because their negotiations with Jenkin meant their actions were not 'wilful misconduct'. When the district auditor wrote to the councils planning defiance on the first of March 1985, warning them that deliberate failure to make a rate could amount to wilful misconduct, the councillors knew that they would have no such excuse. All but the handful of hardliners intended to pull out before the legal risks became too great.

In reality, the no rate tactic was just as much a fudge as deficit budgeting. Key leaders such as Sheffield's David Blunkett and Islington's Margaret Hodge knew that the line could never be held but went along with it because they could not be seen to lead a retreat. This lack of frankness strengthened the hand of the hardliners and maintained what nearly everyone knew was a fiction – that a handful of councils could take on the might of Mrs Thatcher and win.

The attempt to get the government to the negotiating table was hamstrung by the lack of unity. The soft Left wanted an early meeting with a realistic set of demands which would allow them a dignified compromise. The hardliners stalled and upped the demands. By the time a meeting with Jenkin took place, on February 4, it was too late to win the modest concessions sought by the pragmatists. Jenkin had, in any case, learnt his lesson from Liverpool and simply sat back, offering nothing. The pragmatists were stuck out on a limb and were now committed to the 7 March jamboree.

Left in the firing line

The split over legality was exposed right from the outset by the distinct position of the upper tier precepting authorities – the GLC, ILEA, South Yorkshire and Merseyside – which had, unlike the other councils, a legal obligation to set their precept by March 10.

Originally, the idea had been for all authorities to 'go illegal' on March 7 by carrying explicitly illegal motions. This critical decision was fudged because most leaders knew they could not deliver. After the abortive meeting with Jenkin, the leaders had switched their tactic to a policy of joint 'deferral', because simply to defer setting a rate was not, by itself, necessarily illegal whereas to refuse outright to do so was. South Yorkshire and Merseyside immediately opted out, warning that they would set a legal rate on March 7, leaving the GLC and ILEA in the front line. While ILEA's Labour group had passed a no rate motion, the dissenters announced that they would combine with the Tories to vote through a rate.

That left the GLC which, because of its size and reputation, was always going to be the key authority. The appearance of unity within its Labour group had collapsed the previous weekend when a row flared up between the GLC leader Ken Livingstone and his deputy, John McDonnell, backed by Ted Knight of Lambeth, over the question of legality. Livingstone claimed that McDonnell and Knight had told him privately that the boroughs would still go illegal on March 7, despite the agreed switch in tactics to deferral. Livingstone claimed he only discovered the truth when he saw the motions drafted by some boroughs. He also claimed that McDonnell, who was the GLC's finance committee chair, had deliberately concealed the true financial situation. Livingstone had just received a memo from Reg Race, the former Labour MP and key policy adviser, that far from cuts of £140 million, the GLC could go for modest growth within the ratecap thanks to creative accountancy and using its reserves.

McDonnell alleged that Livingstone always knew the true financial situation but that they had both been opposed to any proposals to cling onto office through financial manoeuvres. McDonnell produced a memo sent to Livingstone the previous October in which he had clearly set out the objectives of the

Labour GLC, a strategy which had been endorsed wholeheartedly by Livingstone. It said:

> The whole point of our administration is that we are a challenge to the central capitalist state. To accommodate at this crucial stage would be to accept without challenge our subservience to Tory class rule. We will undermine the confidence placed in us by hundreds of thousands of socialists throughout the country if we are seen to be capitulating to a Thatcherite government or even breaking ranks with other socialist councils and ducking the fight with the Government by cooking the books.

As the deadline approached, McDonnell claimed that he had produced the means of 'going illegal' by obtaining a legal opinion which said that the Tories could abstain on the vote and not be at risk of surcharge When this was debated by the group on March 4, Livingstone proposed a resolution refusing to set a rate, but with the proviso that if the opposition put forward a budget that included cuts, the fall back would be a budget based on the maximum precept and £25 million growth. The group voted 24 to 18 for compliance.

The following weekend, after 23 hours of council meetings, the Labour ranks broke and the councillors set a rate just minutes before the deadline set by its Director-General. Because the Left refused to support Livingstone's fallback, the agreed rate was put forward by the opposition and was 2.7p below the maximum allowed, a fact that was really galling for the Labour councillors and incomprehensible to the outside world.

This feud between Livingstone and McDonnell, who had been good friends, proved a watershed for the municipal Left and began a process of Left re-alignment that was to break up the alliance between the hard and soft Left. Livingstone was one of the architects of the 'going illegal' strategy drawn up by the hard Left alliance around London Labour Briefing and *Labour Herald*. Although the strategy had always been a charade, Livingstone's alleged 'sell-out' and the mutual recriminations which followed meant an irrevocable split with the hard Left. This was a mirror image of what was happening at a national level where the Bennite coalition, which had reached its apogee in 1981 when Benn nearly became deputy leader, was beginning to fall apart. Key left-wing

NEC members such as Tom Sawyer of NUPE, David Blunkett and Michael Meacher were starting to distance themselves from the hard Left represented by Benn and Dennis Skinner. The divisions in the Left generated by the failure of the ratecapping campaign were to hasten this process.

The strain shows

One by one the authorities succumbed as the defiant words failed to be translated into equivalent deeds. The smaller authorities outside London swiftly capitulated, with Basildon, Leicester and Thamesdown all setting rates by the end of March. Lewisham quickly followed when the Tories passed a legal rate while the divided Labour group was meeting outside the council chamber, and in Haringey a rate was made on April 11 when 13 Labour members voted with the opposition. Both leaders, Ron Stockbridge of Lewisham and George Meehan of Haringey, resigned. On May 7, Sheffield, supposedly a leading council in the campaign, caved in with 20 Labour members breaking ranks to vote for setting a rate.

As the collapse gathered momentum, the leaders of the remaining authorities knew they had lost. While Margaret Hodge talked privately of organising a 'balanced and dignified retreat', there was no one prepared to lead it. As the councils crumbled, it was clear that the widespread industrial action which was supposed to back the campaign would not occur. The whole campaign was in tatters. Jenkin merely had to watch as it ran its course. The battle quickly changed course – it was no longer against the government but within the Labour party.

The splits in the Labour groups were heightened by the knowledge that most councils could get by without cuts. Not only had the original scale of the cuts been exaggerated to add urgency to the campaign, the councils also developed a series of 'creative accounting' measures to overcome their financial problems. The GLC, in particular, was found to be awash with even more money than Reg Race had claimed. In Haringey, a gap of £15 million was bridged mainly through a new device that enabled capital receipts from council house sales to be used to finance repairs. Indeed, of the 7 councils left by mid-May, councillors in 5 – Camden,

Greenwich, Hackney, Islington and Southwark – had been told
that they could maintain spending within the ratecap limit without
cuts. In effect, the councillors were now being expected to put
themselves at risk of surcharge in order to make a principled stand
against an unacceptable law rather than to save jobs and services.

Indeed, for the following two years, the left-wing councils were
to run rings round the Department of the Environment. Despite
ratecapping, they increased their spending, took on more staff and
increased their sphere of activities thanks to a flow of funds from
their bizarre bedfellows, the banks and the City who devised an
increasingly exotic range of creative accounting measures. Initially,
the financial tricks, which had already begun to be used before the
ratecapping battle, were relatively simple such as juggling spending between financial years to maximise grant and capitalising
housing repairs, even tap washer replacement, which enabled
authorities to spread the cost over 60 years. Later the schemes
were to become more and more far-fetched. The most lucrative
was the deferred purchase agreement, through which the council
gets a company to buy an asset on its behalf, agreeing to pay for it
in the future. These sort of devices enabled councils to spend far
more than government controls on capital allowed. Islington, for
example, in 1986/7 spent three times more on its housing programme than the government's imposed limit.

It was not surprising that, armed with this knowledge and with
warnings from district auditors and council treasurers that the risk
of surcharge was growing, the councillors started to buckle. Next
to go was Hackney on May 23 amid ugly scenes in the council
chamber. Again, the Labour group split and the leader, Hilda Kean,
resigned. Rates were set in Southwark on May 30, Islington on the
following day, Camden on June 6 and Greenwich two days later. The
divisions within the Labour groups at times led to intimidation, such
as the sending of white feathers in Southwark to those voting for a
rate. The strength of feelings on both sides ensured that these splits
were to dog many of the Labour groups for long afterwards.

Beyond the brink

By early June, only Liverpool, which had not been ratecapped,
and Lambeth were still standing firm and their continued defiance

was to cost 81 councillors disqualification and surcharge, although the councils eventually made rates on June 14 and July 3 respectively.

Liverpool was a special case. Its financial crisis stretched back to the years of hung councils and was rooted in the city's appalling decline. The councillors had been lulled into a false sense of security by the events of 1984. Then they had ignored the repeated warnings of the local district auditor and since he took no action they thought he was a paper tiger. But in 1984 the situation had been very different since negotiations with Patrick Jenkin were taking place. In 1985, Jenkin had learnt his lesson and refused to deal with the rebellious councillors. This time they were foolhardy to ignore the auditor's repeated warnings.

Above all, it was the politics of the Labour party in Liverpool which drove the rebels over the precipice. The influence of the Militant Tendency, especially in the person of the president of the district party, Tony Mulhearn, and the council's deputy leader Derek Hatton, extended far beyond the small numbers who belonged to the Tendency. Militant controlled the district party which made crucial council policy decisions that even non-Militant members felt bound by.

The Liverpool leaders saw themselves in the vanguard of opposition to the government. The mood in the party had coalesced around making a deficit budget as the councillors felt that the imposition of a high rate increase was simply passing the crisis onto poor ratepayers. At the June 14 meeting, the Labour councillors passed a motion for a 9 per cent increase and a budget of £265 million, nearly twice the amount of income that could be generated from that level of rates. Despite earlier doubts expressed by many Labour councillors, they held firm, voting for illegality and potential bankruptcy.

That Lambeth held out for so long was also a surprise to many observers as Labour only had a majority of four. Two Labour councillors defected early on, and it seemed that Ted Knight would soon be humiliated on his home ground as at least a quarter of the councillors were on the centre or soft Left of the party. Despite repeated warnings from the district auditor and the council's lawyers, Lambeth outlasted all the other authorities by almost a month. This was a result of the tremendous pressure exerted by the local party on councillors. Over the previous year,

Labour members who were unwilling to back illegality were asked
to resign and more hardline members joined the council in the
subsequent by-elections.

It was also Ted Knight's powerful psychological grip on the
Labour group which explains this remarkable show of unity. He
managed to convince councillors that the auditor would not act or
that a subsequent case could be won. Knight was wrong. Already,
on June 26 the actions against both Lambeth and Liverpool
councillors were begun. In both cases the district auditor was
under a legal obligation to surcharge councillors if he was satisfied
that losses had occurred because of deliberate action or 'wilful
misconduct'. The main source of losses arose through the extra
interest payments on loans to cover the rate income not collected.
These could not be calculated accurately until the end of the
financial year and instead the auditors identified two smaller losses
– from the refusal of the DHSS to pay subsidies towards rate
rebates until a rate was set and from the delay in payment by the
Treasury of its contribution in lieu of rates on Crown property.
Both sets of councillors failed in their High Court appeals.
Lambeth called it a day and the evening of their court defeat, a
year bar a day after the strategy had been launched, a packed rally
at the Town Hall greeted Knight and his colleagues as heroes. The
rebels had been ordered to pay £126 947 in surcharge plus £120 000
costs and were banned from public office for five years. Liverpool
went to the House of Lords and a year later, in March 1987, they
lost, facing a bill of £106 000 in surcharge and £440 000 in legal
costs as well as being barred from office. The district auditors
subsequently decided to take no action against councillors in
Camden, Hackney, Islington, Southwark and Sheffield after in-
vestigations into the anti-ratecapping campaign in these authorities.

The repercussions

The ratecapped councils could point to some small gains arising
out of the struggle such as their improved ability to campaign and
to put political messages across, and the fact that they had won
over public opinion on the ratecapping issue. However, there was
no disguising the fact that it ended in defeat. The central reason
for this failure was the lack of unity. Throughout, there had been

three groups in the Labour camp. First, there were those who were opposed in principle to illegal action, arguing that Labour's commitment to change society through the ballot box was undermined by deliberate law breaking; the second group were those councillors who took a pragmatic stance on tactics, ready to adopt anything that worked; thirdly, there was a small but vociferous group of hardliners, who actively sought confrontation with the government and saw ratecapping as an ideal opportunity.

The first group included prominent councillors such as Tony McBrearty, chair of housing at the GLC and a Haringey councillor, and the Labour front bench, including Environment spokesman John Cunningham. Indeed, Neil Kinnock himself had, in a speech to the Labour local government conference in February 1985 in Birmingham, made a powerful plea not to get hooked on 'wrangles over legality'. Kinnock called his strategy the 'dented shield' – for Labour councillors to stay in power and do their best to avoid cuts. The councillors in the ratecapped councils were angry that Labour's national leadership and its NEC made no attempt to forge an alternative national campaign against public spending cuts. Such a campaign could have taken on the overall Tory strategy of cuts in spending, not merely ratecapping; it could have taken on Thatcherism outside the ratecapped areas; it could have been led jointly by the front bench and local leaders. Instead of concentrating the argument on the very ground chosen by the Tories, and getting diverted into the issue of legality, it could have focused on the continued damaging cuts forced on local authorities and the health service by the Tories. If the national leadership had given such a lead, the confrontational strategy might have been avoided. Instead, Kinnock lost the initiative and all the running was made by a handful of local leaders.

By far the largest number of councillors belonged to the second group, the pragmatists. They argued that they had now reached the stage where it was not a question of illegality but which law to break – compliance with ratecapping would eventually lead to breaking other legal obligations, a point acknowledged by Kinnock in his Birmingham speech when he said that councils which cut services below the legal minimum would risk being taken to court by local residents. To this group, the strategy was one of creating a united front for illegality that would force the government into collective negotiations and real concessions.

Throughout, the pragmatists were outmanoeuvred by the third group, the hardliners. The pragmatists failed to speak out against the hardliners, in the interests of a false unity, and did not properly pursue their alternative strategy of getting Jenkin to the negotiating table. Because the tactic of confrontation was identified with the hardliners, it was they who paid the heaviest price for the failure of the ratecapping campaign. Coupled with the defeat of the miners and Kinnock's increasingly assertive leadership, there was a new mood of realism on the Left of the Labour party. The hardliners' attempts to purge 'moderate' candidates from the 1986 elections failed as they were reinstated by the London Labour Party executive and the Labour groups elected in 1986 were largely dominated by the soft Left, as demonstrated by their readiness to make cuts following the 1987 general election defeat.

At the national level, the collapse of confrontational tactics was to have dramatic implications for the political climate within the Labour party. The public split between Livingstone and McDonnell, and the growing number of party activists who became openly hostile to the strategy, heightened the divisions within the Left.

A year after the optimistic Sheffield conference, in July 1985 Jack Dromey, the soft Left national secretary of the T&GWU, attacked the strategy at a local government conference in Manchester as 'a fiasco which created bitter divisions in our own ranks and left Patrick Jenkin laughing'. Provincial left-wing leaders such as Manchester's Graham Stringer and Merseyside's Keva Coombs criticised, as Stringer put it, 'the mayhem that had happened in London'. The contrast between the Sheffield and Manchester conferences could not have been greater. The extent of the hardliners' defeat was best demonstrated by Kinnock's dramatic speech at the Labour party conference in October 1985 when he launched a ferocious attack on Liverpool council's tactics which ended in the 'grotesque chaos of a Labour council hiring taxis to scuttle round the city handing out redundancy notices to its own workers'. The rapturous applause which greeted this comment symbolised the collapse of the hardliners' power within the party. The confrontational strategy had backfired with a vengeance.

4 'Working for London'

'The GLC is typical of this new, modern, divisive form of socialism. It must be defeated. So we shall abolish the GLC' (Norman Tebbit, March 1984).

While Labour was tearing itself apart over ratecapping, Mrs Thatcher was busy pursuing the other major element of her second term attack on local government – the abolition of the GLC and the six metropolitan county councils. The GLC in particular stood for everything she disliked about Labour town halls. It pioneered many of the new Left initiatives and seemed to spend money like water. Its leader, Ken Livingstone, proved a constant source of irritation. Above all, it was the flagship of municipal socialism.

This was not always the case. For most of its life, the GLC was a largely remote and obscure body, a matter of indifference to most Londoners. But, just as Herbert Morrison had breathed new life into the London County Council 50 years previously, Livingstone was to put the GLC firmly on the political map.

The GLC's rise to prominence began with two years of consultative meetings by Labour activists leading to a Labour victory in 1981 with the most detailed and longest GLC manifesto. However, it was not necessarily the most left-wing. Indeed, Andrew McIntosh, the leader at the time was quoted in *Time Out* as saying, 'You could call it tough, you could call it radical, but you couldn't call it leftwing'. The 1973 manifesto, 'A Socialist Strategy for London', was in many ways more socialist. It had promised to scrap the proposals for three motorways around London; to reduce fares as a first step to their abolition; the complete municipalisation of private rented housing; and an extensive housebuilding programme and opposition to rent increases. In the event, few of these commitments were implemented by the 1973–7 GLC led by Sir Reg Goodwin. The rate increase required to fund them was not acceptable to the leadership at a time when the Labour government was pressing for cuts in local spending. The key difference in 1981 lay, not in the manifesto, but in the new, more innovative breed of councillor and the determination of Livingstone to leave his political stamp on the capital.

'Fares fair'

The central plank of Labour's programme was the promotion of public transport. A proposal for free fares during the manifesto discussions had been replaced, because of opposition from the London Transport unions, with a commitment to a cut in bus and tube fares of 25 per cent followed by a fares freeze. There was nothing unique or extravagant about this proposal. It was modelled on the low fares policy operated by South Yorkshire County Council since 1975 and several European capitals such as Paris and Rome had cheap public transport policies. The Labour groups which controlled the metropolitan counties from 1981 all had some form of low fares commitment.

The manifesto had openly warned that the cost of 'fares fair' would be met by a supplementary rate of 5p in the £. This estimate, however, had not allowed for Michael Heseltine's more punitive system of grant penalties introduced in April 1981, which more than doubled the cost of the cut. Far from backing off, the GLC persevered with support from all sections of the Labour group. 'Fares fair' conflicted directly with Heseltine's strictures on spending. It also upset Bromley's Tory leaders who claimed that the new policy was unfair to residents in outer London.

Moved also by Livingstone's growing notoriety, the Bromley leaders mounted a legal challenge against the policy on the grounds that it was unreasonable. Few expected Bromley to win. It had always been understood that the Transport Act of 1969 had given the GLC freedom to determine the level of transport subsidy. To widespread astonishment, both the Appeal Court and the House of Lords unanimously declared the fares cut and the supplementary rate unlawful, largely on the basis of a very narrow interpretation of the requirements of the Act that London Transport should be run 'economically'.

This led to disagreement over tactics within the Labour group, and widespread confusion over the legality of different levels of subsidy. In January 1982, the council finally agreed to double fares. A motley alliance of 21 Labour, 3 Tory and 3 Alliance members defeated 24 Labour opponents, including Livingstone, who were pressing for defiance of the legal judgement and confrontation with the Government. Round one in the battle for a radically different London had been decisively lost.

Cheap fares were not the only transport commitment to collapse. The GLC also offered a subsidy to British Rail's fares in a move towards a more integrated fares structure; but the Government vetoed it. The legal judgement, however, did not signal an end to the GLC's transport hopes. In 1983, 18 months after the 'fares fair' fiasco and after the legal ground had been thoroughly checked, the cheaper fares policy was resurrected with a new package involving a 25 per cent fares cut and the introduction of the Travel Card giving integrated bus and tube fares. By mid-1984, fares were roughly a fifth lower in real terms than at the time of the 1981 election.

Other transport policies that were implemented included 230 new bus lanes and the introduction of the 'wheel clamp' for illegally parked cars. Overall, these policies led to a modest improvement in the transport situation. By 1984, the GLC claimed that car travel was down by 15 per cent in central London and passenger usage up by 16 per cent – the first increase since the 1950s.

The GLC also suffered a number of embarrassing defeats on other manifesto pledges, causing rebuke from its Left critics. A plan to cut the price of ILEA school meals from 35p to 25p was dropped following legal advice that it would lead to the surcharge of councillors. The GLC also failed to prevent the government-imposed transfer of its housing stock to the London boroughs and its attempt to revive the housebuilding programme from 35 starts in 1981 to 1500 was blocked by Environment Secretary Michael Heseltine.

Municipal pioneering

Fares fair was not the only radical initiative and its failure had the side effect of providing plenty of cash to pay for the others. The lower fares were paid for through a large rate increase which swelled the GLC's coffers when the fares were reversed and enabled the funding of its new roles (Carvel, 1984).

Here was the window of opportunity for Labour's 'rainbow coalition'. The GLC was always the wealthiest of local authorities, given its huge rate base, and now there was a full purse to finance a wide range of alternative projects. That cash was to enable there projects to take root very quickly. The initiatives, all in areas outside the council's statutory obligations, covered industry and employment, ethnic minorities, women, gays and lesbians and policing. It was the 'patchwork quilt politics' of these areas which was to attract the greatest public attention and contribute to the GLC's eventual demise.

The most expensive, but which attracted least media attention, was the establishment of an industry and employment committee which created a new economic policy department and the Greater London Enterprise Board. The Board was given wide functions of financial support for companies operating in London and aimed to support the establishment of novel forms of public and municipal enterprise (see Chapter 5 for a discussion of its work).

But it was the pursuit of 'equal opportunities' that lay behind the bulk of these initiatives and the GLC's pioneering work was to inspire similar policies among the new Left councils. A well-staffed ethnic minorities committee was given powers aimed at reversing the under-representation of blacks in County Hall jobs and services. The committee had grant-giving powers for voluntary organisations and launched campaigns, such as the anti-racist year in 1984, to raise public awareness of discrimination. A women's committee, the first full committee of its kind in Britain was established, again with a large staff and budget, most of which was spent on childcare provision. The GLC was also first to champion the cause of gays and lesbians with policies to combat discrimination suffered by homosexuals (see Chapters 7, 8 and 9 for an assessment of the success of these policies).

A police committee, again the first of its kind, was also set up to monitor the Metropolitan Police. While all other county councils had such statutory committees to oversee the work of their local police forces, there is no such routine scrutiny in London because the Metropolitan Police is directly responsible only to the Home Secretary. The committee, backed by a police unit with a staff of

20, aimed to increase public awareness of police activity and policies. It campaigned for greater democratic accountability of the police in London. It ran campaigns both against proposed legislation and on individual cases such as Colin Roach, alleged to have shot himself in a Hackney police station, and on aspects of policing such as the failure to take up cases of racial harassment and domestic violence. It also funded police monitoring groups in most London boroughs.

While the issue of greater police accountability for Londoners was relatively simple, the committee immediately found itself enmeshed in far more complex issues in an area where the Labour party's policy, both locally and nationally, was rudimentary. Some staff were hostile to the police, seeing the force largely as an 'instrument of state repression' which harassed blacks and political activists. As one former worker put it, 'some had such a deepset hostility to the police that they had absolutely no idea how to deal with them if they were to change'. Others in the police unit felt that a dialogue with the police was essential in trying to democratise it. The Labour councillors were ill-equipped to handle this debate. Politically, even the left-wing GLC could not be seen to be simply police bashing but neither would the Left-dominated London Labour Party allow it to have too cosy a relationship with the Metropolitan Police.

The police, too, were rather taken on the hop by the creation of the committee; on the one hand offering a place on a Met working party, on the other publicly criticising the existence of the committee. Despite these inherent problems, the unit produced much impressive work and, as a result, was to prove influential in changing the Met's policy on some aspects of its policing. A new bulletin, *Policing London*, provided comprehensive and hitherto little-known information about the Met's work, while individual reports covering such issues as a democratic structure for London's police force were thoroughly researched pieces of work. Interestingly, the Met's policy on all three areas where the unit had been most critical – domestic violence, rape and racial harassment – underwent dramatic changes during the 1980s. The police started to intervene in cases of domestic violence, special suites for the reception of rape victims were opened and racial harassment became recognised as a specific class of offence. While these changes were not solely attributable to the work of the GLC's police committee, the well-researched reports and the media attention attracted to these controversial areas by the committee's work undoubtedly contributed to the Met's change in attitude.

Much of the worst publicity around the new committee centred on the activities of the monitoring groups. Where these had real community support such as CAPA (Community Alliance for Police Accountability) in Tower Hamlets and the Newham Monitoring Project, both of which focused on the serious and widespread problems of racial harassment, they had real success in influencing local policing policies. However, some groups were taken over by hard Left groupings with few roots in the local community and a wholly destructive attitude towards the police.

Because the limitations and frustrations of a simple police-bashing perspective quickly became apparent, in its latter stages the unit moved towards much more practical work on crime prevention and fear of crime, particularly on council estates. This necessarily involved greater liaison with police and it was an approach which gradually came to dominate the work of most of the police committees set up by Labour boroughs. In some boroughs they even became integrated with the police consultative groups, first set up in Lambeth in the wake of the 1981 Brixton riots and later extended to all London boroughs, and which had first been seen by most Labour councillors as powerless talking shops. This was a remarkable compromise on both sides, since originally the police had boycotted many of the borough police committees, while Labour councils had often boycotted the consultative groups.

While the record on all these initiatives was mixed, the GLC's policies on the arts were among its most successful. The Labour Left in Britain has had a somewhat ambiguous attitude to culture. This reflected the party's obsession with 'Labourism' and with class politics in which struggle was assumed to take place at the workplace through the mechanism of mass trade unions, and with the elitism associated with British culture and art. Art too has mostly enjoyed a neutral political status at least when it comes to national funding. The GLC's arts policies had always been largely bipartisan. Influenced by the creative arts policies of councils like Rome and Florence when controlled by the PCI, the Italian Communist Party, and by the success of the Rock Against Racism concerts and the campaigning policies of the Anti-Nazi League in the 1970s, the new GLC set out to break with 'this tradition of Labour welfarism' (Bianchini, 1987, p. 99).

There was a huge expansion in funding. Established centres like the National Theatre, the London Festival Ballet and the English National Opera all benefited but cash was mainly poured into fringe arts as part of a new policy of supporting 'popular culture'. The GLC upset 'the Establishment' by raising the delicate issue of the balance of funding between 'community' and 'prestige' arts. Festivals and free concerts were introduced in a number of parks. The South Bank concert halls were livened up and made more accessible with the introduction of free lunch time exhibitions and recitals which included jazz, folk and calypso as well as classical music. This 'open foyer' policy attracted millions of visitors and helped to reverse the decline in concert attendance at the South Bank theatres and concerts. Annual festivals like Thamesday began in 1981 with an average attendance of 200000 people enjoying free music, dance, arts and exhibitions, childrens' entertainment and fireworks along the riverbank. Although these initiatives were not overtly political, Tony Banks, the Chair of the arts and recreation committee saw their aim 'to project the GLC's image as a progressive, caring and socialist society' (quoted in Bianchini, 1987, p. 100).

Cultural initiatives were also used more explicitly as a vehicle for politicisation. Political festivals ranged from pensioners' days and anti-racist events to the huge 'Jobs for a Change Festival' in Battersea Park in 1985 with an all-day programme of music, poetry, cabaret and visual arts in a challenge to unemployment, and modelled on the *Festa de L'Unità* festivals of the Italian Communist Party. Such events provided not merely a successful campaign forum, but also aimed at giving Londoners a sense of community and social identity and solidarity, and at raising public awareness of the GLC with its new theme of 'working for London'.

The new arts policy also had a clear political objective of endowing certain groups with an independent cultural voice. As part of a wider policy of promoting 'community arts', the GLC also funded new cultural forms from photography and video to pop music and community radio which had been traditionally neglected by the state. Certain groups were targeted including women, gays and lesbians, the young, the disabled and the elderly.

But while access to the arts among these groups was encouraged, by far the highest priority in resources and back-up went to the 'black arts'. The Round House in Chalk Farm was funded as a black arts centre, a festival of Third World Cinema and a Black Theatre season sponsored along with a London-wide programme of seminars, exhibitions and performances. Courses on film and video, radio and print journalism were also established. The 'social engineering strategy' as one observer has called it 'made a considerable impact in terms of rendering London's oppressed minority culturally more visible and also in creating a new climate of co-operation between local Labour politicians and people already engaged in radical and oppositional cultural practices, but often bitterly disillusioned with Labour Party politics' (Bianchini, 1987, p. 108).

The GLC's arts policies were predictably controversial, but they have had a lasting impact. They made London a more exciting capital. They expanded opportunities for groups formerly on the margins of cultural activities. They raised attendances at concerts and theatres and created more open air entertainment. They brought the concept of image and style, of a cultural strategy, to campaigning.

The backlash

From its earliest days, the Labour GLC was highly controversial. Livingstone himself was rarely out of the headlines – most of them highly critical, often vitriolic. This began with stinging attacks from most of Fleet Street over his defeat of the moderate McIntosh. Suddenly Livingstone was elevated from a minor local politician into a public figure. Popular newspapers despatched reporters to burrow in his dustbins and to harass his colleagues and friends.

Much of this publicity surrounded his incursions into 'foreign policy', his attempts to promote his views on wider issues such as royalty, sexual politics and especially Northern Ireland. He declared sympathy for the IRA hunger strikers, called for discussions with the Sinn Fein leader, Gerry Adams, and started campaigning for the withdrawal of British troops. The media latched onto this with increasingly hostile coverage, and Livingstone became more and more unpopular. Although much of the coverage was exaggerated or contrived, he was hardly an innocent victim. He loved the limelight and rarely tried to avoid publicity, or to exercise caution in his views or the way he presented them.

During the height of this publicity in the summer of 1981, he became the subject of widespread criticism within the GLC Labour Group, including the Left, for diverting attention away from council policies onto himself. Certainly Livingstone took a lot of stick for the defeat of 'fares fair'. Many – both Right and Left – believed that without his high public profile and his diversions into 'external politics' the legal challenge would probably never have been made. At one stage it was touch and go whether he would survive as leader.

These attacks on the GLC were not confined to Livingstone and did not just come from the muck-raking tabloids. The GLC's policies, especially on equal opportunities and the police, became increasingly controversial, and many were accompanied by internal friction among politicians and staff which provided easy and juicy headlines.

Other criticisms of the GLC were much more the result of right-wing, trigger-happy journalism. From 1981 to 1984, the funding of voluntary organisations soared from £6 million to over £50 million and the GLC was accused of supporting its political friends. Yet the bulk of this money went to groups which would have been widely seen as worthy and respectable. Of the total grants budget of the women's committee, for example, around 60 per cent went on child care. Opponents singled out grants to groups such as the Greenham Common Peace Camp, the Karl Marx Library, *Spare Rib,* the Gay London Police Monitoring Group and assorted peace groups such as Babies Against the Bomb. Funding of controversial groups accounted for a tiny fraction of the total grants budget, and were a matter of legitimate political judgement. The Gay Police Monitoring Group, for example, received a grant to monitor the incidence of alleged police harassment of the gay community and to give support to its victims.

The GLC also became an increasing source of irritation to the Labour Parliamentary leadership as many senior Labour figures did not share the GLC's priorities and believed that Livingstone's style contributed to Labour's swingeing defeat in June 1983. In turn, Livingstone rarely missed an opportunity to attack Michael

Foot and the leadership when he disagreed with them. Equally important, Livingstone saw the GLC as providing an alternative Parliamentary opposition, a substitute for what he saw as a feeble Labour opposition in the Commons. This further angered Labour's front bench.

The record

To many, the GLC was seen as an inspiration for the whole Labour movement, a model for both local and national government. As Livingstone put it in his book, 'The extent to which the GLC had touched the hearts and minds of Londoners, and the change it had undergone during that process, gave us a glimpse of our potential to transform our society' (Livingstone, 1987 p. 342). This view of the GLC is widely shared on the new Left. As Beatrix Campbell and Martin Jacques put it, 'the GLC stands as the greatest achievement of the labour movement since 1979. It shows what can be done. Creativity and imagination have been in desperately short supply in the labour movement. The GLC has bags' (Campbell and Jacques, 1986).

Overall, however, it is difficult to make simple judgements about the GLC's record. Livingstone and his colleagues believed they were embarking on the development of a new model of local socialism, but like that of other Left councils of the time its record was pretty mixed. The GLC's policies were heterogeneous and developed in a largely piecemeal way, but it is possible to identify three main strands. The first was the development and improvement of existing services. Despite the loss of several powers, public transport was improved, child care places were created, estates forcibly transferred to the boroughs were modernised and repaired and heating systems were installed. Arts funding was greatly expanded. The opening up of the South Bank and other complexes, the growth of festivals, parks, concerts and sporting events meant that London became a better place to live.

This was not just a matter of expansion. There were attempts to give policies a distinctly socialist edge aimed at improving the life and conditions of ordinary people through redistribution. This was true of its grants and arts policies. Resources raised from businesses and the richer boroughs were pumped into the poorer inner cities, particularly through the stress borough programme in the final year of the GLC. Transport, however, best illustrates the ideological character of County Hall and its clash with Whitehall. Labour was committed to the promotion of public, at the expense of private, transport. Since the responsibility was transferred in 1984 from the GLC to London Regional Transport, a government-appointed quango, that philosophy has been reversed. The new body has had to operate on much lower budgets, fares have risen, services and jobs have been cut, and functions have been privatised.

Secondly, the GLC attempted to carve out its own agenda to win the support of new constituencies based on its equal opportunity policies. It established a new set of priorities including gender, race and sexuality which is now firmly on the national political agenda. Particularly significant was the attempt to associate Labour with the cause of gays and lesbians who, for the first time, were identified as citizens with legitimate demands to make of the local government.

Thirdly, the GLC's aims went beyond the improvement of traditional services and pioneering new initiatives. Livingstone claims that the GLC's policies were an attempt to promote a new kind of progressive self-help and power sharing. 'Instead of trying to do everything for people, we broke away from Labour's client group approach to politics and enabled people to begin to do something for themselves' (Livingstone, 1987, p. 345). Others have similarly argued that the GLC was involved in an exercise in participatory democracy, 'an attempt to widen the scope of democracy in London beyond the vote: by providing resources and a political platform for movements and organisations outside conventional party politics' (Mackintosh and Wainwright, 1987, p. ix).

In themselves, these aims are a very important part of new Left thinking on welfare. Post-war welfare was built on a paternalistic model of the state, the 'nanny state' which defined and provided for needs on a mass scale, and which led to vast, undifferentiated housing estates, big and anonymous hospitals, vast schools, a welfare production line paralleling the organisation of industry and its production of standardised products for a mass market. Recent years have seen mounting criticism of this 'Fordist' model as it became known after the mass production systems pioneered by Henry Ford (Murray, 1988).

The institutions which arose to administer this welfare were centralised, hierarchical and inflexible, too often run by professionals for professionals rather than clients. Services were delivered in a remote and uniform way with a lack of sensitivity to the growing diversity and individuality that has characterised people and communities. This in turn has led to increasing public disquiet with traditional, 'statist' forms of welfare, and paved the way for Mrs Thatcher's attempts to 'individualise' welfare through cuts, privatisation and a new emphasis on charity.

Accepting many of these criticisms, the Left has looked to reforms which allow greater individuality and innovation in the way services are defined and delivered but within a collective framework. This has led to a new emphasis on the need for decentralisation, flexibility and self-definition of need. The two main strands of this new approach have been attempts to involve recipients more closely in the process of welfare provision, and a new emphasis on self-help. Increasingly the state's role is being seen as less about direct and exclusive provision and more about enabling – providing the means whereby people can ensure that their needs are met but not necessarily by direct state provision itself. The aim is greater democracy, more choice and more power sharing.

Some of the GLC's policies can be seen as moving in this direction. First, there was the encouragement of voluntary and self-help groups on a large scale through a big increase in funding to agencies helping the homeless, the disabled and the unemployed, to black groups, to nurseries and to sports clubs. These, for the most part, encouraged more creativity and innovation, services better related to need and the empowerment of both workers and recipients. Second, there were attempts at a more open and consultative approach to policy making.

On the whole though, the GLC's development of these ideas was limited. Outside of transport and arts and recreation, the GLC was not responsible for the delivery of any major welfare service, so the scope for experimentation was limited. There were few, if any, examples of the GLC transferring actual responsibility for its existing services to external groups or organisations. Most of the self-help initiatives were in new service areas. The experiments in consultation, although a radical departure from tradition, were not always very successful, and the groups involved were not always representative (see Chapter 5).

In addition, the GLC's commitment to these ideas was only partial. The implied decentralisation of power carried the political cost of loss of power, something which the politicians were reluctant to allow. In essence, the GLC's project was more doctrinaire than democratic, and was much more about mobilising popular support and building political platforms around Left causes. As Hilary Wainwright put it

> The present GLC ... has dared to use its rate base to help sustain the resistance and self-organisation of those whom Thatcherism is trying to break. As a result, Tory councils have faced GLC-funded campaigns against their privatisation schemes; City managers find their clerical workers organised with the help of a City based resource centre funded by the GLC; the Metropolitan Police have faced constant exposure from 'Police Monitoring Committees'; and the government's prize quango, the London Docklands Development Corporation, finds that all its smoothly packaged plans for turning Docklands into a property developer's delight are constantly disrupted by community campaigns – again funded by the GLC (Wainwright, 1986).

County Hall was increasingly used as a wider political platform, and as a launch pad for causes as diverse as gay rights and pensioners' needs. London was declared a nuclear-free zone; 1983 became a 'Peace Year' and 1984 an 'anti-racist' year; a campaign was launched against 'useless' civil defence arrangements. Dubbed 'the People's Palace', County Hall's vast and imposing entrance hall symbolised this new role with its widespread use of exhibitions, extensive free literature and an almost continuous stream of lobbyists.

Whatever the record of the GLC, many councillors argued that it provided a blueprint to which Labour nationally should aspire. Between October 1983 and abolition in April 1986, Labour was performing much better in London than nationally, whereas normally the capital follows the national trend. Livingstone attributed this sustained lead to the popularity of the GLC and has used it as evidence of the potential support for its policies. The truth is rather different. A series of opinion polls commissioned by the GLC from the Harris Research Centre during 1984 and 1985 shows the GLC to have enjoyed a very mixed public reception (Waller, 1988). While the GLC scored highly for 'doing a good job', 'for caring for people like me', 'having a good leader' and on 'fighting government policies', it scored badly on 'spending money sensibly'. There was widespread criticism of the GLC for spending money on 'crazy schemes' of benefit to minority groups rather than Londoners generally. Nearly half the sample (46 per cent) thought the GLC was too concerned with minority groups, most whites had 'little sympathy' for anti-racist policies and there was 'very strong opposition to the GLC's ideas of intervention to further women's, gay and lesbian rights'.

According to Robert Waller of the Harris Research Centre, Livingstone's popularity and Labour's lead in London had little to do with the policies of the GLC, but lay with Mrs Thatcher's decision to abolish it.

> In London, Labour performed far better than its national showing for much of 1984 and 1985. This cannot be ascribed to anything other than the publicity campaign over the GLC abolition issue which led to the council being seen as an embattled victim of an over zealous centralist and ruthless government (Waller, 1988, p. 90).

Abolition meant that the GLC's record was never put to the full electoral test, so the claims of popularity must remain a matter for speculation. Livingstone's GLC undoubtedly represented a bold and imaginative attempt to transform the role of local government and one which proved the main inspiration to other Labour councils in London and elsewhere. Despite this, the claims made by many GLC councillors and its supporters were exaggerated. It did not suffer the problems of many other urban councils. It had few difficult services to manage and after the collapse of 'fares fair' was awash with money. Many of its policy initiatives were pathbreaking, but many were also flawed in implementation. Then just as it was beginning to learn from some of its errors and some of the experiments were beginning to blossom, the GLC's ambitions were brought to an abrupt halt.

Abolition

The decision to abolish the GLC, inserted at the last moment into the 1983 Conservative manifesto, was widely seen as an act of pure political malice by Mrs Thatcher. Neil Ascherson of *The Observer* described it as the 'most disgraceful act in seven years of Conservative rule. Vicious and petty in conception, brutal in application and demoralising in its effects, it brings lasting shame on all those who planned and carried it out'. As Norman Tebbit boasted, abolition was about the 'defeat' of socialism.

Support for abolition had, however, stretched more widely. Ken Livingstone had advocated it himself in 1979. The GLC was unpopular among many Labour borough leaders and London Conservative MPs. In 1977, 31 'abolitionist' candidates had stood in the GLC elections. Initially the idea had not been taken seriously in Whitehall, but this changed as local government assumed more political importance. Abolition was discussed several times in Cabinet. Although Mrs Thatcher's Environment Secretaries, Michael Heseltine and later Tom King, were against it, she viewed abolition as a way of eliminating what she saw as a wasteful and unnecessary tier of government and as a way of silencing Livingstone.

Certainly there were many things wrong with the GLC. Set up by a Conservative government in 1964 in an attempt to end the power of the previous Labour-controlled LCC, it never became a successful strategic authority. Its key role was to plan and co-ordinate the future development of the whole of the capital, but for fear that it would prove too much of a threat to the mainly Tory-controlled outer London Boroughs, it was not given the power to do it effectively. Unrealistic and vague, the Greater London Development Plan had little impact. The GLC also had a poor record in the strategic task of tackling London's acute housing problems. The GLC, under both Tory and Labour administrations, had drawn up detailed plans to relieve stress in inner London by building in the more spacious outer London boroughs. But with inadequate powers, these were easily thwarted by borough opposition. Until Livingstone's attempt to improve public transport, the GLC's record on transport was little better. Proposals in the GLDP for a huge network of urban motorways giving the capital a string of four 'ringways' generated huge opposition and were rejected by the winning 1973 Labour administration. A later suggestion in Labour's 1973 manifesto to revive public transport as an alternative solution to London's growing traffic problems also floundered, this time the victim of the economic retrenchment of the times.

The GLC had not fulfilled the hopes of the 1960s that it could create a solid planning framework for London, develop as a strategic housing authority and prove the ideal mechanism for co-ordinating transport. To many, the GLC had become a bureau-cratic monster desperately looking for a role to justify its exist-ence. By the early 1980s there was a case for a review of the London local government system. All previous reforms of local government have been preceded by detailed enquiries into the alternatives and their merits. On this occasion Mrs Thatcher decided on full-scale abolition without any consideration of its desirability or impact. Her ill-considered proposal to transfer everything to the boroughs was widely condemned by experts and professionals and was soon shown to be unworkable.

Many GLC functions could not simply be transferred to the boroughs but required an all-London approach. The GLC had responsibility for a ragbag of minor services and duties such as running the coroners' courts, providing building inspectors, licensing places of entertainment and ensuring the safety of reservoirs as well as more substantial responsibilities such as the fire service, the disposal of the capital's annual 3½ million tons of rubbish, dealing with emergencies and the control of London traffic that could only be run effectively on a London-wide basis.

The government defended abolition on the grounds that it would bring cheaper and more democratic local government. Initially the government claimed savings of up to £10 million, but these were soon revised downwards, and eventually it was accepted that savings would be slight. The government's second argument on democracy had equally little force. At least half of the GLC's responsibilities went to non-elected quangos run by government nominees or to central government itself. Even before abolition, responsibility for London Transport had been transfer-red to London Regional Transport. Other new quangos created included the London Planning Commission and the London Residuary Body to handle a whole host of functions from pensions to disposal of property. Existing quangos including the Arts Council and the Sports Council took over some GLC roles. Other services which could not be run locally such as the fire service, refuse disposal and grants to the voluntary sector have been run by 'joint boards' consisting of councillors nominated by the boroughs. In practice, these have proved remote, confusing and unaccountable. In addition there was a significant increase in central government involvement in London affairs on issues such as traffic control and responsibility for roads. One study has shown that the complex network of almost 100 bodies that now govern London spends as much money and employs as many people as the GLC did before abolition, and that only 40 per cent of services are now run by elected or indirectly elected bodies (Herbert and Travers, 1988).

The inherent weaknesses of the Thatcher proposals meant that the process of abolition was much more difficult than she realised, and it was to dog her second term time and time again. The first problem was that the GLC and metropolitan county council elections were due in May 1985, eleven months before the councils were to be abolished. To deal with this, the government decided to cancel the elections and substitute councillors, appointed by the boroughs, were to take over for the remaining year. This, how-ever, had enormous constitutional implications. First it involved cancelling elections for a body which had not yet been abolished. Second, its effect would have been to change political control of the GLC from Labour to Tory because a minority of the boroughs was in Labour hands. The Paving Bill to implement this decision had the stormiest ride through Parliament in living memory. It was bitterly attacked by many leading Tories. Edward Heath described it as the 'greatest act of gerrymandering in the last 150 years of British history'.

Meanwhile, taking the Tories' effective use of political advertis-ing as a model, the GLC had launched the brilliant and lavish campaign to save itself. London became plastered with GLC posters with slick and evocative slogans and powerful images. One poster portrayed a mass of red tape with the caption 'What will London be like without the GLC?' Another showed a photo of Parliament asking 'What kind of place is it that takes away your right to vote and leaves you with no say?' Hardly a Londoner was unaware of the significance of the central slogan used throughout, 'Say No To No Say'. Harris's earlier findings about attitudes to the GLC were used to make the main focus of the campaign one of democracy rather than the GLC's record on services. Indeed the campaign was designed to avoid rather than win support for the new Left issues around minority groups. The campaign was a stunning success. Large majorities of the London public were opposed to abolition, and opposition mounted among professional groups, leading Conservatives and the general public. Aided by his own popular television performances, Livingstone was transformed, in the words of *The Guardian*, 'from popular demon to defender of democracy against dictatorial central government'.

The embarrassment for the government was not confined to hostile public opinion and a split in its own ranks. The Lords dealt a devastating blow, passing, by a massive anti-government majority of 48, an amendment to the Paving Bill effectively allowing the elections to go ahead. It was the most damaging defeat of Thatcher's period as Prime Minister, and left the government's strategy in ruins. The government had to allow Livingstone and his colleagues another year in power, and they took every advantage of this stay of execution to exert maximum damage on the government proposals. The GLC was able to embark on just the type of spending spree and asset stripping to the benefit of the boroughs that Mrs Thatcher had been trying to prevent in the Paving Bill proposals.

In the end, the GLC and the Metropolitan County councils were abolished in March 1986, but not without further scares for the government. During the debate on the Abolition Bill in the Commons, the government's majority slumped to 23 with around 100 Tory MPs abstaining or voting against the government on an amendment to replace the GLC with a directly elected authority, a policy that Mrs Thatcher had dubbed the 'Son of Frankenstein'. So after two years of fierce battle and speculation, with the outcome always uncertain, Mrs Thatcher got her way. And with it she brought more centralisation, more quangos, and more instability to urban government.

The GLC in exile

In fact, the GLC did leave behind a successor. Nine London boroughs clubbed together to fund the London Strategic Policy Unit in order to save the jobs of many of the staff of the more contentious committees. The Unit, a last-minute idea of Livingstone's, attempted to continue the GLC's work on its new initiatives such as women, race, gays and lesbians and employment as well as keeping a watching brief on planning and transport. With a budget of £7 million and an initial staff of 300, it was hoped that it would be an embryonic 'GLC in exile' ready to become a fully-fledged London government after a Labour victory at the next election.

Wracked by internal conflict and without the GLC's financial and political clout, the Unit never really got off the ground. It was bedevilled by industrial disputes, mainly around minor complaints of racism and suffered from inadequate managerial control and much grinding of political axes among its largely inherited staff. Useful reports on planning, employment and policing did emerge but this was little to show for an organisation which had more employees than Labour party headquarters. Had a more modest 'think tank' been established, rather than a catch-all for all those made redundant from the units, then it might have proved a viable permanent lobbying weapon for a new London government. Instead, as ratecapping began to bite and the Tories won the 1987 general election, the boroughs withdrew their support and the unit, which had become severely criticised for its ineffectiveness, was wound up on 31 March 1988, exactly two years after the GLC itself. The remaining staff, by then down to 100, were redeployed to the boroughs.

5 'Tool for Change'

'A realisation developed in local Labour parties that local government might develop, once again, into the tool for change which had been so effective in the late nineteenth and early twentieth centuries' (Blunkett and Jackson, 1987, p. 88).

The Left was not just interested in running local councils, it was determined to change them. Local government was, after 1979, the only arena in which Labour activists could exercise power. The Left was determined to use this control to challenge traditional Labour policies, as well as Toryism. As David Blunkett put it, strong local government could be seen as a 'tool for achieving socialist change' (Boddy and Fudge, 1984, p. 244).

Local councils could also be used as a platform from which to raise the issues of democracy and accountability put at risk by the government's policies of centralisation and spending cuts. Many, as Massey and others point out, wanted to use local councils to 'illustrate an alternative both to Thatcherism and to Labourism, [which] is based on the feminist, anti-racist, anti-nuclear and more generally socialist ideas emerging throughout the sixties and seventies – partly as a reaction to the failures of Labourism'. Left councils were seen not only as being outside of traditional government, but as part of an 'alliance in which political, in this case local authority, resources and powers are made use of to strengthen, support and give a voice to industrial and extra-parliamentary action' (Massey et al., 1984, pp. 225–6).

The new councillors had a very different background from traditional Labour politicians. They were determined to turn local government upside down, and to reintroduce 'socialist' objectives in it. This chapter examines this new politics which included a new campaigning role, new functions, new economic initiatives, changes to the decision-making structures, greater consultation and participation, and increasing the accountability of councils to local Labour parties.

Many of the new councillors quoted the example of Poplar, and the radical authorities in the 1920s – and borrowed some of the symbols of the 'municipal socialism' of George Lansbury and Alfred Salter – flying the red flag over the town hall, and boycotting patriotic and military rituals. Indeed, the policies of the radical Labour councils in the 1920s and the propaganda surrounding them would not have looked out of place in the GLC of the 1980s.

The new councillors arrived in their council chambers armed with bulky manifestos, drawn up after lengthy consultation and approved, often line by line, by their local Labour parties. Indeed the local Labour parties saw themselves as the custodians of the manifesto, and were determined to use their new found strength to ensure that it was carried out. The manifestos contained some innovative and badly needed changes. But more importantly they were a statement of political intent – a determination to change.

A campaigning politics

Local councils were also keen to stretch the boundaries of local government and to move beyond simple provision to interventions in every debate or policy area relevant to local people – and some that were not. This represented an important extension of the role of the council as a representative of local people, speaking on their behalf on issues such as local health provision and transport services. Lawyers were sent off to find new powers, and to reinterpret existing ones – to enable the new councils to disseminate information and embark on campaigns. Section 137 of the 1972 Local Government Act, which enabled a council to spend up to the proceeds of a 2p. rate on anything related to the needs of local residents – was used to the full.

The new councils were keen to use their powers to highlight alternative priorities to those of the government, and to raise issues such as apartheid, exploitation in the Third World, the nuclear threat, and to challenge the prejudices of British culture.

Council meetings could be used to raise wider political issues, by transferring bank accounts away from Barclays as a demonstration against apartheid, and by supporting festivals for international women's day or the Greenham Common women. By renaming the Free Trade Hall to commemorate the Peterloo massacre, Manchester council felt it was making an important symbolic statement about the absence of labour movement struggles from the collective historical memory. By risking surcharge to ban the National Front from the use of council halls during election, Southwark councillors demonstrated support for the view that free speech should not be extended to fascists. By inviting Sinn Fein to speak, Camden and Hackney councils demonstrated opposition to the British government's policy in Northern Ireland. And by investing in *News on Sunday*, Southwark, Wolverhampton, Derbyshire, Lambeth, Brent, Cleveland, Haringey and Lothian demonstrated support for a Left press.

New policy initiatives demonstrated a concern for issues traditionally seen as outside the remit of local government politics. These included establishing nuclear free zones. While they did not succeed in preventing the passage of nuclear material through them (indeed Greenwich council's nuclear free zone contains a small experimental nuclear plant at the Maritime museum), or changing government policy, they did publicise the issue of nuclear power. The GLC produced some effective posters highlighting the possible dangers of the transportation of nuclear waste; and increased public awareness of the nuclear trains that pass through London every night. Several councils defied the government by refusing to take part in 'home defence' exercises, arguing that preparing plans for government during and after a nuclear war was a nonsense.

While Metropolitan authorities already had police committees to which local police forces reported, in London the Metropolitan Police is accountable only to the Home Office. Several London boroughs set up police committees and units to monitor the activities of the police and to highlight public concern about allegations of police brutality, and the failure of the police to deal with issues such as racial harassment. In many cases these units and committees were initially hostile to the police, but over a number of years became involved in issues of community policing. While they remained critical of abuses by the police, they have begun to work with them on crime related issues such as improving security and safety at night.

Rituals of civic pride were abandoned, or turned into political occasions. Town-twinning, often regarded as having declined into nothing more than the occasional junket in obscure European towns, was turned into an expression of solidarity. Lambeth, Lewisham, Sheffield, Oxford, Leicester and Manchester twinned with towns in Nicaragua. Others formed links with villages in the coalfields during the miners' strike. The trappings of civic splendour were trimmed. Annual banquets were replaced with tea and cakes, and the size of the 'mayors purse' slashed. In Manchester, the mayor's role was confined to chairing council meetings.

While initiatives on housing, social services and child care were expensive, symbolic campaigning initiatives were cheap and did not challenge the entrenched interests of management and trades unions. The risk was that when symbolic political gestures were made, without real improvements in services being delivered, local people would feel that the Left had got its priorities wrong. In many authorities the time and energy taken up by political gestures was out of proportion to their importance, and some gestures designed to create political awareness of an issue backfired badly. The popular press was always seeking examples of councils neglecting their constituents to concentrate on issues such as anti-apartheid or Northern Ireland. For example, as when Lambeth tried to rename parks and leisure facilities to commemorate revolutionary leaders in Southern Africa, public hostility was so great that the plans were abandoned.

Left councils were also determined to use their resources to campaign against the government's increasingly restrictive local government policies. Some councils developed an expertise in using the media and advertising. The production of good quality leaflets and the use of hoardings did change local public opinion. Councils began to use polling and to carry out surveys. These techniques were also used to publicise council activities and to improve public information, most notably welfare rights advice. Councils sponsored take-up campaigns to encourage local people to claim all the benefits to which they were entitled, such as women who might have been eligible for unemployment benefit. They began to provide debt counselling services for tenants. Information was produced on issues ranging from Aids and registration for British citizenship, to keep fit classes, and lead pollution.

Shaking up the bureaucracy

A major part of this new campaigning politics involved changing the way councils made decisions. Many Labour parties, and often back-benchers, felt ill-informed and excluded from decision making. Many decisions were taken in meetings between committee chairs and officers before committee meetings, or in powerful policy committees, and in some authorities the Labour group was simply expected to rubber-stamp the decisions of the leader.

The new Left changed all this. Many of the councillors who obtained senior positions had been excluded from power under previous administrations, and they were willing to use their new power to bring back-benchers into the decision making process. GLC councillor Valerie Wise wrote in *London Labour Briefing* in July 1981 that the new GLC was going to be more democratic, 'Chairmen do not take unilateral decisions on policy issues, but bring them to the Policy Committee and then to the full Labour groups so that everyone can participate'. Labour group meetings became the centre of policy making, and the most important meetings in the council calendar. The creation of new committees responsible for women, racial equality, police monitoring and so on inevitably shifted the balance of power since there were more chairs and fewer back-benchers. But in addition, back-benchers demanded, and got, more information and a greater role in decision making. The new councillors were not willing simply to accept an agenda dictated by officers and by the six-week committee cycle, and set up policy discussions, seminars and working groups to discuss the direction of policy. Back-benchers were sometimes given responsibility for reviewing policy areas. In several authorities each committee set up its own Labour group, to determine policy before each meeting. Even so, in many councils, while power was shared, responsibility was not, and back-benchers continued to operate as an informal 'opposition', unwilling to come to terms with the realities of exercising power in authorities responsible for thousands of people and an expenditure of millions of pounds.

New Left Labour councils identified much of the failure of the old Right administrations with the absence of any political strategy and the dominance of the professionals over the politicians. Councillors were determined to reassert the political nature of local councils. Leaders and committee chairs began to work full-time at council business, giving up their jobs and relying on attendance allowances. The new councillors were not prepared merely to preside over a structure that virtually ran itself, but sought to be centrally involved in decision making. They were intent on speeding up the dull snail-like pace of their councils, and placed little trust in their chief officers to carry out their plans. Therefore they began to intervene at every level of the council structure – rewriting reports, carrying out their own reviews of council provision, meeting the staff and making detailed suggestions about day-to-day activity. In some authorities, corporate planning, modern management techniques, and officer boards were seen as contributing to the growing power of chief officers. In Southwark the corporate plan was abandoned; in Hackney, as the Arden report suggests (Arden, 1987), basic organisational structures were dismantled in an attempt to reclaim power. The new councillors had learnt from accounts by Tony Benn and Richard Crossman about how officials could sabotage radical policies.

Officers identified as having no sympathy with the objectives of the new Left were encouraged to leave, although this often cost the new administrations generous golden handshakes. Ken Livingstone says candidly: 'Most of the senior officers I was determined to get rid of – because of their simple inability to understand what we were about, their incompetence, racism or Tory sympathies – were gone within two years' (Livingstone, 1987, p. 144).

Many of the senior officers in the new Left councils were indeed antipathetic. Many others were, quite simply, too long in the tooth to tolerate the upheaval. Many senior officers therefore left willingly, to move to gentler pastures in district councils where house prices were cheaper and the pace less strenuous. But it would be wrong to assume there was a major 'clear-out' of old-style officers. In most boroughs the majority of the senior officers remained, and those newly appointed to replace the departed officials were, in the main, traditional professionals, often from the next tier down. Indeed, perhaps one of the reasons for the limited nature of the municipal socialism experiment has been the absence of any root and branch reorganisation at the management and officer level. A new type of officer was introduced to work on the new initiatives. The GLC brought in former left-wing MP Reg Race to head the programme office, and Robin Murray, a left-wing economist, to lead the economic policy group. But most of these initiatives were 'bolted on' to existing structures, which were managed in traditional ways and dominated by supposedly neutral professional priorities. Even decentralisation often led to an extra 'neighbourhood' layer being added to existing large central departments. Few councils actually tried to dismantle the existing officer structures.

The mood in the Left councils did, however, attract a group of younger and more politically sympathetic officers – policy advisers, leader's advisers, and personal assistants for full time councillors. The new units – police monitoring, women, race and campaigns, and departments created to deal with employment and industrial policy and with community affairs – attracted staff with experience of the voluntary sector or single issue campaigns who were often Labour party members or sympathisers.

Many of the new officers brought skill, knowledge and experience that had long been missing. Economic expertise and skills in communication were vital for the role councils were attempting to play. Many of the traditionalists were uncomfortable and unfamiliar with equal opportunities policies, and attempts to involve the local community. Councils needed officers who were willing to find new ways, financially and legally, of achieving their objectives within government constraints. This created two sorts of problems, a confusion over the respective roles of councillors and managers, and the controversy about political appointments.

Officers complained that the constant 'hands on' approach of, often inexperienced, councillors meant that decisions were taken without proper advice. They complained that councillors abandoned any planned implementation of policy, and responded only to the most recent crisis. The chief executive of Lambeth wrote to council leader Linda Bellos in January 1987 complaining about the interference of councillors in the day-to-day running of departments. In the absence of clear objectives within which they could work, managers often simply referred decisions to politicians, and failed to take any strategic view of the direction of council services. 'Some claim that Left Labour councillors have made unacceptable demands on professional senior officers and have appointed political sympathisers to key posts who lack appropriate expertise, or, worse, behave in a way that creates a climate of fear among less politically committed colleagues' (Stoker, 1988, p. 210).

The failure came from both managers and politicians. The professional approach of managers, which had traditionally pretended that their work is politically neutral, made it hard for officers to adjust to the demands for radical change coming from their new political masters. But there has been a long-term failure to understand and respond to the unique nature of local government as a democratic institution, accountable to the local electorate, and to accept the legitimacy of political priorities. At the same time, politicians have failed to entrust experienced managers with the details of policy implementation. The absence of trust between members and officers made the lives of councillors far more difficult, and prevented the development of new approaches to managing democratic organisations. But there has been pressure not to try. The Tory government has tried deliberately to deny the political nature of local government, and has implied that setting local political priorities is illegitimate.

Controversy was aroused over a number of political appointments. The most notorious case was in Liverpool, when a Militant supporter, Sam Bond, was appointed to the post of race adviser, against the wishes of the local black community. The appointment of Ed Atkin, a businessman with no previous housing experience and married to a Labour councillor, Sharon Atkin, to the post of Director of Housing in Lambeth attracted press and community criticism. Mr Atkin resigned within a few months for health reasons. It is clear that all successful administrations have to be free to appoint officers sympathetic to their aims, and equipped with the necessary skills and knowledge to carry them out. The mistake was that in some cases political credentials were accepted as a substitute for professional qualifications or management experience.

Right-wing critics have made the mistake of not distinguishing between mere nepotism, and appointments for posts where political skills and knowledge are a necessary part of the job, such as, for example, the appointment of ex-GLC deputy leader John McDonnell to the coveted post of chief executive of the Association of London Authorities. Tory allegations about the corrupt nature of these appointments were disingenuous, given the extent to which Tory politicians pack civil service, health authority and quango posts with 'their' people. Mrs Thatcher has gone further in politicising the upper echelons of the civil service than any previous Prime Minister. Compared with the use of patronage in the business world, or the pervasive influence of the masons in many areas of public life, the attempts by Left Labour Councils to bring in sympathetic staff were amateurish. The Widdicombe report, commissioned to investigate this area, recognised that the tradition of political appointments was at least as strong among Conservative administrations as Labour ones, and accepted that there was a role for political advisers in local councils as there was in government – merely arguing that these 'political' appointments should have clearly separate roles from other officers who should be seen to be serving the council as a whole, rather than the ruling party. The Widdicombe enquiry was not convinced by evidence that Labour councils had simply promoted a 'jobs for the boys and girls' policy – noting that 'some Conservative councils vet applicants through Conservative Central Office' (Widdicombe, 1986, p. 155). They argued that it was important to ensure that officers had the right skills for the job and were appointed on merit, rather than through patronage, and recommended that the role of senior officers was politically neutral. They did recommend, however, that senior managers in one authority should be banned from holding political office in another, to ensure a distinction between the roles of politicians and managers. The Widdicombe report failed, however, to understand, or respond to the unique nature of management within a democratically accountable organisation. The legislation which resulted from Widdicombe, the Local Government and Housing Act 1989, went much further than the report, by banning any local government officers earning over £13 500, apart from teachers, and many others who have contact with the public, from holding any political office. While some may be able to apply for an exemption, the legislation clearly rules many tens of thousands of people from taking part in political activity and consequently the Act attracted opposition from Tory as well as Labour councillors.

Opening up the town hall

The new administrations were committed to changing the struc- ture of decision making by making local government more open, by increasing the flow of information to local people and by involving the public in decision making. In many cases, committee meetings had been closed to the public until the 1970s, and the full Council, the only public committee, was a rubber stamping body. The procedures of Labour groups and policy committees were often shrouded in secrecy. In Southwark, for example, the leadership of John O'Grady during the 1970s had been particularly exclusive and secretive, with information hard to come by even for its own backbenchers. When the Left took over in 1982, therefore, its manifesto referred to the need to 'inform and involve' local people in all activities; to increase participation in housing and to improve public consultation in the planning process; to provide community resources; and to improve information and advice services. Similar objectives were set out in other contemporary Left manifestos. The approach was spelt out by Graham Stringer, leader of Manchester from 1984: 'We want to bring people in and open up the town hall, ask people what they want and involve them in the decision making process. We want to involve all sorts of different people who are exploited in society and provide support to these people' (*Tribune*, 19 July 1985).

Town halls were opened up as meeting rooms and advice centres, and for crèches and exhibitions. London's County Hall, in particular, became a giant meeting room for women's groups, black groups, community organisations and Labour party activists. Councils began to pay more attention to communication, and to improve the quality of their publications. Leaflets were produced in plain English, and where necessary translated into minority languages.

The planning process had much more stress on local consultation, and was no longer dominated by the assumption that the planners know best. Experiments in community planning, such as Coin Street in Lambeth, allowed local people to plan the development of their areas. Southwark Council created a stir in planning circles by printing its North Southwark Plan on one large coloured and annotated map, instead of producing hundreds of pages of inaccessible documents. Rather than railroading through the plans of developers or professionals, the new councils were far more concerned to reflect the demands of local working people. This brought them into conflict with central government initiatives such as the London Docklands Development Corporation which, for several years, was boycotted by the Labour boroughs.

Tenants were given more say over their housing. They were

consulted over the details of new improvement or repair programmes, obtained seats on local district housing committees and
contributed to local estate management. In some authorities,
tenants are beginning to be involved in the allocation of capital
resources. Tenants' associations were consulted over rent increases, policy changes and decentralisation proposals and
delegates from tenants' associations were co-opted onto housing
committees.

Participation in council decision-making was not restricted to
tenants. As we see in later chapters, local activists were involved in
women's committees, race equality committees and gay and
lesbian committees and several councils created forums for the
elderly, the disabled, and community groups, attended by both
councillors and members of the public. Relations with the voluntary groups improved immeasurably and resources for community
groups mushroomed. Community projects and local organisations
were increasingly consulted about council proposals. Representatives of community groups were invited to meet officers, brief
councillors or give advice to committee meetings. While old style
Labour councillors had been suspicious of voluntary organisations
and felt that only they represented local people, the new councils
(with the exception of Liverpool) saw the voluntary sector as the
voice of important sectors of the community, and as partners in
any project to involve a wider cross-section of people in decision
making. The new Left councillors made themselves more accessible to the local community, and were willing to hear petitions,
receive deputations, and work closely with local groups. Because
more cash was channelled into the voluntary sector, there were
more local and community groups to consult and involve. As
David Blunkett and Keith Jackson put it, 'Many voluntary groups
are volatile and impermanent, nor can they be considered representative in the same way as elected councillors, but they do speak
directly on behalf of their members or users, and the important
task is to give the energy they represent a permanent and assured
place in local politics' (Blunkett and Jackson, 1987, p. 92).

Some Left councils attempted to go even further down the route
of devolution of power to local communities. Basildon, before
Labour lost power in 1987, divided responsibility for services into
three independent neighbourhoods, with area committees run by
all ward and county councillors for the area, self-appointed

representatives from the relevant joint estate management committees and community representatives appointed by the committee itself. The transfer carried no safeguard of support for Labour
policies. In Billericay and Wickford neighbourhoods, there was a
strong anti-Labour majority. But as Hilary Bryan writes, 'the
imposition of socialist control by a phoney local democratic system
was not the aim of the exercise. It was instead the creation of a
workable system of local government which was a genuine and
realistic method of local people actually taking the decisions they
wanted and solving problems in the way they felt best' (LCC,
1988, p. 29).

Islington has also set up 24 neighbourhood forums which will
determine in some limited ways how services are provided and
money is spent in their local areas. However, worries that these
may prove unrepresentative has meant that the council will play a
role in ensuring that they are organised in a democratic, legal and
workable way, and that women and minority groups are represented.

This question of representation goes to the heart of the problem
for Left councils about involving local people. While the Left
shared a commitment to greater involvement of local people, there
was often a desperation to ensure that local people would not
express views that cut across the priorities that had already been
decided. Some sections of the Left were already convinced that
they had correctly identified 'working-class interests'. They were
more interested in using new communication techniques to campaign on policies already decided in the Party, than to listen to
alternative points of view. As Gyford says of Liverpool, 'the
emphasis on "explaining", on "attracting new support", on "drawing together", on "raising morale" and on "listening to the council's
case" suggests that the major concern is to mobilise the people
behind the line already identified as correct by the council, or
more accurately by the local Labour Party' (Gyford, 1985, p. 92).

Perhaps inevitably, the commitment to democratisation was
only partially implemented. Even where there was a genuine
desire to make the council more accountable to the community,
Left councils often only succeeded in opening up and listening to a
very close knit group of community activists, many of whom were
supported by the council in the first place, and who shared its
political culture. It tended to be the younger and more energetic

community activists who were able to attend evening meetings, since they did not have child care or transport problems. There was a cultural divide between the newer, more political, voluntary organisations, and the more traditional tenants and residents associations, and local charities. Left councils have often been wary of decentralising decision-making too far, because of fears about the representativeness of local forums, and, in particular, about opposition to equal opportunities policies. Efforts to involve the local community have demonstrated the extent to which there is no single set of local interests to be represented. Devolving decision-making highlights the differences and the potential conflicts between the council workforce and services users, between young people and pensioners, between people who have bought their council home, and those who have not, and between the older traditional working-class residents and more recent arrivals, including both the black community and the young white professionals. And, as we see below, the attempt to increase accountability to local people did not mesh with another development, that of increasing accountability to the Labour party.

The search for accountability

The councillors selected in 1980/1 were chosen in the middle of the debate at national level about reselection and the accountability of MPs. The Left argued that MPs had betrayed the socialism of grassroots activists. Once safely in office, they ignored the socialist policies on which they had been elected. The way to avoid this betrayal in the future was to make MPs accountable to their local Labour parties, so that they acted not on their own independent political judgement, but as representatives of the political views of their local Labour parties. As Peter Tatchell, Labour candidate in the Bermondsey by-election, put it, 'an MP is no more than someone who is temporarily loaned the authority to speak and act on behalf of their party and constituents' (Tatchell, 1983, p. 146). In that way local Labour parties could continue to have a controlling influence on policy at national level.

While the debate had centred on the reselection and accountability of Labour MPs, it was also extended to the selection of councillors. As Hilary Wainwright puts it: 'Once party members had shown that it could be done, whether to a Cabinet Minister or to a Mafia of local councillors, party activists elsewhere applied it to their own local circumstances' (Wainwright, 1987, p. 94).

In the Labour party, councillors are chosen by individual ward selection meetings from a panel endorsed by the local government committee made up of representatives from all the constituencies within a local authority area. Local government committees are the official Labour party body responsible for borough-wide and local government affairs. During 1981, several local government committees introduced new vetting procedures and many nominated candidates were dropped from the panel for failing to give assurances about supporting the manifesto and refusing to be made accountable to their local parties. In areas such as Islington and Southwark, this took place against the backdrop of internecine warfare between the Left and Right with mutual accusations of packing meetings and fixing delegations. Many of those dropped from the panel subsequently defected to the SDP, confirming the suspicions of local left-wingers. Of those who did not, most were reinstated to the panel of possible candidates by Labour party HQ.

Despite these conflicts, the majority of the new councillors accepted a far higher degree of accountability to their local Labour parties than their predecessors. In some councils, all party members were invited to Labour group meetings as observers, and local government committee delegates were accorded considerable respect. Local Labour parties set up manifesto monitoring groups with representatives from local parties attending council committees and Labour groups to check on the actions of councillors. Individual councillors were expected to attend ward meetings and general committee meetings regularly and to report back on their council work. Councillors were expected to vote in accordance with the wishes of the local Labour parties as delegates rather than as independent councillors.

In Liverpool, the power of the party was absolute. Michael Parkinson explains that 'The district Labour Party has got in the 1980s what it never had in the 1970s, the power to actually determine the council group's policy. When adopted as candidates, members have to agree to follow district Labour party policy, if elected. If they don't agree, they do not become candidates. The group does what the district Labour party tells it to do' (Parkinson, 1985, pp. 26–7). Indeed without an understanding of

the relationship between Liverpool Council and the district
Labour party, it is impossible to make sense of the enormous
influence that Militant had over the council, despite its small
numbers. Derek Hatton pushed the Militant strategy through the
district party, to ensure that the council was committed to confrontation. Throughout Liverpool's brinkmanship, Tony Mulhearn,
the Militant district party chair, not a member of the council,
wielded considerable power from the district party.

   Elsewhere, the influence of the party was made explicit in new
procedures and structures. In some London boroughs, local parties were involved in the annual elections for the leader of the
council and for the key committee chairs. Perhaps the most
advanced institutionalisation of Labour party control was in Hackney, where elections of leader and committee chairs – and
decisions on all substantial areas of policy – are handed over to a
borough conference, which consists of the councillors plus the
local government committee and the three general management
committees of the council. Senior councillors have come to rely for
their base not on the support for their fellow councillors, but on
the support of the local Labour parties. The result was that the
Labour group became less and less important since the major
decisions were taken elsewhere, and it proved increasingly difficult
to get a quorum for group meetings. The shift of power to the
borough conference also resulted in considerable instability. Until
Andrew Puddephatt took over as leader, the borough conference
elected five different leaders in as many years. A pamphlet by the
local Labour Co-ordinating Committee argued that the relationship would fail unless the Labour party also recognised the other
responsibilities of councillors,

   The Labour Group increasingly accepts the decisions of the
   Borough conference and the Local Government Committee . . .
   the LGC should be responsible for helping launch policy and
   discussing policy with the labour group and, once policy is
   decided, for campaigning in the community. . . . What the LGC
   must also recognise is that the relationship with the Labour
   Group must be handled diplomatically and sensitively: The
   LGC is not the Council. Ultimately it is elected Councillors who
   must make the decisions (Hackney Labour Co-ordinating Committee, 1987).

None of these rules were 'constitutional', as any attempt to force councillors to accept party mandates is expressly forbidden by Labour party national rules. The national Labour party could be wheeled in to prevent the disciplining of representatives accused of breaking a mandate. While some councillors defied the decisions of their local government committees or the borough conference, the ethos of accountability has gained strength because most of the new councillors believed passionately in it, and fought strenuously for the principle. They accepted a more participatory view of decision making and were keen to ensure a greater role for Labour parties.

Inevitably, the structures created to involve local people were cut across by those politically more powerful mechanisms designed to ensure that councillors were accountable to their parties. Differences inevitably emerged between the demands of local tenants and community groups, the priorities of the Labour council, and the policies of local Labour parties. These splits did not emerge simply out of political differences, but also from the growing fragmentation of local communities, and the cultural gap between Labour parties and their constituents. Sometimes these were resolved with Labour activists becoming involved in local campaigns and creating strong community links. Other Labour activists, however, refused to accept the possibility of any conflict of interests, because they believed that their particular Left faction was the expression of the natural interests of working-class people. This assumes that Left activists know in advance what working-class interests are – even if working-class people are not aware of them – and it results in suggestions that working people's actual views can be disregarded as a sort of false consciousness. At its worst, such an approach can be seen in the determination of Liverpool council to override the interests of local people who had worked for years to form housing co-ops – and to return their lovingly self-designed homes back into council ownership, because the Labour politicians had decided that co-ops represented 'privatisation'.

A second set of problems was created because, in practice, it was difficult for councillors to involve local parties in the detail of decision making. They found it impossible to convey all the information they had received from council officers to members of the general management committee, or their own ward Labour parties. Discussions of council business frequently resulted in resolutions calling on councillors to follow principled positions, rather than ones which dealt with the difficult trade-offs and choices they were, in practice, always being forced to make. It was often easier for councillors to secure political support from their wards and general management committees through high profile campaigning than through day-to-day decision making on planning applications, rent arrears or staff recruitment. The unwillingness of local Labour parties to override already established policies in the interests of pragmatism meant that councillors played safe by 'sticking to the manifesto' rather than attempting to find constructive solutions to policy problems. Often it was safest to take no action at all. Difficult decisions could be 'referred to the parties' for consultation and delayed for months. While power shifted from councillors to the local Labour parties, responsibility stayed with the local councillors. Thus general management committees could cheerfully vote for a resolution demanding that councillors risk surcharge, and just as cheerfully vote against a resolution calling for Labour party members to share the risk!

Councillors found themselves with conflicting instructions from different levels of the Labour party. Local ward parties, with whom councillors had most contact, might mandate councillors one way, while the constituency general management committee might mandate them another way and the local government committee a third, depending on the balance of power between the Right, and soft and hard Lefts, at different levels of the party. The result was often that the canniest councillors would seek a mandate from somewhere to instruct them in the way they wanted, and would find arguments for disregarding mandates that they did not want to follow. Indeed, later, as the politics of constituencies and wards changed, and councillors found themselves instructed to vote for legal budgets and against confrontation, many of those on the hard Left who made the most fuss about accountability defied their party mandates!

The problems have been created, not by the idea of accountability itself, but by the rigidity of the structures, and the lack of trust between local Labour parties and their representatives. It may be that the party should be more involved in setting out the general direction of policy for their council rather than in checking on the detail. Until the Labour party at local level has found a way of re-establishing links with all sections of the local community and is in tune with local people's perceptions and aspirations, there will always be a danger that accountability to the party will hinder accountability to the electorate.

Economic initiatives

Inner city authorities had witnessed, since the 1960s, the destruction of much of their manufacturing base and growing unemployment reaching more than 20 per cent in some areas. In the 1970s, council attempts to tackle this seldom ventured beyond promotional advertising which sought to lure new firms to the area. The new councils were committed to a much more interventionist approach and economic initiatives were central to new Left politics for a number of reasons.

First, economic decline in urban areas was probably the most important day-to-day influence on local people's lives. Councils had to tackle the social consequences of rising unemployment and poverty, but didn't accept that their job was limited to picking up the pieces. They wanted to use their limited powers to the full to create local jobs, both by expanding council employment, and by shaping the local economy in ways that protected working-class communities. The primary aim was to protect and increase manual industrial jobs, both through rescuing ailing manufacturing concerns and through funding new industrial workshops. In London, though not elsewhere, these policies were backed by the use of planning powers to block office development, since, it was argued, offices failed to provide jobs for local working-class communities with traditional skills.

Second, there was a wider ideological commitment to an alternative economics, initiated by the 'collapse of Keynesian demand management as a strategy for full employment' (Wainwright, 1987, p. 255). The GLC brought in socialist economists like Robin Murray who argued for a new stress on the purposes and nature of production, rather than simply on the creation of jobs.

Third, the new Left councils wanted to challenge the Thatcherite belief in the supremacy of pure markets. Their support for local trade unionists taking industrial action and for workers' take-overs provided trade unionists with resources and information to strengthen their hand in bargaining. The objective was to create specific types of jobs which did not suffer from security, low pay or lack of unionisation.

Finally, the councils attempted to use their economic powers to try to advance social and redistributive objectives, targeted at helping the low paid, ethnic minorities and women. This included training, to give local people access to better jobs, and to provide women with manual skills.

The most ambitious attempt at local socialist intervention was by the new GLC. The brainchild of the chair of its new industry and employment committee, Michael Ward, the GLC produced an *Industrial Strategy for the Capital*, an industrial building programme, a network of co-operative development agencies, and the Greater London Enterprise Board. The GLC was not alone. New economic committees and departments were established in most Labour London boroughs and in Sheffield, Leeds and Manchester with remits to invest in local firms, promote co-ops, initiate training courses and develop vacant industrial sites. Enterprise boards were also established by the West Midlands, Lancashire, West Yorkshire and Merseyside County councils.

GLEB was by far the biggest and most adventurous of these initiatives. It received £60 million from the GLC over three years. Of this, £18 million was invested in 120 enterprises, £16 million was used to purchase property, £10 million went on staff and overheads, and the rest on a variety of projects. GLEB's aims were to rejuvenate the flagging London economy, create and improve the quality of jobs, and widen the control that Londoners had over their working lives. Investment was to be used to give the authority direct involvement in management decisions aimed at persuading firms to commit themselves to remain in London, to abide by health and safety and equal opportunity legislation, to allow the establishment of trade unions and to allow an element of workers' democracy. GLEB also had a number of secondary goals – to promote new forms of social ownership including co-ops and encourage the progressive use of new technology.

In pursuing these aims, however, GLEB had a somewhat mixed record. Originally, GLEB aimed to achieve its goals through a 'sectoral strategy' geared to the restructuring of whole industries. The idea was not simply to help single firms which might have a negative effect on other firms in the industry, but to encourage wider success by promoting restructuring through training, advice on technology, markets and products possibly through sectoral advice centres available to all firms.

A similar approach in promoting successful, prosperous industrial districts had been pursued in the Emilia Romagna region of northern Italy, an area controlled by the Italian Communist party since the war. Here, the Communist party saw the pursuit of socialist goals as going hand in hand with a predominantly private enterprise culture, though one carried out in co-operative rather than competitive spirit. The area is a patchwork of thousands of successful small firms, many of them co-operatives. The economic success of the region has been fostered by the policies of the local state which has developed industrial parks, encouraged loan guarantee consortia which provide and guarantee loans to its members, and initiated special industrial centres which give advice and information on particular industries which could not be provided by the firms themselves. The provision of high quality public services including an abundance of nursery places has also contributed to the very high employment rate especially among women (Brusco, 1985).

Despite valuable and detailed sectoral studies by GLEB staff, however, the sectoral strategy never really got off the ground. The idea was perhaps too ambitious to bear fruit on a small-scale regional basis without a supportive, national economic framework. GLEB was swimming against the tide of the deflationary national economic policy which fuelled the recession in the first half of the 1980s, and of the anti-interventionist stance of the government's industrial policy.

GLEB's investments were, therefore, mainly piecemeal, covering a diverse range of companies in a variety of sectors. Many of the firms supported proved to have severe financial difficulties. Increasingly, GLEB became a lender of last resort, providing finance to companies that were unable to attract funds from elsewhere. Partly this reflected GLEB's largely reactive, firm-led approach. But, according to internal reports circulated after it was taken over by the boroughs, there was also limited commercial expertise in appraising applications and drawing up investment packages. In addition, a lot of investments were taken for wider political reasons rather than on grounds of sound commercial judgement. This was especially true when trade union pressure was brought to bear because of impending redundancies. As a result, there was a high failure rate. According to an internal GLEB report by Tony Millwood, former leader of Hackney council and the chair of GLEB after the abolition of the GLC,

> GLEB has a very weak investment portfolio and very consider-able sums have been spent – neither in supporting investment nor in promoting social objectives, but in funding the ongoing revenue losses of companies for which there was little or no reasonable chance of eventual success or profitability. The great bulk of the money passed to GLEB by the GLC has been lost in this way.

Part of the problem was the failure to separate social from investment objectives. GLEB often expected small firms operating in competitive sectors with tight margins to meet social objectives such as providing staff training and facilities for the disabled, but without providing for the extra costs of doing so. There was a strong ideological commitment within GLEB to social goals but the support of firms often fighting for survival made these im-possible to achieve. Commercial viability is essential to the success of social objectives which in any case can only be achieved over the longer term.

It was always hoped that placing GLEB representatives on the boards of firms in return for financial support would impose pressure for change. But, according to a former academic adviser to GLEB, this was excessively optimistic.

> GLEB lacked clarity as to mission and members worked at cross purposes. From within GLEB came pressure to achieve, by imposition, the social goals that single-issue factions deemed paramount. The implicit notion was that . . . control of the firm could give top management, which included a GLEB official, the power to direct organisational practices at will. At the same time, GLEB board appointees were working alongside manage-ment who saw themselves as caught between survival in the marketplace increasingly dominated by better-organised foreign firms and a band of social reformers seeking to establish a workplace utopia from the security of government offices (Best, 1988).

Similar problems occurred with the idea of 'enterprise plans' under which firms supported by GLEB were to be pressed to allow greater worker democracy through tripartite discussions and union representation on the board. According to one former GLEB official these were a 'complete disaster' and for similar reasons. No more than six plans got off the ground and here the union representatives were often in an impossible position, torn between loyalty to the union and commercial realities. The problem was exacerbated by a lack of the training and back-up essential to its success. The idea of forcing firms to be more open and encourage involvement was sound but proved somewhat meaningless if the workforce lacked the skills to take advantage of the opportunities.

There was also a conflict between the economic and social goals. The stress on industrial regeneration in order to protect existing jobs meant that policies centred on job opportunities for men, rather than white-collar or service jobs for women. The insistence on high-quality, socially useful jobs meant that potentially viable private sector schemes were turned down, and no encouragement given to the development of offices, hotels and shops.

GLEB's performance, however, was far from totally bleak. It was engaged in a number of experimental and pioneering ideas and doing so in a very difficult economic climate with the decimation of large parts of London's manufacturing base. GLEB provided the inspiration for a novel socialist approach to local economic intervention, even if its implementation was sometimes flawed. It aimed at economic prosperity without relying on sweated labour, low wages and dehumanised work. It challenged a purely market-based approach to London's economy and encouraged a closer working relationship between trade unions, shop-stewards' committees and community groups.

While GLEB had only limited success in pursuing social goals in the private firms it backed, it promoted a number of producer co-ops accounting for a total of around 500 jobs and confirming national experience that co-ops have a higher success rate than private start-ups. It also financed a number of successful black and ethnic minority businesses. GLEB established technology networks which brought together the community, workplace groups and academics with the aim of identifying socially useful applications of new technology. GLEB was selected by the EEC Commission to head a three-year multinational project to develop a human-centred computer-integrated manufacturing system, based on the principle that new technology should build on and not replace human skills. The aim was to show that it is possible to combine efficiency with a more human and stimulating working environment. GLEB also established a number of successful training schemes and science parks.

When the GLC was abolished, GLEB was transferred to the boroughs and its funding fell sharply. It was renamed Greater London Enterprises and much of the property portfolio was sold, all at a profit, to keep it afloat. The high overhead and staffing costs were cut and it was reorganised. GLE has retained a commitment to equal opportunities and other social objectives, but these are financed by a separate 'social fund' with separate accounting and monitoring. Investment is based on a more rigorous commercial assessment with an emphasis on raising private capital.

The other enterprise boards all operated on a much smaller scale with more modest resources from their sponsoring authorities, and more limited objectives. There was a greater emphasis on commercial viability and less risk-taking, and they have mostly had a more successful record of local investment. Some have pursued wider goals such as the encouragement of co-ops and an improvement in the position of the unemployed and disadvantaged groups.

The West Midlands committed itself to a sectoral approach to intervention and has commissioned over 20 detailed industrial studies. As well as providing a wealth of vital information, these reveal a history of under-investment, technological backwardness and inadequate skill training. The sectoral approach is designed to tackle these problems and has been most developed in the case of clothing. The clothing study revealed 500 firms employing 20 000 workers, many more than in official statistics, archaic production techniques, poor working conditions and a low-paid and predominantly non-unionised and Asian female workforce.

A central element of the programme to tackle these problems was new investment in selected companies with potential for long term growth and employment creation. By March 1986, the board had approved investment of £14.2 million in 39 companies in the form of equity stakes and long-term loans, financed by the rates and by pension funds. The investment decisions were based on the sectoral studies. Thus four out of the first six investments were to non-competing foundry companies, based on a detailed study of the potential of the depressed ferrous foundry industry. Although one failed within weeks, the other three have proved successful. The investments have applied to a variety of circumstances from growth and expansion and financial restructuring to mergers and management buy-outs.

Other initiatives to tackle these problems have included the establishment of a business advisory centre and training courses for managers and workers, a campaign on homeworking, health and safety and low pay, and the establishment of a clothing resource centre offering specialist advice to all firms on technology, markets and fashion trends and the use of computer-aided design facilities. The West Midlands board has also established a technology transfer centre aimed at the diffusion of new technology, and a unit for the development of alternative products.

In Sheffield, an employment committee and department were set up in 1981 to tackle rising unemployment and regional disinvestment. With a staff of 100, the department undertook sectoral studies, intervened to protect existing jobs, and drew up plans for the regeneration of the local economy. These have included the encouragement of small firms and co-operatives, training schemes and equal opportunity initiatives. A product technology development unit was established by the council and the local polytechnic, and a business and management development programme started. Socially useful products were developed such as adaptations for the disabled.

Sheffield and other authorities also supported local trade unions, and helped establish networks of unemployed and trade union resource centres to provide help and research on industrial restructuring. Good employer codes and co-operative development agencies have also been established. Southwark concentrated on training and established a number of ambitious training schemes with the help of funding from the European Social Fund.

Many authorities introduced contract compliance, practised with great success by public bodies in the US. Labour councils followed suit by insisting that major companies which received funding or were awarded contracts had to meet conditions such as equal opportunities, trade union recognition and in some cases, disinvestment in South Africa. The latter enraged a number of major firms and the Tory government, prompting the outlawing of contract compliance in the 1988 Local Government Act, despite misgivings from many Tories who recognised its importance in creating local employment.

Local economic initiatives are now an established part of a local council's armoury. How successful they have been is difficult to assess with precision. In the first three years, the five enterprise boards outside London invested £25 million in over 200 companies and many millions more in other employment projects. It was claimed that 10 000 jobs were created or saved at an estimated cost of £3500 to £4500 per job compared to £35 000 in the case of national regional policy (Miller and Mawson, 1985). These, however, are gross costs and make no allowance for any displaced employment elsewhere.

The initiatives have had a much wider significance. They have provided a clear Left alternative to the Thatcherite non-interventionist industrial strategy and pure reliance on private capital and markets. They have mobilised additional industrial investment, and exposed the inadequacies of capital markets especially in the case of longer-term investment. They have established the importance of accountability and control so that public money is not a free hand-out. They have shown the potential for combining efficient enterprise and wider social goals. They have focused attention on the need to create local and regional economic strategies as part of a nationally based progressive economic strategy aimed at industrial restructuring, job creation and more socially accountable private industry. And they have been deployed at a time when it is being increasingly accepted that economic globalisation has weakened the power of the nation state, and that some of the state's economic functions should move upwards to the EEC and downwards to the level of the region. In both Italy and the Federal Republic of Germany, regional governments have important powers of economic intervention while some of the smaller European countries with highly successful economies like Sweden and the Netherlands are about the same size as the regions of large countries.

Of course, these models of local intervention have, at the same time, highlighted the problems to be overcome in developing such a strategy. These include the conflict between the need to exercise democratic power at the local level, and the need to concentrate

power in order to wield sufficient power over international companies – the tension between social objectives and profitability.
There is also the difficult choice between maintaining existing
investment and employment patterns against the grain of economic change, and investing to assist new industries which require
different skills and often fewer employees.

Conclusion

New Left councillors refused to limit their activities to simply
providing social services, housing, refuse collection and libraries.
Their enthusiasm for using local power to demonstrate alternatives
to Thatcherism led them to explore new areas for local government
activity – campaigning and economic initiatives. They also challenged established assumptions about the 'non-political' nature of
local government, the neutrality of council officers and the limited
role of elected members. They tried to sharpen the political
direction of local councils by intervening in day-to-day decision
making. Finally, they set out to increase the involvement of local
people in decision making, and the accountability of local councils
to both the electorate and the local Labour party. In many ways
the municipal Left were over-zealous and ill-prepared for these
changes. The failure to create effective decision making structures
often led to crises of inaction. Campaigning initiatives were often
crude, and while they demonstrated the commitment of politicians
did little to win over their communities. Economic initiatives were
too ambitious, and it proved difficult to disentangle attempts to
demonstrate alternative economic objectives, from strategies designed to reinvigorate local economies within the limits of the
market. Nevertheless, Left councils did begin an exploration of a
new and expanded role for local government, one which involved
the 'representation' of local people on a wide range of issues,
working with local people to plan the local area and the local
economy, and responding creatively to new needs and new local
interests. Experiments with neighbourhood forums, tenant management committees and community planning initiatives were the
first attempts to devolve power below the level of the local council.
We have stressed the limited nature of these experiments and the
failure of some Left councillors to distinguish between their own

political preoccupations and the views of their constituents. Involving local people in decision making means recognising and responding to the wide divergence of views and interests in the community. Accountability to the local community often conflicted with the accountability councillors felt to their own party, because of the growing gap between the political culture of inner city Labour parties and the people they represented.

6 Serving the People

'Inefficiency is organised theft from the working class' (Andrew Puddephatt, leader, Hackney Council; interview).

The new Left came to power not only to expand the role of councils into new areas such as women's issues and race relations, but also to change the way that councils provided traditional service. The manifestos on which the new councils were elected were full of detailed policies and while they varied widely from area to area, they had three main themes in common – expansion, challenging the paternalism of previous administrations and de-centralisation.

Expansion

High spending Labour councils were not new. Indeed in the 1920s Bermondsey and Poplar were accused of extravagance in health programmes and 'lavish outlay' on poor relief before such provision was considered a basic prerequisite for civilised life.

Indeed, Labour councils have always tended to provide more services through higher spending than their Conservative counter-parts. Once health provision became centrally controlled, they took the lead in house building and the development of social services. A 1978 study of local authorities found that 'while Conservative councils tend to spend less, Labour ones tend to spend more over and above any difference in their spending needs' (Jackman and Sellars, 1978, pp. 63–73). Labour councils led the expansion in the post-war years that introduced 'bigger, airier and lighter schools, better trained teachers . . . larger more elaborate leisure centres . . . as well as better staffed and stocked libraries' (Stoker, 1988 p. 9).

Initially, the Right's argument against high spending was that money was being wasted by extravagant and inefficient councils. The Tories argued that local services could be streamlined and rates reduced without loss of quality, and flagship Tory councils, such as Wandsworth, set out to prove it.

However, a close look at Wandsworth by Michael Ward, former deputy leader of the GLC, reveals how the council kept its rates down not only by providing a low level of service, but also by ensuring that it obtained the maximum subsidy from the government through the rate support grant system (Ward, 1987). Whereas in neighbouring Lambeth in 1986/7 only 23p in every pound spent by the council came from government grant, in Wandsworth the figure was 75p. Wandsworth, in fact, received more government grant than either Brent or Haringey, both of which are education authorities.

Ward examined seven specific services – child care, services for the handicapped and mentally ill, housing management, bed and breakfast use by the homeless, libraries, home help and meals for the elderly – and in all of these services Wandsworth spent less per head than the average. Some of the differences are staggering. Wandsworth spent just £2.58 per head on physically handicapped people, while the inner London average was £8.27. It spent only £10 on its library service, compared with twice as much even in Tory Kensington and Chelsea and £47 in Camden.

Of course, it is impossible to measure the quality of services by merely looking at spending figures, since Wandsworth would argue that it was simply more efficient. But qualitative measures suggest that the borough provided a poorer service than its neighbours. Wandsworth had fewer libraries, for example, opens them for shorter hours, and bought fewer books, records and cassettes. It also had fewer home helps, and provided fewer home help hours, 16.3 hours for every person over 65 compared with the London average of 20.6 hours. Since the Tories won control in 1978, services have worsened. Meals on wheels to the elderly fell by a half, and the number of nursery places was reduced from one place for every 26 children under 5 to one for 19.

A detailed scrutiny of the services of Greenwich and neighbouring Tory-controlled Bexley published in *Labour Weekly*

(21 February 1987), showed that the Conservative council provided less services and charged more for them. Bexley's meals on wheels were 90p., double the Greenwich price. Greenwich offered 353 day nursery places for under-5s, with another 65 planned. Bexley had just one centre with 45 places. Greenwich had twice the number of home-help hours per person aged over 75 and spent £11.91 per person annually on libraries, over £2 more than Bexley. And Greenwich's pupil–teacher ratio was significantly better in both primary and secondary schools

The debate about quality versus efficiency has often been conducted at the level of rhetoric without firm facts, because of the absence of effective non-financial measures of efficiency which would make evaluation of relative quality or value for money possible. The available evidence suggests that Labour's higher spending buys more. Figures for home helps per 1000 pensioners, for example, showed that in 1985 all but 7 of the top 40 providers were Labour-controlled, and Left councils such as Lambeth, Hackney, Lewisham, Haringey, Greenwich and Camden were all in the top 10 for 1985. Similarly in provision for under-5s, Camden, Islington, Brent, Lambeth, Manchester and Hackney were all in the top 10 for 1985. The Left Labour boroughs consistently come out well in league tables for service provision.

Camden, which had a high spending tradition that predated the takeover of the new Left in 1982, is the highest spender on libraries in the country. A library adviser from the government's Office of Arts and Libraries reported in 1986 with nothing but praise. 'Camden libraries do more than simply issue books; the provision and dissemination of community information in Camden is of a standard not equalled elsewhere in my experience.' The adviser concluded that one reason for Camden's high spending 'appears to be that the service in Camden is better than elsewhere' and therefore it was unreasonable to assess the cost on the same basis as used for other authorities.

The commitment of the Left Labour councils to expansion in the early 1980s stemmed from their emphasis on redistribution. At a time when government spending cuts were hitting the most vulnerable people in society, progressive councils felt their role was to protect them against Tory policies. Unemployed people were losing benefits, but they could be given free passes to leisure facilities, unemployed centres and training schemes. Crèches

could be provided for single parents. Margaret Hodge, leader of
Islington, says that 'compared with the old Right, the new Left of
the 70s did believe in using the council as a redistributive mechanism. We believe in using the rates income to build nurseries, to
provide libraries. The old Tammany Hall politics were low tax,
low services' (interview).

A similar sense of redistribution encouraged councils to expand
their staffs rapidly. Since unemployment in inner city areas was
high, it was felt that the most effective strategy that a Labour
council could pursue was to employ as many people as possible.

Between 1981 and 1986, despite government efforts to enforce
cuts, local authority spending rose by 51 per cent, during a period
when inflation was only 39 per cent. Inflation for councils was
probably higher than elsewhere because of the high wages element, but real spending nevertheless increased overall. Because
these average figures include spending in rural Conservative authorities, in inner-city Labour councils spending increased at a faster rate.
Here, the high spending policy was made to look more extravagant
by the punitive rate support grant system under which an extra £1
spent often cost as much as £3 in rates income. Even so, the increase
in real spending was considerable. For example between 1982 and
1987, Hackney's spending in real terms rose by 114 per cent and
Camden's by 90 per cent. Camden brought in 2000 new staff (an
increase of a quarter), three-quarters of whom were white-collar.

Innovation

Left councils were not merely committed to expansion but also
wanted to provide services in a different way and to meet newly
identified needs.

Camden, for example, developed a highly sophisticated system
of flexible childcare, with a full range of facilities, including day
nurseries, crèches, playgroups and support services to child-minders
– which gave parents in the borough real choice about how they
wished to plan their child care. Islington, over the same period
developed the most comprehensive service for under-5s in the
country, at a cost of £5 million annually. Between the local authority
and ILEA there were 6000 places of some sort of day care in Islington
by 1986, enough, according to Islington, for every child whose
parents wanted to use it. Many other Left councils gave consider-

ably higher priority to child-care provision than had previously been the case in local government.

Southwark set up an ambitious leisure programme, including free facilities for the unemployed, and a positive programme to encourage local people to use community and sports facilities, including basing development workers on local estates. Greenwich developed an imaginative leisure strategy based on using the parks to provide entertainment and music and introduced a very popular concert programme ranging from brass bands to Mozart to rock.

Several authorities invested millions in repair and improvements on the worst rundown estates, using imaginative methods to make 'defensible space' including individual gardens on the ground floor, blocking off through-routes within estates and installing answerphones. Brent managed to improve some of its worst tower blocks by installing a 'concierge' porter system with a reception in the entrance hall. Southwark and Lewisham introduced very popular cheap burial services that undercut local undertakers and alleviated fears of older residents about having a 'pauper's send off'. Greenwich earned a nationwide reputation for the work of its Environmental Health Service in preventing glue-sniffing, and the Environmental Health Department in Lambeth pioneered work on the local environment and pollution control. Manchester became the first authority to employ a 'houses in multiple occupation officer' to help people in bedsits; Southwark employed a worker to look after the needs of carers in the borough; Greenwich was the first to sponsor a worker to find local employers prepared to employ severely handicapped people. Possibly the most astonishing success was when Haringey was commended in 1987 by the London Chamber of Commerce for providing more practical support to local business than any other authority in London. Another remarkable initiative was Lewisham's sponsorship of Millwall football club to the tune of £70 000 per year. In return, the club visits local schools, gives free tickets to people with disabilities, and provides a crèche at home matches. The link has been remarkably successful, helping to improve the image of both club and council, and, unlike so many Left initiatives, was blessed with good fortune when Millwall was promptly promoted to the First Division.

Sheffield, despite a high expenditure (8.6 per cent more per head than the average for metropolitan districts), was constantly being praised by the Audit Commission. John Banham, the Controller of the Audit Commission, said on a BBC radio programme in 1985, 'the best local government is superb and private enterprise could never improve on it, with Sheffield a shining example'. Sheffield did well on various financial criteria: housing rent arrears were 3.4 per cent compared with an average of 4.6 per cent; the cost of cleaning schools was 12 per cent lower than average; the cost of school maintenance was 17 per cent lower than average; and Sheffield bought its supplies cheaper than many Tory boroughs. Nevertheless, the council expanded its workforce by 2000 between 1979 and 1986, and introduced many innovations. One was its reorganisation of services for the elderly. The council created 'elderly person support units' based in local areas to provide a more accessible and flexible service. Run by 'community support workers', the units aim to provide the whole range of services which old people need from occasional help with heavy tasks or relief help to give carers a break, through to a comprehensive care programme, to meet all the day-to-day needs of the frail elderly. The aim is to enable elderly people to have the choice of staying in their homes or going into a home.

Decentralisation

Decentralisation featured strongly in many Left manifestos. The idea had been pioneered in Walsall between 1980 and 1982, where a mildly left-wing administration had dismantled the old housing department and sent about 150 of its 200 civic centre staff out to neighbourhood offices. The direct labour organisation was organised into neighbourhood repair teams and plans drawn up to decentralise other services. The intention was 'not just to provide a better service but to help tenants and residents in Walsall's 42 000 council houses exercise more control over their communities' (Sharron, 1982). The new staff appointed to take over the neighbourhoods were unusual local government officers in that they included community workers and bus drivers who were 'sympathetically minded'. The decentralisation proposals were implemented speedily with little consultation, despite a strike by NALGO. In the end the sheer volume of new jobs silenced opposition from the more senior management staff in the union.

The Walsall experiment was shortlived. Although the neighbourhood offices survived Labour's defeat in 1982 by a Conservative/Alliance administration, the more pioneering aspects such as devolving control of the offices to local people were scrapped. However, the idea of decentralisation was seen by many on the Left as a way of extending power to local people and the Walsall example was quickly followed. The Labour Co-ordinating Committee suggested in a 1982 pamphlet that 'going local' was the 'fundamental response necessary to meet the devastating challenge to local government from the Tories'. Decentralisation was perceived as the way of involving local people in the provision of services and therefore winning their support to defend those services against Tory attacks. It was a way of encouraging tenants and community groups to become more involved in the workings of the council and to break down the bureaucracy of local councils. It was even seen as offering advantages to the workforce since by 'enjoying the effectiveness of working directly with the public, [they] could develop much more worker participation and other democratic management practices'. As the pamphlet put it, 'decentralisation promises to change the provider-consumer relationship between the council and the people' (Labour Co-ordinating Committee, 1984, p. 7).

Decentralisation was not universally supported on the Left. Sections of the hard Left felt that the focus on decentralisation was a diversion from campaigning politics and they argued that the working class would automatically support public provision under threat. They were concerned that restructuring proposals could involve 'cuts in disguise' and would lose trade union support by increasing productivity or changing job descriptions. This ambivalence towards decentralisation did not stop some groups using it as a campaigning tactic. As *London Labour Briefing* put it, 'one of our hopes for decentralisation of council services should be that it will help develop a political awareness among more people that the struggles of council workers and the "community" over cuts in jobs and services are a common anti-capitalist struggle against economic oppression'.

The term 'decentralisation' has been used to describe two very different sorts of projects. The first is the decentralisation of service delivery and administration. The second, where far less progress has been made, is the decentralisation of political control.

Most councils opted for the former through a vagueness of intention and the need to find the line of least resistance from managers and unions. Moreover, the commitment of Left councils to involving the community and the trade unions meant that many initiatives dissolved into a constant stream of vague consultations and a paralysis of decision making. In Southwark and Camden, for example, decentralisation was constantly on the agenda but little progress was made. Baiter, Hambleton and Hoggett (in Hambleton and Hoggett, 1987, p. 87) explain that 'while the London boroughs bent over backwards in their efforts to consult the public and their own workforce, [they] encountered formidable trade union hostility'. They point to the failure of the decentralisation initiative in Hackney, where 'the political and organisational momentum sunk within a miasma of uncertainty' (p. 100). In many boroughs, the plans collapsed under union opposition. In others, such as Lambeth and Lewisham, union determination to protect existing staff conditions delayed implementation, increased costs, and blunted the radical edge of decentralisation. Because of caution from both unions and management, decentralisation has often meant little more than an additional tier of bureaucracy at a local level.

The most successful experiment was in Islington. An ambitious programme to decentralise to 24 neighbourhood offices covering housing services, housing benefits, environmental health, social services, community work and welfare rights was begun in 1982 and completed just after the 1986 elections. While it proved expensive, much of the money has been spent on improving services; for example, the number of homes controlled by each estate officer was reduced from 645 to 450. The waiting time for repairs was cut, often dramatically. The decentralisation was based on widespread public consultation and careful negotiations with unions. The latter did not prevent sporadic industrial action and the council made late concessions in order to win union support, such as the creation of at least 100 extra posts and 100 upgradings, and the abandonment of the attempt to create a truly generic service. However, there was a hard-headed realism and an attention to detail about Islington's approach to decentralisation which was not always the case elsewhere. The offices were designed by staff with a brief to make them friendly, accessible and open plan; and in recruiting staff the neighbourhood offices took on a far higher proportion of women and ethnic minority managers than in the rest of the council. Islington's decentralisation was undertaken primarily to improve service delivery and make it more cost effective. Margaret Hodge said that 'there are ideological reasons for undertaking decentralisation. In the context of Islington, these are important but secondary' (in Hambleton and Hoggett, 1987, p. 32). Perhaps the biggest problem has been the extent to which greater access for the public has resulted in an increased workload and created an unprecedented demand for services.

The trend for decentralising services now goes well beyond the municipal Left and is supported by right-wing Labour councils such as Birmingham, Democrat-controlled Tower Hamlets and even some Tory authorities, such as East Sussex. 'It is now quite difficult to find a public sector housing department with a stock of more than 20 000 properties which is not engaged in a decentralisation initiative of some kind' (Hambleton and Hoggett, 1987, p. 1). Decentralisation is no longer seen as a passing fad, but as a long-term trend in local government. Decentralisation poses a number of problems for the Left when it goes beyond the realms of administration and becomes an attempt to devolve political power. Most fundamentally, is the Left really prepared to allow local people to develop and impose policies which run counter to those of the council? Only in Tower Hamlets, controlled by the Democrats, has there been the creation of virtually autonomous neighbourhoods where political control has been passed to the party with the most seats in the area, resulting in three of the neighbourhoods being under Labour control. Other questions which remain unresolved include whether a move to decentralise decision making can lead to inequalities and differing standards within an authority; and who decides priorities and resources between neighbourhoods; and if councils are not prepared to hand over power, should they not restrict themselves to the administrative model of decentralisation? It is not surprising, therefore, that it remains unclear whether any of these initiatives will develop into a more radical set of changes in the organisation and management of service delivery.

Failures

Left councils will be remembered less for their successes like decentralisation than for their failures because of the astonishing media attention, which led to these mistakes receiving much publicity. Yet, failures are not confined to Left Labour councils. There have been scandalous examples of bad management and poor political judgement among Right Labour councils and Tory-controlled councils – including the infamous sale of Tory West-minister's cemeteries for £1. Many of the problems faced by the new administrations had little to do with left-wing politics but were inherited from mistakes made by their predecessors.

However, there was a series of failures which highlighted the fact that the service delivery problems faced by these councils required a more complex analysis of the tasks facing local government than the Left had identified. They had criticised previous administrations for sloth, lack of imagination and failure to meet local needs. Yet, at times, the new administrations provided less efficient services than their predecessors, and sporadic industrial relations problems and management failures resulted in offices failing to open and promises not being kept.

Lambeth's housing benefit service is a vivid illustration of a service that was in a state of collapse for a long period. Housing benefit was transferred in April 1983 to local councils with very little time for preparation resulting in enormous administrative difficulties. Some councils, such as Camden, overcame these difficulties to deliver an efficient and popular service. In Lambeth, by contrast, many of the poorest members of the community were finding that benefit was not paid, or was paid only after enormous delays. Private tenants often faced eviction before they received their benefit. A report commissioned by the new council leader-ship in 1986 listed 29 reasons for the collapse of the service, including lack of interest among the councillors. As the report put it 'housing benefits had a lower than necessary priority in the organisation of council business'.

Some problems stemmed, not from lack of goodwill, but from a failure to make sure policies worked at the point of delivery. For example, despite the major expansion of under-5s' care by Islington, the council failed to ensure that places were taken up. An independent auditor's report commissioned by the man-agement found that of the 680 places, only 386 were on average filled, despite a substantial waiting list. The number of places available had already been restricted to 680 by a ratio of four workers to one child which was more generous than DHSS guidelines recommended. The ostensible reason for the low take-up of places was that staff did not take on extra children during periods when there was a staff vacancy at the nursery, but in reality the problem went deeper than that. There was, according to one councillor, 'a culture at the centres in which there was a marked reluctance of the staff to allow parents to leave their children for the periods they wanted to. The staff simply didn't want all these children running about' (interview). The staff had banned any part-time places, although in practice parents did leave their children there part time. Relations between staff and management were bad and there had been a strike in 1984–5 when an admissions ban contributed to the low attendance. Again, councillors had paid little attention to the actual running of the under-5s centres, although they had been instrumental in increasing the provision. There was also a failure to collect fees, 60 per cent of them remaining unpaid. While collection of the money was set out as part of the job description of the nursery organisers, neither management nor councillors had ensured that this task was carried out.

In Hackney, two independent reports showed how the administration of services had reached crisis point. One, undertaken by barrister Andrew Arden (1987), had originally been intended to investigate the influence of masons. Finding little, he was allowed to extend his brief to cover all aspects of council performance. The second was by the local deputy district auditor and was a review of the council's management in the light of its 'worsening financial position'. The two reports revealed wide-ranging problems of poor management and inefficiency. The council had a very high rate of empty properties because it took six months to re-let vacancies. The library service was expensive, and open very long hours, but was badly used. The nursery service showed that places were not taken up because of staff shortages, despite a waiting list of over 600. The auditor criticised the imposition of a rent freeze which had lasted several years. He pointed out that much of the burden of a rent increase would fall to the government through housing benefit payments, while a simple increase in line with inflation would release £8.5 million. Because two-thirds of the council's tenants were on benefits, only £1.4 million would come from them. The capital programme was also in difficulties. The council had failed to manage the existing programme of £40 million, yet it was intending to increase this by a further £50 million through creative accounting. The auditor commented, 'there is little prospect . . . that the present system could cope satisfactorily with a massive and relatively sudden increase in the programme'. Andrew Arden sums up Hackney's problems as being due to 'inadequate attention paid to basic administrative practices at Hackney over a prolonged period, and to the detriment of the people for whom Hackney Council exists to provide services'.

The Audit Commission's criticisms

The existence of these management failures was seized on by the Tory party to demonstrate the alleged failure of the municipal socialism experiment. Critics were given new ammunition by a report written by John Banham, the controller of the Audit Commission, in January 1987 (Audit Commission, 1987).

The report selected eight inner London councils, all controlled by the Left – Brent, Camden, Hackney, Haringey, Islington, Lambeth, Lewisham and Southwark – and compared them with two other groups: eight other London boroughs, reckoned to have 'similar levels of housing deprivation' – Greenwich, Hammersmith and Fulham, Kensington and Chelsea, Newham, Tower Hamlets, Waltham Forest and Wandsworth; and the eight 'most deprived' provincial authorities – Birmingham, Bradford, Coventry, Kirklees, Knowsley, Manchester, Sandwell and Wolverhampton.

The report started from the premise that inner London suffered from problems that, if action were not taken, could become as bad as those of the Bronx or south Chicago. It stressed, however that 'increased investment only makes sense if it can be managed effectively: one of the lessons of the past is that "throwing money at the problem" all too often simply means more waste'. It went on to identify inefficiencies which it believed could not be explained solely by the social problems of inner London. By examining performance on housing management and maintenance, social services for children in care and the elderly, refuse collection and vehicle maintenance, it showed that the eight councils were spending twice as much per head on these activities as the outside London authorities and 50 per cent more than the other London boroughs. The Commission accepted that the higher expenditure could partly be explained by policy differences, with Labour councils in inner London providing a wider range of better quality services, but still argued that 'inner London authorities tend to have costs for an apparently comparable standard of service well above the most deprived Metropolitan districts'. The report singled out the cost of rent arrears, and the high cost of some services such as refuse collection, which it was said was 'at least 10 per cent more expensive than it need have been ... bonus arrangements had not been subjected to detailed scrutiny for ten years or more'. The Commission argued that while expenditure per person in Inner London was 'notably different from elsewhere', rising by 20 per cent since 1981, consumer satisfaction, according to a MORI poll carried out for the Commission, was much lower.

The Commission was not entirely critical. The report praised the high level of provision in inner London authorities for the mentally ill and the mentally handicapped and the efforts to place children in foster homes rather than residential care. But this was scant consolation compared with the criticisms.

The Banham report fuelled the attacks on Left councils yet was recognised to have inherent weaknesses, even by Banham's colleagues who were concerned at both the fact and the timing of its publication. For example, Tower Hamlets, until 1986 run by a right-wing Labour group, was included in the group of supposedly well-run boroughs, and yet it had a very poor reputation in local government circles, particularly in relation to housing. Its Housing Investment Programme was consistently underspent for several years despite the fact that the borough had some of the worst housing conditions in the country. By including Tower Hamlets in the 'efficient' group, Banham was able to single out only Left councils for criticism and to avoid reducing his figures for average costs across the eight boroughs. In fact, Tower Hamlets was a classic example of the argument that low spending does not necessarily mean efficiency. It can simply mean neglect.

The report did not sufficiently take into account the concentrated problems of poverty, unemployment, crime and poor housing facing the Labour inner London boroughs. The argument that the comparative group had similar levels of housing deprivation does not stand up – while there are pockets of bad privately-rented housing in Kensington and Chelsea, it is not comparable with the poor housing conditions of a large proportion of the population in Hackney or Southwark. Odran Steed, finance director of Brent, argued that the independence of the Audit Commission 'is clearly brought into question by the issue of this paper' since it 'draws conclusions on extravagance and inefficiency based on comparison of the groups without adequately reflecting or taking account of the level of need, or the quality or quantity of service being delivered' (*Local Government Chronicle*, 27 March 1987).

The Association of London Authorities, to which all the councils attacked by the report belonged, used measures such as homelessness, housing deprivation and percentage of black people to demonstrate that the problems facing the eight left-wing boroughs were much greater than those of the other eight. It argued that the extra needs created by growing unemployment and homelessness, the greater housing deprivation in inner London, cuts in the health service and changes in government policy such as the 'care in the community programme for the mentally ill and handicapped' were disproportionately concentrated in inner London.

Many of these were not related to the politics of these authorities but to the fact that the Left had predominantly taken control of inner city authorities with huge social and economic problems. Nevertheless, there were problems which need to be understood in the context of the politics of the Left councils, in particular those related to industrial relations.

Workers and consumers – the hidden tensions

The new Left councils were committed to improving the terms and conditions of their staff and to creating a closer relationship with the workforce. The wage rates of manual workers in the public sector are notoriously low. In 1985 the Low Pay Unit estimated that 45 per cent of full-time local authority manual workers earned less than the Unit's definition of low pay – two-thirds of median male earnings. One third of non-manual workers in local authorities were also on low pay. The large proportion of women employed in low status manual and administrative jobs is an important element – 70 per cent of these women workers could be categorised as low paid. There is also evidence that ethnic minorities are concentrated in the lowest grades of local authority service (Stoker, 1988). Left councils looked sympathetically at claims for regrading, and several of them introduced minimum wage policies directed at the lowest paid workers. The ALA response to the Audit Commission report pointed out that 'the "target" authorities are not apologetic about their desire to improve the pay and condition of their employees'. But since the major cost of any local authority is staffing, the policy of improving the lot of their employees obviously resulted in higher costs. While the authorities were quite justified in trying to improve the employment conditions of their workforce, particularly in view of the problems in recruitment faced by some, there was a price to pay. As a Labour Co-ordinating Committee pamphlet put it, 'any improvement in terms and conditions of work, without improved efficiency and flexibility are bought at the expense of consumers of council services: shorter working hours mean fewer opening hours. In the context of resource cuts and central controls on raising rate income, there is nowhere for improvements in staff conditions to come from, except the pockets of the local community' (LCC, 1988, p. 21).

Left councils conspicuously failed to address the problem of, let alone resolve, the tension between the interests of producers and the interests of consumers; or to develop clear priorities between policies to improve service provision for the local community and measures to better terms and conditions of staff. This was in part because the rhetoric of the Left constantly confused the two. The struggle that councils were engaged in was 'to defend jobs and services' which were seen as inseparable. The uncomfortable reality that services could be protected while jobs were lost, or vice versa, was not confronted. At the most simplistic level, sections of the hard Left identified their interests entirely with those of the town hall unions because they saw them as the key local representatives of the working class.

In councils such as Southwark and Liverpool, this logic was extended to argue that only the manual trade unions were the authentic representatives of the working class. In both authorities close links between the manual trade unions and key councillors and activists were established that were untypical of the Left councils. Indeed, the 'workerist' view that manual trade unionists were true representatives of working-class people, while blacks, women, Nalgo members and professionals could be dismissed as 'fringe' or 'middle class' had more in common with the old right-wing Labour parties than with the 'rainbow coalitions' of the new

Left. Nevertheless, the scandal uncovered at the Nye Bevan Lodge old people's home in Southwark, and the discovery that a 'special relationship' between the unions and the councillors led to the covering up of widespread ill-treatment of the old people reveals the dangers of informal relationships taking over from accountable structures.

As early as 1979 during the administration of John O'Grady and the old Right, allegations had been made about ill-treatment of old people at Nye Bevan Lodge. The place was likened to a 'concentration camp' by one resident. There were allegations of old people 'helped to die' by staff leaving windows open, of faeces being put into the mouth of an incontinent resident, and of sexual assaults and misbehaviour by staff and councillors at a bar at the home. Even when these allegations came to light, reports remained 'confidential' and the extent of the maltreatment was covered up by the council which initially allowed the trade unions to block the establishment of an independent enquiry. It was not until the election of a new council in 1986 that an enquiry, under barrister Jocelyn Gibbs, was established. Its report, published in July 1987, reveals the extent to which the trade unions, and the manual branch of NUPE (the public employees' union) in particular, were able to influence and even take over the decision-making process of the council. The management at Nye Bevan Lodge and at social services headquarters was in permanent fear of the union officials who made threats of industrial action if there was any challenge to their conduct. One union official was singled out by the report as having a 'roving commission' that allowed him to turn up at Nye Bevan Lodge 'on the slightest pretext'. At one time, when a complaint had been made against him, he went down to the Lodge and called an immediate stoppage until a councillor agreed to call a meeting of the powerful Industrial Relations Emergency Sub Committee to discuss, not the complaint, but the possibility of action against the officer who had made the complaint!

The special relationship between trade unionists and a group of councillors who came to be known as the 'workerists' found visible expression in the local Labour club. Decisions made there became *de facto* decisions of the Labour group and subsequently of the council. The trade unionists had two routes to power – as workers and trade unionists they were able to negotiate with councillors on matters affecting their employment conditions. As prominent members of the Labour Party they were able to influence what policies the council took to those negotiations, because they dominated Southwark's Local Government Committee which sets out the policies to be followed by councillors. There were other examples of poor service delivery because of this relationship. Measures agreed in 1983 to improve the efficiency of the refuse service were not implemented for three years. As the auditor's report put it, 'the problem of running an authority such as this is that members' sympathies would (normally) be with the men rather than management'.

The Gibbs report on Nye Bevan points out that 'some of the people who spoke to us believed that some of the difficulties encountered by the managers stemmed from an inability on the part of some members to come properly to terms with their new roles (as employers). They supposedly found it strange to act as employers with ultimate responsibility for the benefit of the local electorate as a whole.'

Southwark is a special case, and it is important not to deduce that similar problems lurk under the surface in all Left authorities. Ironically, one of the reasons for the overriding commitment to the interests of manual workers came from the larger than average number of Southwark councillors who were manual workers themselves. In most Left councils, the vast majority of ruling councillors were white-collar workers.

Nevertheless the approach of Left councillors, party activists and town hall trade unions to the issue of management and industrial relations has wider implications. The politicisation of town halls created a crisis of roles, since traditional assumptions behind local government career patterns were disrupted. Values of neutrality and professionalism, strongly held by many career officers, were challenged by a new stress on change and task-orientation. The highly political strategies adopted by Labour local authorities forced many officers to choose between a quiet life and a committed one. Officers in central positions were now perceived as active participants in policy making, especially in new areas such as equal opportunities, employment and industrial strategy, and campaigns against central government. Only the tiny minority who had specifically joined these authorities because of personal sympathy with their aims did not feel this conflict.

Union officials also felt inherent conflict in their new role. On the one hand they were being asked to join in joint campaigns with the council. On the other, if the campaigns failed, then the resulting cuts would affect their jobs and they would have to fight the council. As a result, they felt torn between political solidarity and a need to keep their distance in case they had to take industrial action against their employers. The unionists were also wary of the more informal relationships between councillors and staff and the new structures set up to campaign because they breached the traditional employer/worker relationship. Participation in Labour group meetings was not the same as negotiation with managers and it was no longer clear which was most effective. Many union organisers were also active party members and supported the use of industrial action to try to influence the political decision-making of the council. The relationships between the unions and the council were complicated by the increasing number of representatives of the council workforces who were elected to senior positions in the constituency Labour parties, resulting in an increasing influence over council decisions by the very trade unionists who stood to benefit directly from them. This could paralyse negotiations, since the union side, rather than having to accept compromises with senior managers, always had the alternative of using their influence on the local Labour party to mandate councillors to give in to union demands!

The genuine desire of Left councillors to improve working conditions for staff, combined with their inexperience in negotiations, made them appear a 'soft touch'. Added to this was the political commitment of the Left to an alliance in struggle with trade unionists against the government. They therefore expected to be able to call on the trade unions to demonstrate or call industrial action at the council's whim. Inevitably this led the councillors to soft pedal on unpopular decisions. The sympathy of many councillors for any union action, however unwarranted, meant that they were unwilling to retaliate or even to punish unions for industrial action. Industrial action became virtually 'cost free' for the unions and their members who did not even usually lose pay. The unions exploited this weakness by increasingly using industrial action as a first tactic, instead of negotiating. Throughout the period 1982–6, for example, the unions in Hackney were always ready to take industrial action as they knew the council never retaliated. For example, Hackney's libraries were frequently and unpredictably closed because the staff had unilaterally set staffing levels. When staff shortages or illnesses occurred, they shut the buildings without warning, but the councillors took no action against the staff concerned.

The fiasco over Lambeth's housing benefit, outlined above, also had its origins in the fraught relationship between councillors and the local authority unions. The report of the consultancy team which had been asked to investigate the problems reveals that figures on the backlog of payments to private tenants were 'no longer updated on Nalgo instructions as they are thought to be meaningless'. The report refers to 'apparent union intractability and inflexibility' and suggests that the unions had been allowed to create a culture in which they had an effective right of veto over decisions.

So, ironically, the new Left councillors often had a worse industrial relations record than other authorities. The national social workers' strike in the early 1980s hit the Left councils hardest because the union knew there was no fear of retaliation. In the run-up to the 1985 ratecapping campaign, there were strikes among social workers in Southwark, nursery staff in Islington and housing workers in Camden, Sheffield and Lewisham. Newly-elected Left councils found themselves immediately at the wrong end of disputes. Ealing suffered a four-week Nalgo stoppage in 1987, a few months after Labour's election victory, over a demand for extra London weighting, and a few weeks later, in Waltham Forest, also newly-Labour controlled, social workers walked out over a similar demand.

Initiatives undermined

It was the new policy initiatives of the Left councillors which provoked the greatest number of disputes. Decentralisation and changing methods of service delivery frequently cut directly across the vested interests of staff and their unions. There are many examples of progress being stymied by union resistance and by workforces unwilling to relax any of their restrictive practices even when the councils were expanding their workforces and there was no question of redundancies. In most cases 'local government unions have tended to resist all attempts at decentralisation over the last few years' (Hoggett, 1987).

The unions were concerned that, at a time of cuts, frontline staff would be given extra responsibilities but no extra powers and that neighbourhood offices would become a buffer zone between a dissatisfied public and the council. But by opposing moves towards greater flexibility in job descriptions, unions undermined initiatives designed to improve the quality of services to consumers. By refusing to accept flexible opening hours or open plan offices, by insisting on existing lines of accountability and demarcations between different tasks and by defending existing hierarchies, unions blunted the impact of decentralisation initiatives.

In 1983, for example, Hackney's plans for decentralisation were first blocked, and then killed off by the resistance of the workforce and the management to the radical changes proposed. After a lengthy but vague public consultation period, a three-way row developed between the tenants, the councillors and white-collar workers. At first the staff union boycotted all work on decentralisation, and finally, when that dispute was sorted out, the council decided not to fill various vacant posts, since decentralisation meant that they might be deleted. Nalgo took this to mean a cut in staffing and demanded that the decision be reversed, effectively ending negotiations on decentralisation. Three years later, the newly elected Labour administration of Hammersmith and Fulham suffered the same fate, abandoning its decentralisation plans in the face of opposition from its workforce.

In St Helens, a left-wing administration faced similar problems in 1983. Its attempts to reorganise the council provoked an eight-week strike by all 1800 Nalgo members. The objective of the reorganisation was to collapse a number of hierarchies and, according to the local Nalgo district officer, it would have a bad effect on many members' career prospects by creating 'a huge number of dead ends right through the ranks'. The strike started when computer staff in the Treasurer's department refused to co-operate with a move to the Chief Executive's department, claiming insufficient consultation. The council argued that it had discussed the move with the workers' trade union leaders but the results of this consultation had not been passed on. The new administration said that they were prepared to talk, but they were unwilling to allow Nalgo the power of veto it had exercised over previous reforms. Even the chief officers came out. Here the dispute was not about cuts or redundancies, but ostensibly about a right of consultation. Sharron (1984) argues that the strike is best seen as 'a reaction by frightened staff who put their career interests, and a concern to maintain their professional preroga- tives, before consideration of efficiency or more accessible or accountable services'.

Similar issues were at play in a housing dispute in Sheffield. The council was trying to introduce new technology in the face of opposition from Nalgo which had, some years previously, won an agreement that said, rather confusingly, 'A status quo will apply to all applications covered by this agreement'. This type of woolly wording was typical of agreements which on the face of it gave unions the power of veto. Here there was also, according to two of the Sheffield strikers, 'a small group of activists from the far Left [who] worked very hard to assist the strike' (*New Socialist*, March 1985). The *Socialist Worker*, the newspaper of the Socialist Workers Party, called on Sheffield workers to intensify their action: 'Escalation is the key to winning the dispute, as both Nalgo and the council will realise.'

The role of the SWP in promoting industrial action has been highly publicised, not least by the SWP itself. The pages of *Socialist Worker* often implied that the organisation was running revolutionary struggles in most of the Labour authorities in the country. Of the Islington nursery workers' strike, the paper said: 'The escalation, which will involve social services, housing depart- ments and computer operators, is a big step forward, but it must be used to build for an all-out strike.' Of course, the SWP has its own agenda. As the major Trotskyist party, which has refused to get involved in alliances with Labour party members, it has a vested interest in demonstrating the failures of initiatives on the Labour Left and the consequent necessity for an all-out revolu- tionary strategy. For SWP members there is no delicate balance to be achieved between the interests of the workers and those of the tenants and ratepayers who are the consumers of council services. They argue that local government employers are indis- tinguishable from their private capitalist counterparts. By escalat- ing strikes, and forcing Labour councillors to respond, the SWP aims to show up the limits of reformist politics and to win people to their cause. During a dispute in Liverpool in 1984 the paper said: 'Unless local authority unions remain independent of their councils, members' interests will be sacrificed for a spurious unity.'

It would be a mistake, however, to exaggerate the role of SWP members in Town Hall disputes. Often they were simply an irritant, to trade unionists as well as to council managers. They were less influential than those union activists who were also active Labour party members and who saw accelerating industrial action as a way of mobilising workers and preventing 'cuts'.

Underlying all this was the central unresolved problem for public sector trade unionists of organising where the boss is not a capitalist company intent on maximising profits, but a democratic- ally accountable public body attempting to provide collective services for local people. In many cases the taxpayers for inner city councils, and the customers of the services it provides, are poorer and more powerless than the workers. Yet trade unions have tended to insist on treating industrial relations within a council as identical to those at ICI or Ford, without recognising the extent to which improving their conditions may affect service delivery, nor the effect that poor service delivery will have on public support for collective versus private provision.

Union members were drawn into industrial action because the combined effects of cuts in government grant and radical reorgan- isation plans from Left councils led to a general sense of anxiety and low morale amongst staff. Where reorganisation plans failed, it was often because the majority of staff did not feel involved or consulted, and saw only that changes would worsen their working conditions and career structures. There was no clear culture of identification of the needs of service consumers and staff did not always feel enough confidence in councillors and managers to be sure that changes would improve the quality of provision.

Absence of management

It would be wrong to simply blame town-hall unions for the problems faced by Left councils. The responsibility for balancing the demands of service consumers and producers rests squarely with politicians The problem was that councillors often failed to come to terms with the possible conflict of interest between the needs of consumer and producers. Many of the Left councillors

were decidedly uncomfortable about their new roles as managers
of very large organisations and particularly uncomfortable about
the need to set priorities. Indeed, because there were established
channels of communication between the workforce and the councillors and no equivalent forum where consumers could express
their demands, it was easier for councillors to understand the
needs of a badly paid workforce than those of service users.

Many councillors saw clearly the need to improve service
delivery. But many of their innovative policies were stillborn or
damaged by failures of political direction and failures of management. New and inexperienced administrations often made vast
numbers of policy decisions without thinking through the managerial consequences, creating impossible problems for officers.
Councillors spent a lot of time discussing issues and consulting
with a wide range of people but at times this process substituted
for a clear decision making process. An internal Haringey report
said that:

> Haringey has plenty of policies but no policy system. Haringey's
> policy system is characterised by drift: postponement of de-
> cisions; vagueness; excessive involvement of members and
> senior officers in day-to-day decisions; lack of detailed attention
> to implementation and indeed lack of implementation; lack of
> monitoring; separation of policy and budgeting; and a con-
> sequent policy vacuum filled by bargaining and fiefdom
> (Haringey, 1987).

Some of the problems related to the speed of expansion without
the management or structures being geared to handle it. In several
authorities there was no mechanism by which the quality of
services could be measured, no complaints procedure and no way
of assessing consumer demand. Expansion took place with the
emphasis on more spending rather than more effective spending.

There were more fundamental management failures. Local
authority managers were often ill-equipped and unskilled at implementing change. They clung to traditional methods and were
reluctant to accept the need for upheaval. There was no history in
public sector services of measuring efficiency, performance indica-
tors, generating innovation, or involving consumers in service
delivery. In some instances, there was no absence of goodwill but

the administration was so ineffective that decisions to improve the service could not be implemented. In others, managers were not equipped or prepared to translate policy decisions into workable changes. Unsympathetic officers at times blocked initiatives by inaction. Alternatively, the implementation of changes became bogged down because managers were unused to problem solving and they referred any difficulties to councillors. Industrial relations were made worse by the absence of training programmes and proper communication with staff, so that the intentions behind policies were not communicated. Without clear objectives and proper monitoring, it was difficult for staff to know what they were supposed to do or for managers and councillors to find out whether or not they were doing it.

Dave Sullivan, leader of Lewisham council between 1985 and 1987, was highly critical of the failure of Labour councils to manage and the councillors' neglect of their role as employers. He wrote in a paper to the local parties: 'The issue of management has nothing whatsoever to do with ideology or philosophy. All ideologies and philosophies have to be implemented in an effective way.' He suggested that in Lewisham the councillors had not managed effectively because Labour's view 'assumes that somehow the need to manage can be replaced by concepts of workers' control or industrial democracy'. Yet, Sullivan argues, 'the ultimate in industrial democracy still requires that decisions taken by the workers have to be co-ordinated and organised by the managers'. The failure by the Labour councillors to recognise this led to 'policy indigestion' and poor industrial relations. The former results in the council's initiatives 'sinking slowly into a quagmire of bureaucracy'; the problem with the latter, he says, is not really strikes and disputes, but the real issues of industrial relations – 'absenteeism, high sickness levels, high staff turnover, low productivity, flexitime abuse, excessive overtime, poor quality work, low self-esteem and low public esteem'. He argues that while Lewisham was successful in fending off the attacks on its resources by central government, this deflected the council from its real function of providing services into a defence of local government. Therefore, he concluded, 'we must urgently begin the process of transforming this authority into one that truly serves the interests of working people by using efficiently and effectively the large sums of money we take from their pockets'. Not to do so, he says, 'is nothing less than a rip-off' (Sullivan, 1987).

The Left councils' stated reason for not addressing these problems sufficiently was that they were not only engaged in internal change, but in external campaigning. There was only so much political energy to go round. The Association of London Authorities argued that 'it has to be admitted that the struggle to maintain existing services has diverted councillors' time and energy away from the kinds of problems of service delivery highlighted elsewhere in this report. This is an inevitable consequence of rate-capping and other punitive measures such as cuts in grant' (ALA, 1987). Margaret Hodge, the ALA leader, also critical of the limited impact that Left councils had on the provision of services, said

> We had to fight on too many fronts at the same time. We have had to face a whole onslaught of attacks on us by central government through the removal of grant, rate-capping, the abolition of the GLC and the met counties and so on. We were into campaigning and 'opposing'. It was Labour local authorities that provided the real opposition to the Tory government during its first two terms and there was very little energy left to do other things we should have been doing . . .

But, she continued,

> The campaign did mark the beginning of the realisation that the services we provided were not good enough. We realised that you couldn't dream up a political slogan in a Labour party committee room and expect a groundswell of support for it. We have to be honest. One of the clear messages we received is of the failure of local authorities to inspire support. One of the reasons Thatcher was able to exploit their unpopularity was because they were seen as bureaucratic, inefficient, unresponsive and paternalistic by many of those people who are dependent on what we provide (interview).

The fact that these criticisms were beginning to be made following the 1987 general election defeat illustrates how much the Left had learnt from the municipal socialism experiment, mainly through bitter experience. In the Left councils, there were some welcome expansions in basic service provision, and some important innovations, especially in relation to child care, care of the elderly and greater client consultation. Decentralisation, in several boroughs, stands out as a major achievement. But elsewhere, policies to decentralise services were blocked, or seriously truncated because of union opposition. The revolution in the relationship between the council and the people never happened. The cost of this failure, in political terms, was very serious. The new Left administrations were committed to winning the support of the users of council services in their fight against the government. Consumers often recognised and appreciated the attempts Left administrations were making to find out and to respond to the choices and preferences of the local population. But this was often combined with deep frustration about the councils inability to deliver effectively, as a result of both their own failings and the government's increasing restrictions. The failure to turn increased spending into a visible improvement in service delivery, cost the Left councils the wholehearted support of local people.

It meant that when the Tory party and the press renewed their onslaught on Left Labour councils as inefficient and profligate, their arguments made partial sense to service users. Moreover, it strengthened the government's hand, when they decided to intervene not merely to cut local authority spending, but to try to enforce the transfer to the private sector of many of the services that councils provided.

7 The Race against Racism

'This was exemplified in the autumn of 1979 when the principal race advisor and the race advisor in management services were given a hostile reception at a shop stewards meeting in one of the large predominantly blue-collar directorates. Their instant view of the Race Relations Unit and the Equal Opportunities Policy was encapsulated in a statement made by one of the stewards: "We know what you're up to. If you think you're going to turn up with a truck load of niggers on a Monday morning and tell us we have to take them on, you've got another thing coming!"' (Ouseley, 1983, p. 170).

This chapter and the following two examine the municipal Left's initiatives on equal opportunities for blacks, women and gays and lesbians. The roots of these initiatives lay very much outside the traditional Labour movement, stemming from the single issue campaigns and community action of the 1970s. Disenchanted with the limitations of this kind of pressure group politics, and growing weary of internal splits, many of the activists joined the Labour party and attempted to broaden its concerns away from traditional issues. Some became councillors themselves. So, gradually, these new concerns crept onto the political agenda.

The interest in equal opportunities originated in and was always much greater in London than outside, where, with the main exception of Manchester, the influx of new councillors was still dominated in the early 1980s by the more traditional Left. Sheffield, for example, while by no means opposed to the importance of this new thrust, continued to give higher priority to traditional Labour concerns such as housing, social services and jobs, and the council never established separate race or women's committees. The Militant dominated Liverpool council was openly hostile. Militant has seen the pursuit of sex and race equality and gay rights as diversionary and subordinate to traditional class objectives, and was always scathing of what Derek Hatton had described as the 'yuppie' style of the London Left. 'They were more concerned with image than reality. The Labour boroughs in London, with their obsessions about anti-racist and anti-sexist issues were . . . more concerned that we called the chairman the chairperson, or a manhole cover a personhole cover, than they ever were about the real issues' (Hatton, 1988).

The Left's interest in equal opportunities, however, can be seen as extending the traditional pursuit of equality beyond that of reducing old class and economic divisions, to one of reducing wider social inequalities. It is about spreading opportunities to those who have been denied them in the past, who have been excluded from the mainstream of social and political life. It is therefore deeply rooted in Labour's primary concern with equality and justice.

But as well as fitting basic socialist principles, these initiatives have also come to have a wider political imperative. Since the war, industrial change has led to a steady decline in the size of Labour's traditional constituency – the male, manual working class. In the process, the Labour party, as well as finding its natural support dwindle, began to lose touch with popular concerns. Most people no longer identify themselves primarily as workers, but according to their gender, their race or as consumers and individuals. The means of political expression for these new concerns came, not through the traditional Labour movement, but through what have become known as 'new social movements' – the peace movement, the women's movement, anti-racist groups and, more recently, the ecology and environmental lobby. Society is now more complex and differentiated with a diversity of interests and new historic needs beyond those which socialism attempted to tackle in its earliest days. Some have defended these new policies as not only consistent with Labour's traditional concern with the disadvantaged, but as a crucial element in rebuilding Labour's support. They have argued that it is possible to build a new coalition of interests out of these fragmented and heterogeneous groups, a 'Rainbow Alliance', among minority and other disadvantaged groups who may not have traditionally voted Labour. While the potential for winning power through such an alliance alone is slim, these changes have created a new political agenda, new constituencies and priorities, including a concern with equal opportunities.

Racial equality

The first of these new initiatives to emerge was the pursuit of racial equality. From the late 1960s, report after report had pinpointed the widespread social and economic disadvantages suffered by Britain's black, and especially Afro-Caribbean, population. Since the large wave of Caribbean immigration in the late 1950s, black people have suffered higher rates of unemployment and poorer housing and education than whites.

This was the joint product of the relatively disadvantaged economic position of the black population and of discrimination. Although legislation in 1965, 1968 and 1976, which outlawed individual acts of discrimination, succeeded in eliminating the more blatant examples of racism such as the 'no blacks' accommodation and job advertising, it did little or nothing to remove the much more subtle, widespread and deep-rooted forms of discrimination.

From the late 1960s, a variety of government measures sought to tackle urban decline, including the urban programme and educational priority areas. Only one of these was aimed specifically at the black population – section 11 of the 1966 Local Government Act under which local authorities could claim grants to employ extra staff to meet the special needs of 'Commonwealth immigrants'. In the case of the other programmes, it was assumed that the alleviation of urban deprivation would help black and white equally.

Gradually, however, this 'colour blind' approach began to be questioned and pressure mounted for a more direct approach. Some inner city Labour parties with large black populations grew concerned at the lack of black involvement in the Labour party and their lack of representation on councils. During the 1970s, there were only a handful of black councillors and no black MPs.

The second half of the 1970s also saw the growth of the National Front as an electoral force. They fielded 90 candidates at the

October 1974 general election. In 1976, Martin Webster polled 16 per cent for the National Front in a West Bromwich parliamentary by-election, and the party was getting similar votes in local elections. This led to the rise of organised opposition through the formation of the Anti-Nazi League and the 'Rock Against Racism' concerts and to violent clashes during National Front marches. While the initiative for this opposition came largely from outside the Labour party, and especially from the Socialist Workers Party, the effect was to push race firmly onto the local political agenda.

During the 1970s several councils had paid lip service to the need to take account of black people's needs in the provision of services and jobs. In practice, this had rarely meant more than funding local community relations councils and 'worthy' black community groups, and the appointment of special social workers and teachers. In Lambeth in 1977, the local Community Relations Council challenged this 'colour blind' approach in a report which called for the establishment of a race relations unit at the town hall. Lambeth had one of the highest proportions of black people in London, around a quarter, yet there were no black councillors and relatively few black officers. Nevertheless, this proposal was rejected by the then Labour administration, though the council did appoint a race adviser in housing in February 1978 to investigate claims of discrimination in the housing department.

In the 1978 borough elections, Labour's manifesto said, 'Labour will not tolerate any form of discrimination against black people. We will establish a procedure to review all aspects of Council policy, to prevent any possibility of discrimination, direct or indirect'. After the elections, a race relations unit was established, the first of its kind. The author of the Community Relations Council report, Herman Ouseley, was appointed the head of the unit, additional advisers were appointed in social services and personnel and a new Community Affairs Committee was established with responsibility for tackling racial disadvantage.

These steps set the pattern for race policies elsewhere. The race unit was given unprecedented political clout with direct access to the council leader and committee chairs, the chief executive and departmental directors. Advisers could submit reports direct to committees unaltered by senior officers. Previously, only directors had enjoyed such independence and access to power.

The role of the unit was to develop policies to tackle discrimination and to improve access to jobs and services by reducing both individual and institutional racism. The first major change was the introduction of race record keeping. New application forms were introduced and a staff survey undertaken to determine the racial mix of all departments, to identify black under-representation and to monitor the impact of the policy changes.

Committees began to draw up 'positive action programmes', a term coined from the USA where anti-discrimination policies had been pioneered over a decade before. The programmes were designed to redress past imbalances, promote equal opportunities and ensure that any special needs of the black community were met. To overcome the serious under-representation of black people in the allocation of housing, especially in the more popular properties, for example, a target of 30 per cent was adopted, a figure which mirrored the black population of the borough. In social services, records showed that a majority of children taken into care were black, and in order to reduce the need for institutional care, the council promoted a new programme to recruit more foster and adoptive parents from the black community. Advertising, selection and promotion procedures were changed to remove barriers to fair recruitment. Advertisements were placed in the black press and applications, short-listing and interviews were monitored by the race advisers. Job specifications and the need for formal qualifications were reviewed to check that they did not inadvertently discriminate. Compulsory race awareness training was introduced for all management staff with recruitment responsibilities.

At every turn, the policies encountered opposition and hostility. The 22-strong Tory group regarded the race unit as political gimmickry, a waste of time and money, and consistently opposed its recommendations. Although in public the Labour group unanimously supported the development of explicit policies on race, some on the Right were very lukewarm about the proposals.

There was also considerable suspicion among existing staff. The changes challenged the power, status, prospects and the comfortable way of operating among senior officials. To give them clout and status, the race advisers were paid at levels above the responsibility of the job, which caused resentment. Although many officials were sympathetic to the new policies, others were openly critical and there was inevitably some dragging of feet.

Among junior and manual staff opposition was often much more overt.

The introduction of race monitoring and targets was particularly controversial. Many officials took the view that there was no discrimination problem anyway. Others saw these moves as a threat to their own jobs and promotion prospects, particularly in a period of cuts. These fears were fuelled by the policies being widely, and often deliberately, misinterpreted as positive discrimination in favour of blacks. As a result, the first voluntary headcount had only a 30 per cent response, with the lowest responses from manual workers.

Despite this resistance, the policies were successful in giving black people a fairer deal. Black staff increased from an estimated 8 per cent in 1978 to a quarter in 1985. Highly sought-after manual posts such as dustmen and building apprenticeships, traditionally filled through nepotism and therefore almost exclusively white, were opened up to black people. There was a substantial rise in the proportion of black staff given secondment to professional social services' courses. The monitoring of housing allocations showed that black people obtained a fairer share of the popular properties after the introduction of targets and new allocation policies. New and more relevant provision was made for the needs of particular black clients such as the black elderly in old people's homes.

Inevitably, there were limits to the pace of change. The white dominance of middle and senior management remained largely intact. The new policies coincided with the ever tightening squeeze on town hall spending, and low recruitment slowed the rate at which the racial imbalance in the workforce could be changed. And, however radical the policies, they could only touch the surface of the backlog of racial disadvantage suffered by local black residents.

While Lambeth pioneered many of these policies, it was not alone in taking new race initiatives. Other councils which introduced similar measures at the time included the London boroughs of Haringey, Camden, Lewisham and Hackney. They were later joined by the GLC and, after the 1982 local elections, by Brent, Newham, Southwark, Islington and Greenwich. Councils with anti-racist policies outside the capital included Bradford, Leicester, Coventry, Nottinghamshire, the West Midlands and Greater Manchester.

These councils varied widely in the policies adopted and the degree of commitment. Most appointed race advisers; some established new committees with responsibility for race, and introduced some form of ethnic monitoring; others introduced the concept of the 'race dimension' into policy making, introduced equal opportunity training, and altered the disciplinary code to outlaw discriminatory behaviour; nearly all declared themselves 'equal opportunity employers'. The handful of most committed councils, including Lambeth, Brent, Haringey and the GLC, adopted all these policies (Ouseley, 1984).

Some councils with large Asian populations such as Brent, Newham and Bradford drew up new plans to tackle the growing problem of racial harassment. This included a tougher policy on evictions for tenants found guilty of harassment, the translation of literature into ethnic minority languages, the introduction of record keeping of all cases of harassment, pressure on the police to take the offence more seriously and the funding of special advisers and counsellors. Manchester employed a graffiti squad to deal with racist graffiti on school premises and public places.

Some education authorities, concerned with the problem of serious under-achievement among Afro-Carribbean pupils, introduced multi-cultural elements into the curriculum aimed at reducing the previous white and Eurocentric emphasis but this often meant little more than 'adding black history and culture to the margins of the curriculum' (Ouseley, 1984, p.149). The number of education authorities with multi-cultural policies rose from only two in 1981 to 80 in 1988, more than two-thirds of all authorities. Other councils such as the ILEA, Brent and Haringey initiated policies to recruit more black teachers, secured anti-racist declarations with teacher organisations, removed racist publications from schools and attempted to recruit more black parents as governors.

There were also attempts to involve more black people in decision making. Some councils like Greenwich and Hackney co-opted blacks onto committees, while Lewisham set up a Joint Working Party on race relations. The GLC initiated special consultative forums on issues such as youth, health, the elderly and the arts. A consultative conference on the 'Challenge of Racism in London' in March 1983 attracted more than 850 people. As we have seen, the GLC and other Metropolitan councils introduced contract compliance, by which they agreed not to trade with firms refusing to comply with reasonable requirements to pursue equal opportunity policies, including the recruitment of black workers.

There are now few Labour councils in areas with a significant ethnic minority population which have not moved beyond the 'no problems here' attitudes of the 1970s. The initiatives were broadly welcomed by other organisations with similar objectives such as the Commission for Racial Equality and the Runnymede Trust. Even some hung councils under dominant Conservative control such as Hammersmith and Fulham and Bradford developed similar policies.

Following the riots which exploded in St Paul's, Brixton and Toxteth in the Spring and Summer of 1981, and the subsequent publication of the Scarman Report, the early momentum gathered pace. The number of black councillors soared from only a handful in 1978 to 165 across the country by 1986. In 1987, three London boroughs had black leaders – Linda Bellos in Lambeth, Bernie Grant in Haringey and Merle Amory in Brent. Inner city Labour parties began to give increasing recognition to the importance of the black vote in securing power. In the 1987 general election, four black Labour MPs were elected to Parliament. Added to this, there was increasing pressure from black activists. The growing body of race advisers and professionals began to develop their own methodology and allies in pursuing anti-racist policies. The very success of the policies in recruiting more black staff led to the establishment of black worker groups in many town halls. Some local Labour parties, against the opposition of the national Labour leadership, formed their own black sections.

The tabloid attack

Although aspects of these race equality policies were always controversial, initially the rows were contained within the town hall. Race policies rarely hit the headlines. The main sources of anti-Labour propaganda or 'loony left' attacks at the time were high rates, unguarded remarks and 'red flags'.

Gradually, however, Labour's anti-racist policies became a major source of 'loony left' attacks. Throughout 1986, the *Sun*, the *Daily Mail* and the *Mail on Sunday* ran a series of bizarre allegations about London boroughs, most of which centred on race. It was claimed, for example, that 'Bernie Grant's Haringey' had banned the use of black dustbin liners as racist; that Hackney, Haringey and Islington Councils had banned the nursery rhyme 'Baa Baa Black Sheep'; that Brent had paid for free trips for unemployed black youths to go to Cuba; that Camden had banned the word 'sunshine' as racially offensive; that Haringey was committed to teaching West Indian dialect in schools.

A study of ten of these stories by the Media Research Group of Goldsmiths College, London, found all to be either inventions or deliberate distortions. The 'black bin liners' story was entirely fictitious. Days after the article appeared, Haringey accepted a tender from a local supplier of black liners. Despite this, the *Mail on Sunday* continued to publish letters on the issue such as 'am I a racist in the eyes of Bernie Grant as I am the owner of a black cat, a brown dog, a red car, a yellow canary and several boxes of white typed paper?' The story about freebie trips to Cuba for black youngsters paid for by Brent Council was also false. The less sensational facts were that a local community group called Caribbean Exchange had held a series of fund-raising events to finance some trips, but the Council had refused financial support.

Other stories were heavily distorted. The 'Baa Baa Black Sheep' story surfaced in Hackney in February 1986 and ran for more than a year in a large number of national and local newspapers from Carlisle to Ipswich. Far from banning the rhyme, the truth was that an independent parent-run nursery in Hackney, the Beevers play group, had for some time sung 'Baa Baa White Sheep' as an alternative humorous version of the song. The story then resurfaced in Haringey in October 1986 with a different slant that the Council had ordered playgroup leaders to attend a race awareness course where they were instructed to ban the rhyme as racist. The facts were that playgroup leaders in the borough had requested the course, that attendance was voluntary and that there was no such ban. In February 1987, the same story appeared in Islington, and despite council denials, the story nearly featured in an SDP party political broadcast by John Cleese until it was withdrawn at the last moment, on legal advice.

The product of rumour spread by Tory councillors who fed stories to the press, of anti-Labour staff and tabloid journalists searching for sensational copy, these stories were very damaging to the London Labour party. Indefensible as these lies and distortions were, however, Labour councils were not always the innocent victims they liked to claim. They had often helped to create the kind of climate in which it was possible for such stories to thrive.

In addition, the response by councillors and press officials in the boroughs concerned sometimes added to the confusion. In the case of the 'Baa Baa Black Sheep' story, for example, Hackney council, without checking the facts, issued a statement to the *Sun* in support of the nursery and of the parents' right to ban the song.

Moreover, not all such stories were fictitious. Several officials were disciplined for the use of language defined as racist, such as when a senior GLC personnel officer was accused of racism for use of the term 'jungle drums' in reference to the internal grapevine. In other instances, councils scored massive own goals. Just prior to the London borough elections in May 1986, for example, Lambeth Council's Amenities Committee voted to rename 28 council parks, libraries and other facilities after international black politicians and cultural figures. One of the most well known parks in south London, Brockwell Park in Herne Hill, was to be renamed Zephania Mothopeng Park after a black South African leader serving 30 years in gaol. Streatham baths was to be called Mangaliso Sobukwe pool after the late founder of the African National Congress.

The scheme was the brainchild of Councillor Sharon Atkin. A longstanding black activist, she was subsequently dropped by Labour's NEC as a parliamentary candidate just before the 1987 election for a public attack on the Labour party as 'racist'. These proposals were greeted with incredulity even among those sympathetic to the council's anti-racist objectives. Even the local Left-dominated Labour party was horrified at what it saw as an entirely tokenistic and counter-productive proposal, and suicidal so close to an election. The ruling Labour group quietly dropped the idea.

Turning sour

Moreover, while the anti-racist objectives were entirely justified, this was not always true of the means. Often the success of anti-racist policies was measured more by inputs – the number of race advisers, their status, the level of grant provided to black groups, than outputs – the number of black people who benefited and the introduction of fairer recruitment and allocation policies.

Serious concern began to grow among some committed politicians and officers about the direction of the anti-racist strategies. This applied particularly to the much tougher approach to allegations of racism by individuals. As well as tackling institutional racism, most councils had also tightened up their disciplinary procedures for rooting out individual racism. As a result, the number of accusations of racism mushroomed. In some instances, the accusations were dismissed, as in the Camden case, of an official taken before a disciplinary hearing for allegedly calling his black manager 'sunshine' in a derogatory manner. The worker claimed the word was common cockney parlance and the hearing found the use of the word was not racist. Dealing with allegations of racism is inevitably plagued with the problem of subjectivity. Often it is also a matter of one person's word against another. Resolving such disputes can be time-consuming, long-winded and the source of much bitterness.

More seriously, accusations of racism were sometimes the product of simple personal ambition. The 'race card' was played to obtain an unjustified promotion, to hit back at managers or colleagues or for protection against disciplinary action. One senior, white and widely-respected housing manager in Lambeth, for example, found himself on a disciplinary charge of racism for reprimanding a black worker for persistent absenteeism.

The tougher approach to racism also fuelled the tension created by the new policies within town halls. Supporters of the new stance felt it was justified in the promotion of greater equality, but the price was often an uncomfortable atmosphere in which accusations of racism could be made on the slightest pretext. Even committed officials began to talk of a 'climate of fear' and witch-hunts.

Clapton Park Nursery

The kind of problem generated by accusations of racism is illustrated by a long-lasting, bitter dispute, involving a Hackney council nursery in 1985. The dispute began over a minor issue. Sue Warner, the matron in charge of Clapton Park Nursery, on the advice of senior management, took disciplinary action against a new black nursery nurse, Veronica Wade. A Jehovah's Witness, she couldn't carry out parts of her job description such as taking part in religious festivals or birthday celebrations. Wade was cleared but because the problem of her duties was not resolved, she was switched from her normal teamwork to other duties. As she considered this to be a demotion, her case was taken up by the Nalgo black workers' group in Hackney.

In response, senior management directed Warner to let Wade resume normal duties. But the matron refused claiming that management was simply ducking the problem, and Warner was suspended. Her union, Nupe, then called a strike at the nursery, during which it was kept open by parents and local black activists. The four-week strike became increasingly bitter with accusations of intimidation on both sides. Following a mass picket and a week-long occupation of Hackney Social Services headquarters by Nupe members, Warner was reprimanded but reinstated.

The black activists who had kept the nursery open were opposed to Warner's reinstatement, demanded her replacement with a black matron and re-occupied the nursery to press their demands. What had begun as a dispute over a job description had escalated into a matter of principle about racism. The occupiers believed that the nursery, in which the great majority of children were black, should not have three white senior managers. They accused the white managers of unspecified racism; accused the council of paying only lip service to racial equality; and demanded the appointment of black staff at the nursery and a general enquiry into the racial balance of senior staff in Hackney's nurseries.

The dispute continued for nearly a year. The council attempted several times to launch an enquiry to settle it but had difficulty in persuading anyone to sit on it. Eventually it was only settled when Paul Boateng, a black solicitor and now MP for Brent South, agreed to a one person review of the dispute.

The dispute left a bitter trail. The matron and her deputies, all white, were subjected to considerable personal abuse and hostile local publicity, and felt that they were effectively hounded out of their jobs. The black activists believed that they had a powerful case – that an almost all-black nursery should not be run by all-white management with the few black staff in junior positions.

The dispute illustrates another phenomenon in councils committed to vigorous anti-racist policies – the creation of a momentum for change, a 'frontlash'. The act of commitment creates expectations. Early success in expanding the number of black staff increases the likelihood of accusations of racism, and leads to pressure for faster change than is feasible. Black activists believed that in the Clapton Park dispute the council was dragging its feet, yet their pressure inevitably met with resistance from the workforce who saw their own interests at risk. The white nursery managers were unwilling to step aside to make way for new black managers, and were backed by colleagues in a similar position. The dispute led to sharp divisions between the unions involved, with NALGO backing the black activists and NUPE backing the reinstatement of the nursery staff.

Squeezed between these opposing forces, the council was unable to resolve the dispute. Because of its commitment to racial equality, it was unprepared to back the nursery managers, although they argued that they were innocent victims of the dispute. If the council could have afforded to expand its workforce, it would have been easier to have created more jobs for black staff without arousing hostility among existing white workers. But the arrival of equal opportunity commitments coincided with cuts in government grant.

Maureen McGoldrick

Of the many disputes around anti-racism, the Maureen McGoldrick affair had the widest ramifications. It led to a prolonged and bitter public row which plunged Brent council into turmoil, did enormous damage to the Labour party and raised fundamental questions about anti-racist policies.

Maureen McGoldrick was the headteacher of Sudbury Infants School in Brent, which was 85 per cent non-white. On the last day of the summer term of 1986, she was suspended by a senior education official. McGoldrick had phoned to try to sort out a longstanding problem of four staff vacancies. A junior official, Sheila Szulc, proposed an Indian teacher.

What happened next remains unresolved. Szulc alleged that McGoldrick said that she didn't want any more black teachers.

Because of the council's strong anti-racist commitments,
McGoldrick was summoned to explain herself and seen by Gordon
Mott, a senior education officer and Szulc's immediate manager,
Richard Twining. McGoldrick was accompanied by John Poole,
the secretary of the local NUT, the Brent Teachers' Association
(BTA). In a stormy meeting, McGoldrick denied the remark,
claiming that she had simply expressed concern about the pro-
posed teacher's lack of relevant experience, but was suspended.

A month later, the school governors, after investigating the
allegations, unanimously backed the head and recommended reinstatement. Unmoved, the council decided to press ahead with a
disciplinary hearing. This led to a strike by teachers at Sudbury.
The BTA won a High Court injunction to stop disciplinary
proceedings on the grounds that the council had acted improperly
after McGoldrick had been exonerated by the governors.

This judgement, however, appeared to conflict with the prece-
dent set in the Court of Appeal a year earlier in another prolonged
legal wrangle over the Ray Honeyford case in Bradford. In order
to clarify the law, Brent council lodged an appeal and refused to
lift the suspension. Following the threat of a strike by the NUT
throughout Brent, the council agreed in October to reinstate
McGoldrick but to proceed with the appeal. In November, nearly
four months after the suspension, the Appeal Court upheld the
council's right to hold a disciplinary hearing, but in response to the
national uproar the council dropped the case.

The dispute was accompanied by intense hostility. Throughout,
the council refused to budge, and gathered the backing of the
Brent Black Teachers' Collective, the Socialist Teachers' Alliance
and several local headteachers. McGoldrick, on the other hand,
was backed by parents and governors at the school and the BTA.
Later, she gained the support of the most moderate of the three
local constituency Labour parties, Brent North, and Neil Kinnock.

The dispute was portrayed by most of the press, and much of the
Labour movement, in a rather simplistic way as a witchhunt by a
Left-dominated, stubborn and unreasonable council against an
innocent victim. Certainly, McGoldrick was an unlikely villain.
Unlike Ray Honeyford, who was a vigorous Right-wing opponent
of anti-racism, she had a good track record on race with testi-
monials from parents, teachers and governors.

However, if a dispute of this magnitude was going to surface anywhere, Brent was the most likely place. At 60 per cent, it had the highest proportion of black people of any local authority in the country. For years there had been growing concern nationally among black parents about the poor educational performance of their children. This dissatisfaction was particularly strong in Brent, where confidence in the local education system was low.

Up to 1982, Brent council had only limited policies on race. After the borough elections in 1982, that changed when the number of black councillors increased from 3 to 13. The new council immediately introduced anti-racist policies and set about increasing the number of black staff. This involved a much greater degree of interference from the centre, including an involvement in shortlisting candidates and the attendance of race advisers at interview. These policies reflected the view that the roots of black under-achievement lay in 'racism' of both teachers and wider society.

The white-dominated BTA resented this interference. It alleged that the council had announced the new measures without prior consultation. More fundamentally, the BTA saw the new pro-posals as a threat to the power and independence of headteachers and refused co-operation. It showed its antagonism to them by boycotting a study commissioned in 1983 by the council into black children's 'failure' in the school system which was chaired by Jocelyn Barrow, a black governor of the BBC.

This power struggle was intensified by the new politics in the borough. The council and the local party, as elsewhere, had moved to the Left. Voicing the anger and frustration about the education system felt by many black parents, especially the imbalance between white teachers and black pupils, many of the new black councillors wanted rapid change. As one leading black member of the Education Committee is quoted as saying in the Jocelyn Barrow report, 'When I see in the south of Brent, 80 per cent of children but only 5 per cent of teachers come from the ethnic minority community, I say that's wrong. I say its morally indefensible'.

Eighteen months after the elections, Labour lost control when a maverick black councillor, Ambrosine Neil, who had campaigned unsuccessfully for an all-black school, switched sides to the Tories. The Tories formed a shaky administration with the support of two Liberals. Ironically, this did not stop the pursuit of vigorous anti-racist policies. The Tories had always opposed the race initiatives, but the Liberals supported them, and forced the Tories to go along with this. In fact, because of the lack of interest of the Tories, the newly-appointed, zealous race advisers were left more or less to their own devices and enjoyed even greater influence.

The pressure for change was also encouraged by black activists. The most infamous was Kuba Assegai, a member of Brent South Labour party. A governor of two schools, he had intervened in lessons and had several furious exchanges with white teachers. An outspoken critic of the white dominance of the BTA, he helped to raise tension both before and during the McGoldrick affair. According to one parent at a meeting of black parents at McGoldrick's school, 'he shouted down everyone who disagreed with him. People were really scared of him'. Assegai's wife, Janet Hope-Bogle, was a junior official in charge of the council's supply-teaching pool. She, too, had antagonised teachers by her remarks in a report in 1985 for her previous employer, Brent Council for Community Relations: 'The black community is being more than generous by continuing to send its children to Brent schools to allow their minds to be brutalised by racist individuals in racist institutions.' The new education race adviser, Soonu Engineer, was also a powerful figure in the department.

An alliance of black activists, Left councillors, zealous new officials and black teachers set about making race a central issue and hastening the appointment of black teachers. While both aims were widely supported across the Labour group, the methods used were much more contentious. Under the new policies, teacher recruitment had to conform to a new code of practice, known locally as the 'little red book'. As well as laying down guidelines to prevent discrimination, the Code allowed race advisers full access to the appointments process including shortlisting and the effective right of veto. Many teachers suspected that it was used to fix shortlists and overturn appointments, and the new procedures developed a bad local reputation.

Many interviews were dominated by questions about race and concern grew that professional judgements were neglected and that black candidates were too often promoted or selected over more experienced white teachers. There were allegations that references were altered to give a more favourable impression of black candidates. The council seemed to become obsessed with racism. Accusations of racism against teachers and officials were commonplace. The exercise of professional judgement became increasingly difficult for fear that any form of criticism, however constructive, might be wrongly construed. There were no checks on the abuse of power in this climate. Demoralisation was widespread.

Before the McGoldrick case exploded, two senior officials, Mott, the education officer for schools and Robin Richardson, a senior adviser and race relations expert, were under threat of an internal departmental enquiry. They had been criticised, though not directly by name, in a report to the Education Committee by Soonu Engineer. She accused them of dragging their feet over bids to the Home Office for new grant-aided multi-cultural teaching posts and of threatening the future of the whole scheme. At the same time a press release was issued by the Brent Black Alliance, an organisation supported by Kuba Assegai, calling for the sacking of both Mott and Richardson, accusing them of being 'white supremacists' who had sabotaged the anti-racist policies.

The tension that haunted the implementation of race policies was further fuelled by the publication of Jocelyn Barrow's report in 1986. It concluded that the education system in Brent was 'permeated with racism both overt and covert'. Politicians, teachers and administrators were all seen as guilty, 'outright racists, patronising, biased, ethnocentric or simply naively ignorant of the racist context in which they work'.

Despite lots of positive suggestions, the report had severe limitations. Since teachers had refused to co-operate with the enquiry team, it had been unable to visit schools, and had based much of its evidence on the views of black parents alone. Its inadequacies were later outlined by one of the members of the enquiry, Raj Ray, in a strongly-worded article in *The Times Educational Supplement*. Nevertheless, the council gave the report its full backing, widening the gulf between teachers and the council.

Both the report and the council missed the message coming from black parents – concern with low standards. This is why so many black parents send their children to supplementary weekend schools – private schools where they get a very formal and traditional training. While anti-racist policies aimed at raising teacher expectations are important, they are not a substitute for

ensuring basic standards are high. Other education authorities also
committed to anti-racism seem to have, sometimes belatedly,
accepted this. The ILEA which had pioneered many race initiatives in schools changed its priorities by giving greater emphasis to
raising traditional standards overall. This is a crucial lesson for
all Left councils committed to high profile anti-discrimination
policies. The task of ensuring that black children achieve well in
schools is a complex one.

The element of anti-racist policies which was to prove almost as
heated as the McGoldrick saga was the appointment of 170 new
teachers in Brent, with responsibility for encouraging race equality. Part of the drive to bring a multi-cultural curriculum and
encourage higher expectations of black children, the new post-
holders, all teachers, were to have responsibility for advice on the
curriculum, staff and general school development. The scheme
had all-party support and was born during the Tory/Liberal
coalition before the McGoldrick case. The posts were to be part-
funded by the Home Office.

In the wake of the McGoldrick publicity, the scheme proved
another boon to the tabloids. The new posts were variously
dubbed as 'race spies', 'commissars in the classroom' or 'thought
police'. Senior teachers were divided about the value of the new
scheme. But by now, even teachers sympathetic to the objectives
of the council were becoming increasingly frustrated by the
atmosphere in the borough. As one secondary school head of
department put it, 'It's not that the council's aims are wrong, it's
the way they are going about implementing them. It doesn't do
any good to go into schools and tell teachers who've devoted their
whole careers to working hard for black and white kids that they're
racist.' The education department was in a state of permanent
crisis. Teachers and heads left in droves, and posts were difficult to
fill. A quarter of parents, both black and white, opted for schools
outside Brent. In 1986, five senior officials, including the director
and two assistant directors, quit the council.

The McGoldrick affair caused untold damage to race policies.
The relentless publicity threw a cloud over many of the positive
aspects of Brent's policies. The climate could hardly be less
conducive for the implementation of radical change. The saga
helped to fuel the 'loony Left' label coined by the tabloids and
some Tory leaders. Brent was subsequently dubbed the 'looniest

council of the year' by the *Sun* in its ongoing campaign against Labour town halls. The issue proved a turning point in Labour's fortunes in London. Labour had done well in the 1986 London borough elections. From then its support started to slump. It was certainly one of the key factors in the 'London Effect', the anti-Labour feeling in the capital attributed to council policies by Patricia Hewitt, Neil Kinnock's press officer, after the disastrous loss of the Greenwich by-election in March 1987. The reaction of Neil Kinnock and the Labour leadership throughout was entirely dismissive. Yet politically embarrassing as the affair was proving, an approach which attempted to draw attention to the very real problems of racial disadvantage with which Brent and other councils had to grapple might have initiated a much-needed constructive debate on the issues.

While the row was at its peak, Kenneth Baker, the Education Secretary, ordered a hurried enquiry into education in Brent by Her Majesty's Inspectors, hoping to make political capital out of what was expected to be a critical report just before the local elections in May and the general election in June 1987.

Baker's expectations were not entirely fulfilled by the report, but he immediately used it to condemn the council. Overall, the education service came out badly. Lessons were found to be dull and boring, expectations of children were low, discipline and management poor and morale low. The bleakness of the report was rare for the HMI. But the council's race policies were largely exonerated. They were found to have 'widespread support' among parents and schools and went with the 'grain of local opinion', though there was widespread criticism of the way they were implemented. The inspectors found little evidence that work was 'being distorted by improper practices to do with anti-racist policies' or that the quality of school work had deteriorated because of them. Rather they found that the policies 'had a generally helpful effect in the classroom'.

In the final analysis, it is irrelevant whether Mrs McGoldrick made the fateful remark or not. In most other areas the incident would have been resolved in a low key way, perhaps with a chat between officials and a union representative. In Brent, however, the underlying tensions and the pressure on officials to take a hard line on race ensured that the incident snowballed into one of the *causes célèbres* of the 1980s.

No one comes out with much credit. The council showed incompetence and mismanagement. Many actions of the black activists, pressure groups and some of the council's own race relations staff only inflamed the situation. The professionalism and sensitivity needed for the success of anti-race policies seemed absent. Throughout, the BTA batted largely for its own self-interest. The tragedy was that as a result of the affair, many Brent parents, both black and white lost confidence in the local schools, teachers left in droves and the schoolchildren suffered.

Dewsbury and Manchester

During 1987 and 1988 there were two other major rows – in Dewsbury and Manchester – over race relations and education. In Dewsbury, a group of parents had wanted to send their children to a predominantly white school but they had been allocated places by Kirklees council in a school where 85 per cent of the children were Asian. They withheld their children and, after educating them privately for a year, the parents won a court case on a technicality and were allowed to send them to the school of their choice. The policy of sending the children to the predominantly Asian school was not inspired mainly by the council's anti-racist policy but was an attempt to maintain the level of admissions at the school following a reorganisation of age groupings. Yet the parents were to become a *cause célèbre* in the tabloid press which wrongly attributed the decision on allocation to the Labour coun-cillors when, in fact, it was an all-party decision of a hung author-ity. The affair also raised fears that the provision in the Education Reform Act to lift ceilings on school numbers would encourage racial segregation between schools, not by planning but by default.

In Manchester, the row started over the tragic case of a racist murder at Burnage comprehensive school. An Asian boy was killed by a white schoolmate in the playground. The 120 000-word report into the incident revealed serious flaws in the application of the school's anti-racist policy which had exacerbated divisions between communities. This was shown most notably when white pupils trying to go to the boy's funeral were prevented by the headmaster from getting on the bus. The anti-racist initiatives had failed to take account of the positive role that white people could take in them, and had simply alienated many white children and parents. As a result, they did not feel any responsibility for working out strategies to combat racism and felt that blacks were being afforded special privileges.

The school was described as badly managed with an 'ethos of male violence'. Racial attacks were common and the small minority of black staff felt isolated. The report, written by a committee of three blacks and a white chair, immigration lawyer Ian Mac-Donald, did not criticise anti-racist policies themselves. Indeed, MacDonald argued that such policies were essential to ensure a decent education for all. 'All the work of our schools should be informed by a policy that recognises the pernicious and all-pervasive nature of racism in the lives of students, teachers and parents, black and white, and the need to confront it' (*Guardian*, 10 May 1988). Instead, the report was damning about their dogmatic and ill-thought-out implementation.

Anti-racism assessed

As these cases reveal, anti-racist policies have not always been pursued with complete success. In both Brent and Manchester, the policies suffered from bungled and zealous implementation which fuelled rather than alleviated racial divisions.

But these failures cannot simply be blamed on incompetent administration. The pursuit of racial equality inevitably involves difficult dilemmas and choices which have sometimes been ignored or brushed aside. There was a lack of clarity about whether the aims 'were to reduce the worst excesses of discrimination or to achieve for the black community a proportionately equal share of jobs, resources, access to services and involvement in decision making' (DOE, 1983, p. 8). That is, were the policies about equality of opportunity or equality of outcome? Since quotas and positive discrimination are illegal in Britain, councils have relied on pursuing equality of opportunity, but this has never been sufficient to redress the large backlog of racial disadvantage. Although they have contributed to a fairer deal for blacks, they have inevitably failed to guarantee equal access.

By not being more circumspect about the policies' potential, councils raised expectations which could not be fulfilled. Under constant pressure from local Labour parties and black activists, race was given a priority which too often ignored the inherent constraints and dilemmas. Benefits for one group, particularly at a time of heavily constrained budgets, can be at the expense of other groups or at any rate perceived as such. Of course, some clashes were inevitable. The race policies challenged existing power structures and were bound to lead to what Russell Profitt, the principal race adviser in Brent, has described as 'creative tension'. Such potential tension might have been contained if there were greater efforts to carry the white population along instead of simply attacking them as unreasonable racists. Instead, attempting to impose these radical policies on an electorate and workforce which was not prepared for them and which at times was made hostile to them by the media sometimes proved explosive. As Ouseley, by then Chief Education Officer at the ILEA, put it, the challenge is how 'to convince those who are better off . . . that a political and social response to one section is not against the interests of any other, but is, in fact, in the best interests of all' (Ouseley, 1988).

The starting point for any attempt to tackle inequality must be an understanding of the nature and pervasiveness of racism. This imposes enormous limits to the speed of progress in tackling a problem which extends well beyond the concerns over which councils have a direct remit. A failure to appreciate this contributed to the disputes involving education, since, without the involvement of parents, anti-racist policies are bound to have a limited impact.

There was also at times an excessive concentration on tackling individual instead of institutional racism. According to A. Sivanandan, Director of the Institute of Race Relations, this carries the danger that 'the fight against racism sometimes takes on the dimension of a personalised fight against an individual – as though to change the person is to change the office, the institution. When such confusion is carried over into policy, it tends not so much to alter the course of racial injustice as to damage the larger fabric of natural justice' (Sivanandan, 1988). This in turn led to too much emphasis on the use of race awareness training. Such training is based on the assumption that the problem can be tackled by forcing white people to confront their own inherent racism. The sessions are like encounter groups in which white people are expected to confess their racism, often under heavy pressure from the trainer. These techniques can be psychologically overwhelming and disturbing, and have been criticised by the Institute of Race Relations and other groups.

In Brent and other education authorities, unnecessary tension was also fuelled by the over simple diagnosis that the roots of black under-achievement lay in the individual racism of teachers and in the institutional racism of schools, without tackling the wider problem of overall educational performance. As A. Sivanandan has put it, 'while one way of helping black children to gain confidence in themselves and in their schooling is by employing more black teachers', the battle in Brent 'ended up as a fight about the right to employ black teachers rather than as a fight to improve the education of all our children' (Sivanandan, 1987).

On occasion, the pursuit of anti-racism also became embroiled in wider political and personal power struggles in which the policies were exploited for ends that had little to do with fighting discrimination. The anti-racism cause was sometimes hijacked in the rampant power struggles being played out in the town halls. In some London councils the race card was used by hard-Left-dominated Nalgo executives as a powerful weapon for putting pressure on Labour groups or as part of a wider political strategy for promoting disruption. Factionalism within the Labour group itself or within the local Labour party also played a role.

The drive for racial equality initiated by many Labour councils from the late 1970s had its roots in a genuine concern about racial injustice. Labour local government moved to meet a need which central government, even Labour, had ignored. For the most part, the policies have been implemented fairly and progressively, contributing, albeit slowly, to fairer recruitment policies and delivery of services. As a result of the Left's initiatives, the number of black staff has increased, black people enjoy better access to services, and there is greater awareness about the problems of racism. Race policies are now firmly on the political agenda and have gained growing acceptance. Race monitoring, one of the first initiatives, and other policies have been adopted by some nationalised industries, Whitehall departments and even some large private firms. Despite Brent and the tabloids, and the slowness of progress, there is an emerging consensus of the importance of such policies for the promotion of greater racial equality.

8 Making Space – Bringing Feminism into the Town Hall

'Local government . . . has never been a comely place for poor women or mothers. The demands of local government depend on leisure – the luxury of the affluent or of those who carry little or no responsibility for the lives of those with whom they live' (Bea Campbell in *New Socialist*, November 1984).

Women's committees were set up in an attempt to counter the under-representation of women in local government. They were inspired by a critique which saw the state as reinforcing discrimination, neglecting women's demands, and transacting its business through structures over which women had no control. The women's movement which gathered strength during the 1970s forced the Labour Party to give belated recognition to the discrimination suffered by women, through the Sex Discrimination and Equal Pay Acts. The attention of the women's movement focused on central government, in campaigns over abortion or women's rights, and on trade union struggles. No one thought women's rights had much to do with local government. During the 1970s, even progressive Labour councils had pursued 'gender-blind' policies. Slowly, however, feminists began to point out the discriminatory implications of 'treating everyone the same'; and to draw attention to the failure of local councils to meet women's needs.

It is not really surprising that women's views and needs have

142

been neglected by local councils, since so few councillors are women – in 1976 a survey had shown that 83 per cent were male. In 1986 Widdicombe still found that only 19 per cent of councillors were women. Even in 'progressive' London only 22 per cent of councillors were women (Widdicombe, 1986, p. 27). Women are under-represented at all levels of politics, in local councils as well as in parliament and the civil service. They are far less likely to be senior officers, directors and chief executives. And even trade unions, tenants associations and community groups are seldom represented on decision-making bodies by women, despite the fact that a large proportion of the membership are women. Without special initiatives to involve women in the decision making of local government, women argued that it was unlikely that their views would be heard.

The failure to recognise, let alone respond to, women's demands in local government can be seen by the structure of service provision. While well-meaning male councillors and senior officers felt they were providing adequately for everyone's needs, the evidence contradicts this. Without the distinctive experience and perception of women, impractical, clumsy and downright discriminatory decisions were made, even by the most progressive Labour councils. Housing estates were designed without play areas for young children, without adequate lighting or security and with long, dark, dangerous passageways. Tenants' halls and community halls had bars, but nowhere for women with young children to go. Adult education classes, sports activities and community facilities lacked crèche provision and therefore excluded single parents who perhaps needed them most. Support services for those looking after the elderly, the disabled or young children tended to be provided only as a last resort, and social services were often withdrawn if the handicapped or ill client had a mother, wife or daughter to take over. The service for children under 5 which is especially important to women – full-time day care – was underdeveloped even in the best Labour councils. In London while there is some provision, public or private, in playgroups and nurseries, or with child minders for over a third of children under 5, there are only places for 25 children in every 1000 in local authority full-time nurseries. Women are the primary consumers of a wide range of council services and yet they have rarely been consulted.

The origins

By the end of the 1970s, women who had gained experience within consciousness-raising groups and women's campaigns, began to move back into the traditional labour movement with new confidence and a determination to raise the profile of 'women's issues'. Nationally, Labour women had begun to raise new demands, and to organise a vociferous lobby at Labour's annual conference, demanding a more powerful role for the Women's Advisory Conference, including the election of the five women's representatives on the NEC from that conference, and the presence of at least one woman on every shortlist of candidates when selecting MPs. Local women's sections, reinforced by new young feminists, abandoned jumble sales and refreshments, and began to campaign around sexism within the Labour party. And as Left-controlled constituency parties began to turn their attention to local government, women in local Labour parties began to ask, 'what's in it for us?' In 1981 women's sections began to get involved in the new democratic manifesto-making process, and wrote in commitments to equal opportunities policies, nursery provision and new services for women.

As far as the mainstream (male) Labour Left was concerned, these policies were a bit of an afterthought; the GLC manifesto in 1981 did not propose any special women's initiatives. Indeed, the idea of a women's committee did not originate with the Labour party, but with a determined group of women community workers in Lewisham, who persuaded the progressive administration under Andy Hawkins to create the first local authority 'women's rights working party' in 1979. The Lewisham initiative inspired other women councillors and candidates, who began to take up the idea of special committees devoted to developing and monitoring provision for women.

A year after the Left took power in County Hall, the GLC began to take up the idea of equal opportunity initiatives. In spring 1982, a young and determined Valerie Wise piloted through the establishment of a full committee of the GLC, and a women's unit to service it. The committee began on a modest scale, with three staff and a £300 000 budget. With the 'windfall' money available to the GLC because of the defeat of 'fares fair' (see Chapter 4), and backed by Ken Livingstone, it soon grew. By abolition, it had an annual budget of £10 million and a staff of over 70. Although no other council could afford anything on that scale, the GLC's women's committee became a model.

The Left councils elected in May 1982, with more or less enthusiasm, followed suit. Camden, Islington, Southwark, Hackney and Greenwich set up women's committees or sub-committees. Within the next five years Lewisham upgraded its working party to a women's committee and new committees were set up in Brent, Lambeth, Newham, Hammersmith and Fulham and Haringey.

It would be wrong to see the establishment of women's initiatives as a litmus test of 'Leftism'. The idea struck a chord among many Labour councils that would not have described themselves as part of the Labour Left. By 1987 there were 42 women's committees or sub-committees, in councils as far apart as Kirklees, Middlesbrough, Newcastle upon Tyne, North Tyneside, Nottinghamshire, Leeds, Derbyshire, Lothian, York, Bristol, Brighton, Oxford, Birmingham, Edinburgh, South Glamorgan, Wolverhampton, Stirling and Aberdeen. There was no pattern.

In some councils the committees were composed solely of women, in others men sat on them. Some set up working groups while others invited women's groups to attend the full committee. Some co-opted members of the public. Except in the GLC and Camden, the units set up to service the committees were tiny, with at most three or four staff, and a budget which paid the wages and left a few thousand for grants. The GLC had millions to spend, while the South Glamorgan women's committee had a budget of just over £2500 a year. The committees seldom had direct powers or direct authority over the main spending committees – their role was to advise, monitor and provide reports. Perhaps the greatest point of similarity is that they were all broadly set up by the determined effort of a handful of women councillors, in the face of benign apathy from most male colleagues – and opposition from others.

Into action

Women's committees began with their own councils' record as an equal opportunities employer. Good practice and experience already existed, and councils such as Camden had already begun to develop 'equal opportunities' employment policies. Good employers, however, were vastly outnumbered by those who had added, 'we are an equal opportunities employer' to their job adverts, while doing nothing to change their practices. Women's committees and units were involved in developing new employment policies covering recruitment, promotion, advertising, maternity and paternity leave, and several set up workplace nurseries. Training programmes were introduced. Southwark, Lewisham and Greenwich provided child care for manpower Services Commission training schemes in non-traditional manual skills. Southwark funded a special training course in manual skills, and ran a special project to encourage girls in school to consider council apprenticeships. Lewisham set up a pilot project to research the training needs of women manual workers and established a training programme for cleaners. Birmingham and other women's committees established comprehensive training programmes for women with management potential, training for women administrative staff and made assertiveness training more widely available.

A second concern was to ensure that local services provided what women needed. To discover women's views and to assess their needs, the committees pioneered a much more consumer-based approach to service provision, by commissioning surveys and questionnaires and setting up public meetings and local discussions. The GLC held public meetings throughout London, to discuss services and to find out what local women wanted. This was followed up by a number of open working groups. Southwark carried out an initial questionnaire through the council newspaper to identify work priorities and followed up with a major leisure survey on the sport and leisure provision women wanted. Lewisham held women's days to consult women about priorities. Islington employed a market research company to carry out a survey of women's views in the borough and then drew up a 'borough plan' for women, setting out problems and possible solutions. Even South Glamorgan with its tiny budget set up working groups on the under-5s, health care, women and the arts, education and disabilities.

Women's committees began to monitor service provision and to research the ways that existing services fail to take account of women's needs. As a result, housing allocation policies were found to discriminate against households headed by women. A study in Southwark, for example, revealed that single parents were disproportionately allocated flats on the least desirable council estates. Single women with one young child were only allocated bedsitting rooms, which they had to share with their children, while couples with children were automatically entitled to two bedrooms. Surveys and meetings showed the need for changes in public transport, and improved bus design, for better play facilities and for safer walkways, and better-lit streets and subways. Women's committees also addressed long-neglected problems, including those facing women caring for elderly, people with disabilities or dependent relatives. Women's committees in Greenwich, Lewisham and elsewhere brought carers together to discuss their needs, carried out surveys, set up support and advice networks and recommended the provision of relief care services.

The third task was to increase the representation of women in local government. In a sense that was done immediately by the very creation of the committees – since they were always chaired by women, the number of women senior councillors automatically increased. But the aim was also to give women better access to the political process. Local women were encouraged to attend and contribute to the committee meetings. This often meant changing the structure of meetings, providing more information, making meetings more informal, providing crèches, babysitting allowances, and even transport. Lambeth women's committee held meetings at different times of day and in different parts of the borough. Committee papers were diverted from other council committees to the women's committees to give women from the public a chance to comment. The full meetings were often backed up by working parties involving women from local groups. The attempt to involve women in local government was taken a stage further through co-options. To redress the predominantly white middle-class nature of the committees, places were reserved for blacks, lesbians, older women and trade unionists.

The fourth area of work was aimed at supporting and funding local women's groups. The intention was to enable women to organise themselves, and to encourage new community projects for women, in order to redress the balance of voluntary sector projects. Several committees set up women's centres, produced newsletters and directories of women's activities, and gave small grants to local groups. The vast majority of the groups funded were community nurseries and playgroups, health projects, teenage advice services, women's cabaret and special projects for unemployed women and single parents.

The success rate of these objectives varied. Perhaps the most successful policies have been those directed at the council's record as an employer, where there has been widespread acceptance of the need for change, and new policies and procedures were introduced within a relatively short timescale.

In other areas of policy, progress has been less rapid. Women's committees have been good at finding unmet needs, but they seldom had the power to meet them. The results of research and surveys have been turned into recommendations for other committees, but these did not always share the same priorities. In some instances, women's committees have been forced to demonstrate that there was demand for a particular sort of service by providing it themselves – before other departments and committees would take them seriously. For example, many boroughs found that there was a demand for women-only swimming sessions. In Southwark, the women's unit, unable to persuade a sceptical leisure department of the need, set up its own women's sessions at a local training pool. After several months the sessions were so popular that the leisure department agreed to set up four weekly women's sessions.

In general, however, the small women's units have been limited to asking questions, providing information and monitoring the work of other committees. Because changes in service provision depended on the support of other committees and, as we shall see, there was no direct link into the centres of power in a local authority, token gestures too often replaced real changes. Some of the most visible successes related to increased childcare provisions. Many Left Councils gave increasing priority to under-5s provision, and funded a range of provision, including day nurseries, community nurseries and support services for childminders. Other social and leisure services were improved during the high spending years, but after 1985, financial constraints prevented major service improvements. There have been small changes, however. Housing policies have been rethought to take greater account of problems of security and safety at night. Several authorities have changed policies towards women suffering from domestic violence, and set up victim support schemes. Birmingham women's committee persuaded a housing association to establish a new hostel for homeless women. Planning schemes have been changed to give more emphasis to childcare, shopping and public transport needs, and dial-a-ride schemes have been introduced.

While other councillors talked in the abstract about extending local democracy, women's committees went out of their way to open their doors to local women. Inevitably, as critics have pointed out, the committees tended to involve young, middle-class, articulate and committed women, often from feminist or political groups. Leading councillors and officers were aware of this problem, and perhaps more than other council activities, women's committees experimented with ways of reaching those who did not usually have access to the local authority – holding daytime or local meetings, and providing childcare and transport. While not wholly successful, they did involve a wider cross-section of women than had usually been seen in town halls, including lesbians, black and Asian women, women with disabilities, teenagers and pensioners. Many of the controversies faced by the new committees were a direct result of these attempts to involve local women in their activities. Through trial, and a fair degree of error, they encountered and attempted to deal with some of the difficult questions about representation and accountability.

Finally, the attempts to support and fund women's organisations formed part of a more widespread Left commitment to community groups, and helped to provide a wide range of new activities, organisations and projects in areas which had previously had little or no provision for women. The GLC alone funded hundreds of women's projects across London, and in its last year spent £6.5 million on child care. But the fact that women's committees also gave grants to more controversial projects – which seemed part of the feminist fringe rather than the mainstream of women's concerns – provided ammunition for a vitriolic campaign by the press and the local Conservatives.

Women's committees have been important both in raising issues that affect women, and in making space for women in local government. The idea of new initiatives for women has

commanded considerable support, despite the intensity of opposition whipped up in the media. A London survey in 1987 (London
Strategic Policy Unit, 1987) showed that two-thirds of the women
and nearly half of the men thought that things would be better if
there were more women as local councillors, and 64 per cent of
women agreed that their council could do more for women. A
MORI poll in Greenwich in 1984 showed that 57 per cent of the
population thought that the council should be promoting equal
opportunities for women, and GLC polling showed similar results.
The idea of special women's initiatives is not new. Elsewhere in
Europe, women's committees and departments have been fully
accepted as part of the process of government – even the European Parliament has a women's committee. Perhaps part of the
reason for the intensity of opposition has been because women's
committees were challenging very longstanding traditions and
structures.

Trouble and strife

The opposition of local Conservatives to women's committees was
in most cases almost hysterical, although some Conservative
women councillors found secret common cause with their Labour
sisters over issues such as cancer screening and safety at night. The
Tories seemed determined to protect the traditions of local government against any compromise with women's needs. When Deirdre
Wood, a GLC councillor, brought her baby into a meeting, the
Tories objected that only 'members' were allowed into the Chamber. Tory Central Office combed the lists of GLC-funded groups
to find those – such as the London Women's Liberation Newsletter
Collective, *Spare Rib*, the English Collective of Prostitutes and
Babies against the Bomb – which could be publicised as evidence
of loony feminist activity. They were equally vociferous in their
opposition to equal opportunities policies, training courses for
women and grants to local women's groups.

From the beginning the tabloids treated women's committees
with derision. Fleet Street couldn't get enough of silly season
stories about banning beauty contests, Punch and Judy shows, pin-
ups and renaming manhole covers. Yet many of the media stories
about women's committee activities were false, or taken out of

context, in a deliberate attempt to discredit them. Lynda Lee Potter in the *Daily Mail* accused women's committees of 'concentrating their energy and venom on trying to abolish everything that is enriching, entrancing, fun and innocently frivolous in our lives'. The *Daily Mail* and the *Sun* unleashed a particularly nasty campaign culminating in *Daily Mail* reporter Gloria Stewart's attempt to con a grant and a flat out of Islington council by dressing up in 'feminist' jeans and calling herself 'Islington Women's Collective Against State Oppression in Holloway Prison'. No matter that no firm offer of a grant or flat was ever made – no matter that council officers rumbled her as soon as they met her, the *Daily Mail* still ran a story claiming that even the nuttiest feminist could jump the housing queue.

Sensitive initiatives on sexual harassment at work, or refuges for battered women were treated with equal abuse. In May 1987 the *Daily Mail* attacked a women's health month organised in Islington, because a single workshop referred to fertility and pregnancy problems and included advice on artificial insemination. The *Sun* ran an unpleasant story entitled 'Loonies put ban on wife jokes' belittling Camden's policy on sexual harassment at work.

The women involved in these initiatives were young and often inexperienced and made easy targets. In some cases the failure to work out clear objectives meant that committees tended to react to every issue that affected women and did so without the painstaking work needed to take a conservative population with them. In some London boroughs women's committees were caught up in an intolerant preoccupation with political purity which led to gestures rather than real changes. There was a failure to grasp the unpopularity, among local women, of a gesture such as the banning of a Punch and Judy show, or an invitation to Sinn Fein women to address a meeting. The campaigning work of the committees was often taken up with broad political issues such as supporting the women of Greenham Common and protesting against strip-searching. But these campaigns were not those where the committees could make a local intervention, and they diverted attention from the more difficult and important task of tackling the services and structures of the council.

Women councillors underestimated the extent of resistance, not only from the press and public, but from the town hall trade unions. The attitude of the unions was ambivalent. While, in theory, they supported equal opportunities, the reality was often different. They were often uncomfortable about positive action policies emanating from employers, and jealous of their control over terms and conditions. They were uncomfortable about staff taking grievances direct to women's units rather than to the union. In particular, proposals to eradicate low pay, or to encourage women to work in non-traditional areas challenged established demarcations and hierarchies.

Manual union representatives were predominantly male, and had long represented the interests of male staff – dustmen, carpenters and caretakers – more effectively than those of women care assistants or meals on wheels staff. This unease was made worse by local authority inexperience, poor industrial relations and by attempts to move more quickly than the cautious union structure allowed. In other cases it was caused by a combination of workerism and chauvinism on the part of union representatives – who used their trade union positions to try to prevent initiatives of which they personally disapproved. The Greenwich ACTSS branch twice took industrial action *against* the women's committee. The first time it blacked the women's unit in response to a decision by the women's committee to support women staff in the town hall if they objected to page three-style pin-ups in their departments. In July 1987 they again voted for an indefinite boycott of the women's unit after Labour councillors decided to increase its budget by £80 000. An ACTSS spokesman was quoted in the local press as saying that 'its wrong to expand the women's unit when front line jobs are at risk'.

Within the Labour groups, the support that could have enabled women's committees to make solid achievements in service provision was not always forthcoming. Labour groups suffering from acute 'manifesto-itis' supported the establishment of women's committees in order to demonstrate their accountability to the party, but gestures of support were not always translated into hard work or hard thinking. As with the initiatives on race, many of the older councillors were downright hostile. Supporters of Militant and romantic aficionados of the machismo politics of class war argued that these initiatives merely concerned privileged middle-class women, and had nothing to do with the practical problems of the socialist struggle. In Southwark, the council's male chauvinist pig was lightheartedly nominated every year as 'chair' of the women's committee, and women councillors were subjected to constant personal abuse.

Women's committees were victims of the overall failure of Labour groups to set priorities. When the activities of different sections of the council clashed, attempts were seldom made to resolve the deadlock. Difficult decisions were never taken. The 'bolt on' approach to equal opportunity initiatives meant that women's committees and women's units were expected to carry unrealistic workloads with insufficient staff and very few resources; they were seldom integrated into the management and organisational structures of the local authority, they lacked back-up facilities, and their initiatives were seldom taken up and made part of the central direction of the council's work. Committees in Southwark and Brighton have understood this and attempted to develop a council-wide strategy which takes account of and responds to women's needs.

The women's units which serviced the women's committees in most authorities also had problems. Staff were recruited primarily from the voluntary sector and women's organisations, because few local government officers had any relevant experience. Their know-how was based on voluntary sector and women's movement methods – non hierarchical and informal – and these sat uncomfortably on top of crusty council bureaucracies. Women's units were not just unused to established local authority ways of doing things. They set out to challenge them. But most of the women councillors and their officers had little experience of management, of local government, or of power battles with senior officers and senior councillors. With tiny units, isolated from the rest of the authority, changing the town hall bureaucracy from the inside was an impossible task.

The difficulties facing women's units were sometimes internal as well as external. The GLC women's unit, in particular, was racked by internal dissent and was the centre of controversy. In some ways the GLC unit was always the most likely to come under pressure because of the almost exponential growth of its workload and of the staff to handle it. The rapid expansion from a staff of 3 to a staff of 70 created huge tensions. Most of these were recruited from the feminist or voluntary movement outside the GLC, and many had strong views about the unit's organisation. Instead of a hierarchical approach associated with most male-dominated workplaces, a collective approach was instituted. But the pressures led to collapse in 1984 amid accusations of inefficiency, bad management and institutional racism. Louise Pankhurst, the head of the unit, came under attack in a confidential internal enquiry report commissioned to investigate the unit – but after legal advice left with a tax-free payment of £30 000 and a public statement of exoneration.

The report highlighted the pressures generated by huge work-loads, new and inexperienced staff, poor communication, insufficient planning and badly thought out strategies. It said the unit was given 'almost limitless workloads' and 'from its very inception the unit has been running to keep up with its own and member's aspirations'.

It was also critical of the lack of support from the rest of the authority. The report commented that 'the perception of the women's unit as an "afterthought" may have encouraged a tendency in the council's "establishment" to marginalise its requirements and evade some of the conceptual challenges it posed'. The unit had to monitor the administration of other departments, to develop new relationships with the voluntary sector and the public, to set up entirely new initiatives and to do so within a new structure of collective management. The new staff were recruited on the basis of 'proven contribution to women's issues' but had little experience of local government and lacked basic training.

By far the most serious problems arose over allegations of institutionalised racism within the unit. The truth is obscured in accusations and counter-accusations, but it is probable that the very commitment of the women's unit to deal seriously with the issue of racism, and to ensure the representation of black women, meant that many of the issues that remain buried in other organisations came to the surface.

The internal report itself was subject to criticism for letting councillors and other senior management off the hook. In her 100-page report on the unit Louise Pankhurst had described it as 'nightmarish'. She was especially critical of the confusion caused by the day-to-day intervention of the chair of the committee and of the failure of the enquiry to substantiate many of the allegations. But the report also failed to examine one of the key issues at the base of the unit's difficulties – the tension between traditional local government practice, and the determination of many of the feminists recruited into women's units to challenge the practice of local authorities. There was a conflict between the approach of women trained as neutral local government officers, and that of activists recruited because of their very partiality but who were uncomfortable within the bounds of the 'local state'. There were divisions too – between the priorities of radical separatist feminists and those of the more cautious Labour politicians. The units often sat uncomfortably between the local government hierarchy and women's groups outside the council, attempting to challenge the workings of the former, but often with closer links with feminist networks than with the women on local council estates or using traditional council services. As a result of the internal enquiry, the GLC women's unit was divided into four sections, traditional line management structures were introduced and new senior staff appointed. Despite its continued growth, this new structure seemed to enable the unit to function effectively.

Women's committees also stumbled on the internal contradictions involved in extending community involvement in council activities and, in particular, the difficult question of who can 'represent' the community. Despite the efforts of committees to involve a large cross-section of women in their activities, and to remove some of the disadvantages faced by women with young children and older women, those most able to get involved were young, middle-class and articulate. Inevitably, too, the majority of the women who attended meetings were from women's projects and feminist groups, and sometimes in organised political groupings. Many of these groups had unrealistically high expectations of what the committees could achieve, in part fostered by the self-image of the women's unit workers and councillors. The committees were sometimes portrayed as pre-figurative, feminist structures, and as a structural framework for the local women's movement – rather than as a committee of a local authority with limited powers and resources. The women outside the committee saw women's committees as a conduit into the local state, as a point of access to 'real power', and found politicians with mixed loyalties and limited influence. Feminist councillors were torn between their wish to respond to, and to feel part of, the local women's movement, and their need to be accountable to their Labour group and the Labour party. Feminists involved in the GLC women's committee conceived the notion of 'feminist democracy' – with emphasis on

accessibility, participation, maximum involvement of the maximum number and 'for women themselves to make decisions'.

But the process of co-opting additional people onto the women's
committee highlighted problems of representation and accountability. Councils who held open elections at public meetings found
occasionally that organised groups were able to take over all the
available places by a simple process of packing a meeting and
voting for a tight slate. In Camden and at the GLC, Wages for
Housework, an obscure radical feminist group was able to capture
the majority of co-opted places. In Lewisham, far greater disarray
was caused in 1985 when a group of Tory women were able to
capture all the non-reserved places by the same process. In
Hackney, an expensive borough-wide ballot only produced 300
completed ballot papers.

Even when the selection of co-optees was managed without
incident, the new representatives were expected to shoulder an
unrealistic burden of accountability. Not only did they find themselves thrown into the complexity of council business and committee procedure without proper training or support, but women
elected from open meetings found that people to whom they
reported back changed at each meeting. Representatives of
women's groups such as tenants' groups and mothers' and toddlers
groups found that they didn't meet regularly enough to guide one
member of the group to speak for the rest. And women selected
for their race or their disability or their sexuality found it totally
impossible to 'speak' for whole groups of very disparate women.

Women's committees sometimes failed to create support among
local women for their activities, and alienated some groups in their
attempts to make new provision for black women, and lesbians.
These difficulties cannot simply be written off as loony Left
extravagance. They reveal real conflicts within the community that
remain hidden when some groups are excluded from access to
local government. Conscious attempts to combat discrimination
and to confront the oppression of black women, lesbians and
women with disabilities put women's committees at the forefront
of the conflicts that resulted. Women's committees brought
together disparate groups such as black women, and lesbians, who
had previously been excluded from access to local authorities, and
gave them a channel for their anger and frustration. However,
because of their relative powerlessness, the committees were often

unable to deliver anything in return; and merely added to the frustration. At the same time the involvement of new black women's groups, Asian women's groups and lesbian groups created considerable tension with traditional white communities who were not prepared to have their prejudices confronted so directly. Other tensions were caused by the fact that working-class women often felt out-of-place within the intellectual debates among feminists. At times the politicians felt the need to override the views of the co-opted members, which caused resentment. As Sarah Roeloffs put it in *London Labour Briefing*: 'Came the time when the women (in the advisory group) decided, but the GLC elected representatives disagreed, the women were reminded in no uncertain terms who called the tune and paid the piper – the GLC and the GLC alone' (April 1983).

In the past few years, many women's committees have learnt from the early experiences, and have concentrated on work which can bring together women from widely different backgrounds – such as housing, childcare and employment.

Do women's committees have a future?

Despite their small scale, women's committees explored a number of issues to do with extending participation, and changing the way councils work. The problems they encountered have been partly to do with the 'gesture politics' style of the London Left, but also in part because they have tried to do difficult things, and have encountered some very real political dilemmas. While some committees have proved successful, professional and effective, others have foundered through the naivety, confusion and political intrigues of both officers and members. Many of the silly mistakes were learnt from, and as women's committees became an accepted part of the local government framework, badly-needed skills and expertise began to develop.

The aftermath of the Greenwich by-election and the general election defeat in 1987 led to a backlash against women's committees and their initiatives. The women's committees set up in authorities which did not see themselves as part of the 'new Left' became the most vulnerable, although there have been attempts to scale down or abolish women's initiatives elsewhere. In councils where Labour lost control in 1986, such as Nottingham, the women's committee was soon scrapped. Aberdeen, a solidly Labour council, closed down its women's committee in 1987 and replaced it with a more general equal opportunities programme. In May 1987, Birmingham followed suit, although the surprise in that case was that veteran right-wing leader Dick Knowles had ever allowed it to be set up in the first place! The Birmingham women's committee had been established in May 1984 as a result of a manifesto commitment, with an advisory role. It had a budget of £70 000 for training and an additional £24 000 for promotional work as well as the unit's running costs. An attempt in 1986 to take away the committee's role in promotion and training activities failed, but in May 1987 the women's and race committees were absorbed into a new personnel and equal opportunities committee. Knowles explained that this was not an attempt to undermine the women's committee but to strengthen equal opportunities by ensuring that 'policies which we have advocated for the past three years are carried out through a committee which would give better co-ordination', and which it would be harder for an opposition party winning control of the council to unscramble. Women critics say that the move was part of a backlash in the context of Tory accusations of 'extreme feminism'. The new equal opportunities committee had a membership of 14 men and 2 women, and both chair and vice-chair were men.

Most male councillors have tended to see equal opportunities as a relatively limited process of removing overt discrimination, and to see its main role as related to internal employment strategies. Women's units and women's committees have, however, involved themselves in a far wider range of issues; from campaigning and research to listening to women's views, encouraging women to involve themselves in wider political decision-making and improving service delivery to meet women's needs. Women's committees have often failed to set priorities, and have concentrated their efforts on fairly futile gestures and on very abstract campaigning initiatives, instead of concentrating on the key issues of service delivery and women's representation. But these are not problems exclusive to women's committees. They were part of the politics of some Left Labour councils during the 1980s. If that changes, there should be scope for establishing proper objectives and priorities, and for beginning to make real progress on equal opportunities for women.

As the pressures to cut spending and rationalise bureaucracies gather momentum, women's committees and units may find themselves tidied up into all-purpose equal opportunities units or even swept away. Of course, there is nothing magical about one sort of structure compared to another. Indeed, where the political will and administrative abilities to run an effective separate committee are missing, more may be achieved through central equal opportunity programmes. There is a good case for strengthening the policy-making power of such committees by making them the sub-committees of powerful policy committees. There is a lot to be said for transferring policies that deal with employment practices within the authority into a central personnel unit. It is important to have specialist officers to monitor and develop policy within service departments such as housing, leisure and planning. But despite this, the danger is that the expertise and skills developed in women's committees will be lost, and the initiatives which they began will be abandoned. Without a special committee of women thinking about, and listening to, women's needs, those needs will be neglected. Ironically, while particular policies relating to employment practices and a few service changes are taken on board, it may be the consumer-centred, listening approach pioneered by women's committees that will be lost.

9   Glad to be Gay?

I looked up the 'Book of Genesis' again . . . 'But the men of
Sodom were wicked and sinners before the Lord exceedingly.'
And the Lord destroyed Sodom and Gomorrah. I thought of
altering those words and saying 'But the councillors of Haringey
were gay and corrupted the children of the borough exceedingly.' And I should like to add after this Bill 'The Lords
destroyed those councillors.' (Lord Denning, House of Lords,
November 1986).

Like women's issues, gay rights was not on the Left's early agenda
when they took control of the first wave of Labour councils.
Indeed the more establishment figures on the soft Left, such as
David Blunkett and Margaret Hodge have always treated the issue
with circumspection, cautious that a high profile might undermine
support from the traditional working-class communities, while
sections of Militant and the 'workerist Left' have positively
espoused the hostility and prejudice which they assume the
'working class' would feel. Several factors led to a growing concern
by the new Left with lesbian and gay rights. First, there was a
wider concern for civil liberties and equal rights, aimed at tackling
discrimination. Second, feminists were challenging assumptions
about the 'normal' family and proposing changes in service provision which reflected the needs of a diverse range of household
types, including single parents, single people and extended families. Trying to meet the needs of lesbians and gay men was
necessary to reverse past exclusion and, it was argued, councils
should cease to regard any household structure as normal, or to
enforce conformity to any particular lifestyle. At the same time,
sections of the Left believed that a new politics could only be

160

constructed by abandoning a simple reliance on the traditional working class, and constructing instead a 'rainbow alliance' of oppressed groups, which would also include women, blacks, young single people – and lesbians and gays – groups which, added together, would form a majority for socialism.

Inequality

Politicians had paid very little attention to the issue of lesbian and gay rights since the 1960s. There had been a tendency to assume the problem was 'solved' by the 1969 repeal of the legislation which had made all male homosexual acts illegal. The 1969 Act, however, only legalised homosexuality in limited circumstances – between consenting males in private – and it did not legalise any public expressions of affection. An uneasy compromise had been established, whereby lesbians and gay men were permitted a tenuous legal existence as long as they kept out of sight. The compromise established in the 1960s fell far short of an expression of equal rights for lesbians and gay men, and was based on tolerance as long as they did not attempt to celebrate their lifestyle or 'challenge family values'.

However, discrimination is deeply rooted in both the laws and the practices of the police and the judiciary. The age of consent is 21, compared to sixteen for heterosexuals, and every year on average 40 men are imprisoned, some for as long as four years, for having a consenting sexual relationship with men aged 16 to 21. It remains illegal for two people of the same sex to show affection in public – gays can be arrested merely for kissing as 'an affront to public decency'.

At the same time, it is still legal for a lesbian or a gay man to be dismissed from employment simply because of their sexuality. Indeed the Lesbian and Gay Employment Rights Group has dealt with over 200 cases of gay people being harassed at work or dismissed. The law doesn't recognise a same sex relationship so, for example, homosexuals cannot succeed to their partner's tenancy. Lesbian mothers are still unlikely to gain custody of their children in contested divorce hearings. The campaign within the Church of England to declare homosexuality a sin has intensified; and lesbian and gay Christians are now under attack. Public morality laws are frequently used against lesbians and gay men – and are used to seize books destined for gay bookshops such as 'Gay's the Word', regardless of content. Indeed the irony is that books about Aids and 'safe sex' have been seized as obscene. Police harassment affects gay clubs and pubs and it is considered a productive use of police officers time to act as agent provocateurs to entrap and arrest gay men.

The beginnings of the Gay Rights movement can be traced to San Francisco in the late 1960s. By the 1970s a 'gay pride' movement had emerged in Britain, with the Gay Liberation Front celebrating 'gay style' and organising flamboyant stunts. CHE, the Campaign for Homosexual Equality, was the more respectable and more influential arm of the gay movement, concentrating on lobbying, legal advice and self-help projects. CHE never attached itself to any political party, and indeed looked for all party support. The more liberal social atmosphere of the 1970s, combined with the challenge of the women's movement to the 'normality' of traditional family structures, made it easier for lesbians and gay men to 'come out', although that was probably always easier in London than elsewhere. While the pattern of gay clubs and businesses that developed in San Francisco was never replicated here, there was during that period an expansion of social, political and economic links between homosexuals. While a single 'gay' community never developed, primarily because of the huge political gap between feminists and some gay men, lesbians and gay men became more visible, and more confident.

Labour wakes up to gay rights

During the 1970s gay rights was seen as a non-party, single issue campaign. Certainly the Labour party was no more progressive than other sections of society. When Peter Tatchell stood as Labour's candidate in the Bermondsey by-election in 1982, he was subjected to a gutter press campaign and a stream of hate-mail and abuse because of his homosexuality. Not all of the anti-gay feeling came from outside the Labour party. One of his opponents was John O'Grady, formerly leader of Southwark council, who ran a barely disguised anti-gay campaign. Frank Chapple, then leader of the Electricians' Union was quoted as saying on BBC's 'Any

Questions': 'what we didn't need in the House of Commons was a gay draft dodger from Australia, and we don't need them in the Labour Party either.'

The treatment of Tatchell exposed the intensity of anti-gay prejudice, and awakened Left interest in the issue. More lesbians and gay men joined the Labour party, and, perhaps more importantly, felt able to raise the issues of equal rights in new ways. In 1981, Tony Benn spoke at a press conference to launch an NCCL booklet called *Gay Workers: Trade Unions and the Law* and called on the Labour party and trade unions to take a lead in the political battle for gay rights. In the same year the Labour NEC endorsed a comprehensive discussion document entitled *The Rights of Gay Men and Women*. Attitudes in the Labour party were changing, and gay rights became one of the issues taken up by both soft and hard Left groupings.

The second catalyst was the determination of Ken Livingstone and fellow councillors such as Valerie Wise, to open up the GLC to the issue of gay rights. The GLC set up a gay working party and spent £1 million in grants aiding lesbian and gay services such as phone advice services, police monitoring and employment rights. Behind the headlines, the GLC did a lot of sensitive and careful work to challenge prejudice, and to develop new policy approaches and structures, which began to build confidence among lesbians and gay men in the capital. In a small way, by providing social events, information, concerts and venues, but also by relaxing and changing the prevailing ethos, the GLC made London a better place to live for many lesbians and gay men. Ken Livingstone was voted personality of the year by London's *Capital Gay* magazine, and many lesbians and gay men were brought into politics for the first time through campaigns to save the GLC.

The campaign for lesbian and gay rights gained widespread support among the Left, and even the centre. In 1985 the Labour Party conference agreed a new policy which called for the repeal of all discriminatory criminal laws, a new code on public morality, an equal age of consent, prohibition of discrimination on grounds of sexuality in employment and housing, and action to prevent police harassment. The policy also called on Labour local authorities to adopt properly-monitored equal opportunities policies, end discrimination in housing and to give financial support to phone lines, youth groups and centres. Chris Smith, MP for Islington

South, made history when he 'came out' as gay at a public meeting in Rugby. Neil Kinnock sent a message to Lesbian and Gay Pride 1986 which read: 'Discrimination against gays and lesbians is still too prevalent in our country. It reminds everyone that there is still much to do to rid society of the fear and guilt that has victimised gays and lesbians. It reminds everyone that we must strive to defeat prejudice and the ignorance in which it is rooted.' Larry Whitty, Labour's General Secretary, wrote to all Labour councils in March 1986, drawing attention to Labour's support for equal opportunities policies and initiatives to end discrimination.

Despite official Labour party endorsement for local council efforts to tackle discrimination, apart from the GLC, Manchester, and a handful of London authorities, little action was taken. Even where policies have been developed, they have been small scale. Lesbians and gay rights were scarcely mentioned in the Left manifestos of 1982. Even in 1986, while several made reference to equality for lesbians and gay men as part of their equal opportunities policies, only a few developed specific policies. Camden proposed the setting up of a lesbian and gay working party, and policies to end discrimination in the provision of jobs and services, to support the rights of lesbian women in custody cases and to monitor police treatment. Ealing suggested the need to 'end discrimination towards lesbian and gay students and staff in schools'. Islington proposed to provide community facilities for lesbians and gays 'on the same basis as for heterosexuals' to help to challenge attitudes and to dispel ignorance. A lesbian and gay committee was established to ensure the needs of lesbians and gay men were not overlooked and to provide information on gay organisations such as the Terrence Higgins Trust. Lambeth proposed to improve information and advice services and 'take steps to redress discrimination', while a number of authorities, such as Oxford and Sheffield, supported individual projects without setting up formal structures.

When policies have been implemented, they have been guided by a concern with civil rights, equal opportunities and the challenging of prejudice. In practice, the Left local authorities found themselves tackling issues such as housing, where lesbian and gay couples have often been discriminated against in allocation policies, and employment, to ensure that lesbian and gay men have equal access to jobs. In order to educate their members, Nalgo

and Nupe have produced literature, for example on Aids, to try
to stop workers refusing to work alongside gay people in case they
are Aids carriers. With patient negotiation, some local authorities
have developed good equal opportunities policies alongside the
unions. A number of councils formed monitoring projects to
examine problems of harassment by the police force, and to
develop consultation with the community and build bridges.
Others funded new voluntary organisations. The GLC, for example, funded the London lesbian and gay centre, and gave advice
to switchboards and counselling services. In the process they
grabbed the headlines, and created widespread controversy. Some
councils held back and shelved plans for new centres because of
the local opposition.

The most difficult policy area to tackle has been education.
School is, after all, where young people's attitudes are formed,
and any attempt to counter prejudice has to start there. Young
lesbians and gays can face confusion, depression and appalling
isolation in trying to come to terms with their sexuality among
classmates who use 'poofter' constantly as a term of abuse. Local
authorities face a difficult juggling act, trying to balance the need
to consult and reassure the wider community with the equally
genuine need to prevent discrimination and promote an atmosphere of respect for civil liberties and human rights. The ILEA has
treated the issue of gay rights with circumspection, and was
accused by activists of backsliding. The ILEA never endorsed the
GLC's more radical policies, particularly that of challenging
heterosexism. Nevertheless huge press stories were developed
over the availability of books within ILEA schools, including the
controversial *Jenny Lives with Eric and Martin* which was never
freely available to children, but only to teachers as a counselling
aid.

Positive images

However, a wider political controversy was generated by attempts
to move beyond a 'civil rights' approach to one which attempted to
use the local authority to challenge and change attitudes to gay
people by creating 'positive images' and to counter 'heterosexism'.
The GLC was in the forefront of an approach based on encouraging

the idea that there were real choices of lifestyle available to everyone. There was a concern to treat homosexuality as in every way equivalent to heterosexuality as an alternative lifestyle. The GLC's gay and lesbian working party produced a report *Changing the World, a London Charter for Lesbian and Gay Rights* and the women's committee produced a sister publication entitled *Tackling Heterosexism*. 'Heterosexism' was defined as 'the portrayal of heterosexuality as the only "normal" and "natural" form of sexuality (which) limits the options which are available to everyone'. The concept of 'heterosexism' aroused considerable controversy; partly because it was so abstract – indeed Conservative politicians constantly confused the words heterosexism which implies discrimination against those who are not heterosexual and 'heterosexuality', the sexual proclivity of most of the population. More seriously, the idea of heterosexism was used, by some, not only to defend homosexuality as an acceptable lifestyle, but also to attack portrayals of heterosexual families. Perhaps the most foolish was an attack by a London Labour party executive member, Sarah Roeloffs, endorsed by the London Labour Party, which accused Nick Raynsford of running a 'heterosexist' campaign during the Fulham by-election in 1986, because he used campaign photographs of his family.

The controversy eventually centred on Haringey, the only borough to adopt explicitly a policy on heterosexism, and one of the few left-wing authorities with responsibility for education. Haringey's women's committee had produced a manifesto prior to the 1986 elections which had said that 'Labour will prioritise the need to counter heterosexism. We will promote positive images of gay men and lesbians from nursery through to further education.' The women's manifesto was disowned by the local Labour party as soon as opposition parties began to draw attention to this section, and the Labour party issued a statement saying that 'the Labour Party does not propose to promote gay rights within schools. The Labour Party will not force this issue on you or any other community in the borough.'

However, soon after its 1986 election success, the Labour council in Haringey set up a lesbian and gay committee largely composed of non-elected gay activists and Labour party members. The committee adopted the GLC's approach. As councillor Davina Cooper argued, 'heterosexism is all pervasive . . . there are different ways of living, there are different kinds of sexuality you can express. Each as valid as the other.' The committee set up a new unit which began amongst other work, to a 'positive images campaign'. As part of the attempt to develop develop this campaign in schools, and without referring the decision to the politicians for backing, the unit wrote to all the heads in the borough, asking them what policies they were pursuing to implement the borough's policy. Haringey councillors have since admitted that they had not really thought out the implications of the policy they had nodded through, and that the enthusiastic amateurism of the unit should have had far more support and guidance from experienced local government staff. But then, no one expected the scale of the outcry which erupted.

The backlash

Parents began to organise in opposition to the new policy, and some withdrew their children from local schools. Organisations on the 'moral' Right swiftly took advantage of the row to promote their own propaganda, and to attempt to organise Haringey parents. A group called the New Patriotic Movement, functioning from an address in the West End, suggested that Haringey's gay rights policy was part of a conspiracy to subvert society. The hostile campaign in Haringey was led by Peter Murphy, a Tory councillor who won a traditionally Labour seat in 1986 on a platform of opposition to initiatives designed to promote racial and sexual equality. His first leaflet ran 'We are protesting against plans to introduce HOMOSEXUAL EDUCATION throughout Haringey'.

Meanwhile, the Right, both inside and outside the Conservative party has abandoned any pretence of tolerance or fair-mindedness, and has played increasingly on anti-gay feeling and the Aids scare. It has been joined by some elements of the press in successfully representing Aids as a gay plague, and in fanning an ever more hysterical reaction of fear and loathing. The gay monitoring group reports a dramatic increase in the number of attacks on gays, and an intensification in discrimination. Workers refuse to work alongside gay colleagues because of the fear of Aids, while pressure to close down clubs and gay organisations has intensified. *Capital Gay*, a London newspaper, was burned down in an arson attack in 1987.

The Aids scare has been used by some right-wing thinkers to make a more general attack on the experimental lifestyles and diversity which developed in the 1960s and 1970s, in an attempt to re-establish strong normative ideas of convention, 'natural' behaviour, 'moral' principles and 'family life'. Single parents, group households and gay and lesbian couples are all treated as equivalently deviant, and subversive of proper family life. We are not far now from a reassertion that it is 'normal' for every woman to be economically dependent on a man. Mrs Isabella Mackey, of the 'Concern for Family and Womanhood' recently blamed 'the rising divorce rate, abortion, child-molesting and rape' on feminism and went on to say that 'a married woman should not have a job because being a wife is a job in itself'. There is a close link between the radical Right's stress on returning to pre-feminist family structures and their attack on homosexuality. If a new 'normality' is to be enforced, then tolerance for alternative lifestyles must be brought to an end. The Conservative party's approach, while couched in more moderate language, has had a similar theme. Family values and Victorian morality must be reimposed, and social, political and cultural authority should be brought to bear to curtail the possibilities of diversity. By June 1987 even the Conservative election campaign was using the issue of Left Labour councils 'promoting' homosexuality in schools in election posters showing gay books with the slogan 'This is Labour's idea of a comprehensive education'.

Local authorities took up the issue at the same time as the tabloid press and the Conservative party were whipping up a backlash against freedom of sexuality and of lifestyle in general, and the freedom of lesbians and gays in particular. They saw the ability to combine an attack on 'loony Left councils' with anti-gay prejudice as giving a boost both to anti-Labour feeling and to the 'moral' Right. Not all the papers joined in the hysteria. The *South London Mercury* went out of its way to defend the initiatives. Lewisham council had encountered opposition to its plans to review policies to ensure that there was no discrimination against lesbians and gays. The *Mercury* lead its front page with a piece that ran:

A major row has raged in this newspaper for weeks over Lewisham Council's decision to give gays and lesbians the same rights as any other member of the community. And a lot of ill-informed and dangerous rubbish has been spouted by people who ought to know better. Worse still, it seems many politicians want to jump on the bandwagon to cash in on the fear and ignorance the rubbish-talkers are spreading. Well, the *Mercury* has decided its time to stop sitting on the fence. We don't believe the council's policy comes under the heading 'loony left' ... On the contrary we commend Lewisham Council in its determination to stamp out prejudice and discrimination.

However, it was a lone voice. The tabloid press felt increasingly free to exploit anti-gay prejudice. The *Star* in June 1987 referred to Camden council's plan to set up a lesbian and gay unit as intending to 'employ four full-time woofter apologists', and in July described Islington as looking for a special sort of social worker: 'woofters will assuredly receive a limp-wristed welcome ... and must understand the dynamics of racism and the different cultural influences'. It was, however, the educational policies that took up the most column inches. In July 1986, the *Daily Mail* reported that schools in Hackney had been 'flooded with books, videos and other resources advocating homosexuality as a viable alternative way of life for children to consider'. The *Sun* in August reported a story about a little boy who was allowed to dress up in girls' clothes at nursery school. Terry Dicks, MP for Hayes and Harlington, was quoted as saying that 'Haringey are encouraging children to turn into transvestites. The nutcases who put forward these ideas will mark the youngsters for life.' In July, the *Sun* ran a leader under the headline: 'Gay's the way in a Haringey': 'The Labour council bosses in this London Borough have ordained that courses in homosexuality are to be introduced in 78 schools. In the view of Tory councillors the aim is to make the abnormal seem normal and the normal seem abnormal. The *Sun* offers its deepest sympathy to the children and parents of Haringey.'

The policy of promoting positive images in schools seemed to arouse deep-seated fears about influencing children during a particularly vulnerable phase of their lives, and the press were full of spurious stories about 'teaching' homosexuality. The Earl of Caithness was quoted as saying 'a week's exposure to propaganda of this kind could have an insidious and unhappy lasting effect on some impressionable young people', while Lord Boyd-Carpenter said that 'The promotion of the idea in schools that homosexuality is a way of life of equal merit to the moral normal habits and standards of our fellow countrymen is most dangerous'. But, as Sarah Benton wrote, the question is

> Where do these fears come from? The fear that heterosexuality has such a frail hold in the human psyche that an ILEA teacher, stumbling through a sex education class, might unseat it altogether? The fear that the family is so fragile that those who refuse to live in it (homosexuals) will destroy it? The fear that without laws forbidding public expression of homosexuality, the human race will be seduced into suicide? (Benton, 1988).

The real impact of a 'positive images' approach may never be tested, because almost no schools, despite the press hysteria, ever got as far as putting these policies into practice. Moreover, the new government introduced legislation in the form of section 28 of the Local Government Act to try and suppress such initiatives.

Section 28 began its life with an amendment in the House of Lords to the 1986 Local Government Bill, which would make it illegal for councils to 'promote homosexuality'. The amendment was lost in the Commons, but was soon followed first by a Private Member's Bill which was lost because of the time pressures on Private Members' Bills, and then in a new government amendment to the 1988 Local Government Act. The new clause provided that a 'local authority shall not promote homosexuality or publish material for the promotion of homosexuality; promote the teaching in any maintained school of the acceptability of homosexuality as a pretended family relationship, or give financial assistance to any person for either of the purposes referred to above'. The opposition front bench in committee accepted the original amendment, arguing unofficially that to oppose it would play into the hands of the Right, and that there were votes to be won from appearing to share the public's concern about initiatives to promote lesbian and gay rights. However, under pressure from the party, the front bench tabled amendments to the Bill to reduce its scope. These amendments were lost, but a government amendment was tabled which merely altered the clause to say that no local authority may 'intentionally' promote homosexuality, or publish material 'intended' to promote it.

The government, under pressure from an influential campaign of artists and actors, argued that it is not their intention to prevent, for example, the staging of plays by Oscar Wilde or Joe Orton, or the inclusion in libraries of books by E. M. Forster, or Virginia Woolf. But they can neither anticipate nor control the decisions that will be made by the courts. Right-wing pressure groups were preparing soon after the legislation was passed to try and close down services to lesbians and gay men. However, plans to use the new law in Haringey, to secure the closure of the lesbian and gay unit, abolish the curriculum working party of teachers and councillors, delete all references to homosexuality in statements of Council policy and cut off grants to a community bookshop which includes lesbian and gay literature, precipitated a split within the ranks of Tory councillors. Fifty local Tories, including local MP Hugh Rossi, signed a statement disassociating themselves from the antics of Peter Murphy and expressing their opposition to 'schemes for exploiting the clause in ways which would hinder the borough from the proper provision of services to all its inhabitants' (*New Statesman*, 13 May 1988).

Several Left councils are continuing to fund centres and counselling services, and to develop equal opportunities policies for lesbians and gays arguing that they do not 'promote' homosexuality, they are merely countering discrimination. Indeed, legal advisers to local authorities have advised that the Bill is so ill-defined and vague that, as Michael Barnes QC put it in an opinion to the ALA, 'it is open to serious doubt whether it will render unlawful many actions or decisions'.

Perhaps the most serious danger to lesbian and gay initiatives is not legal action, but self-censorship. Inevitably, cautious council lawyers may well warn against any actions likely to infringe the law, and councillors and council officers may find it easier simply to avoid the issue. Those councils which had not begun any initiatives on lesbian and gay rights are less likely to start now. Councils are also theoretically responsible for any grants that they give to organisations which break the law and this may lead some councils to try to undermine equal opportunities policies in local voluntary groups as well as the local authority. Strathclyde Regional Council's deputy director warned colleges in May 1988 to ensure that grants to student organisations comply with Section 28, while the London Boroughs Grants Scheme which took over the

GLC's role insisted that all grant recipients sign an agreement to comply with the law. Self-censorship will perhaps be the most serious problem in schools, where teachers attempting to teach sex education, or to discuss the problems of Aids, or faced with students coming to terms with their own sexuality, will no longer feel able to provide the honest counselling which young people need.

Too far too fast?

Despite a continuing centralisation of power, this is the very first instance when local councils have been legally prevented from 'promoting' a particular lifestyle, and when a particular section of the community has been singled out and prevented from receiving funding for social centres, advice services or pressure groups. It is based on a view, expressed clearly from the Right, that the unspoken compromise – where homosexuals were tolerated, but not heard – was an acceptable one, and that any claim to normality or equality subverted that compromise and challenged the status quo.

The Labour party and Left councils attempted to extend civil liberties and equal rights in a challenge to that compromise. In practice, however, little has been achieved. Where councils have acted, those actions have had only a limited impact on reducing prejudice, and have often been grossly distorted by opponents. Labour councils have simply underestimated the potential backlash from the initiatives, and failed to recognise the scale of the prejudices and deeply held attitudes which they were confronting. In doing so they exposed a dilemma between pursuing a 'safer' approach to equal opportunities based on winning support for the basic rights of lesbians and gay men, and a much more radical attempt not merely to challenge prejudice, but to promote the idea that homosexual lifestyles were as positive and rewarding as heterosexual ones – and to encourage a consciousness of the real choices that they presented. The former approach connected to the slightly more liberal approach to sexuality and a range of lifestyles which has evolved during the past two or three decades, and which includes greater tolerance of homosexuality. But the positive images approach, and the attempt to challenge 'heterosexism', was altogether a more difficult proposition, since it involved a fundamental change of public attitude, not just one which implied tolerance of difference, but one which argued for the equivalence of different lifestyles, and challenged the 'normality' of heterosexuality. Such a challenge could not be undertaken through a process of peremptory policy changes and gestures. It required a longer time-scale, and a far more sophisticated approach to the process of changing ideas. Chris Smith MP has expressed strong views about the effects of a failure to understand this:

> It is absolutely right that we are committed as socialists to full equality for lesbians and gay men, and to ending the day-to-day discrimination that continues to exist. But instead of presenting that crystal clear case to an often sceptical electorate, we have overloaded our commitment with a lot of language about heterosexist attitudes and a series of gestures that don't really benefit the lesbian and gay community. The overloading has instead served to alienate people – it's done a basic disservice to the basic cause (Chris Smith, *LCC Newsletter*, Spring 1987).

The problems for Left councils were increased when the issue was adopted, mostly for opportunistic reasons, by elements of the hard Left. It was, at times, hitched onto the Labour Briefing bandwagon, and the Labour Committee for Lesbian and Gay Rights was temporarily hi-jacked by an obscure revolutionary group called Workers Power. As a result, a commitment to 'positive images' sometimes became a litmus test of Left credibility, with gestures replacing carefully worked out strategies. The very sensitive issues of changing local attitudes, particularly on very important issues such as Aids, attacks on the gay community, and policy in schools, need to be prepared with a great deal of care. Instead they were sometimes bounced by inexperienced and zealous staff, and nodded through by politicians unwilling to be seen to question them. This was particularly dangerous when dealing with an issue which confronted so many deep-seated fears and prejudices among Labour's traditional voters. It can never be proved whether these clumsy interventions and the attempts to impose gay rights policies on a hostile community led to a loss of support for Labour and the undermining not only of the Left councils, but of the campaign for gay rights. Despite the inept way some Labour councils promoted the issue, it is clear that the acceleration of fear and hostility towards lesbians and gay men had been happening for other reasons. The Right and the tabloid press were delighted to be able to combine attacks on loony Left councils with fanning deepening public hysteria about homosexuality and a growingly conformist public morality.

10 The End of a Dream

'The days of flying banners from town hall windows and hoisting up red flags on the roof are over' (Margaret Hodge, leader Islington Council; quoted in Wolmar, 1987).

The Tory manifesto for the 1987 general election made terrifying reading for Labour councillors. Its policies on education, housing, the poll tax and compulsory competitive tendering for council services were designed to reduce their power to use local government as an engine of social change. Moreover, this onslaught had been partly inspired by their activities. Although the proposed measures affected all local government, it was Labour councillors in authorities controlled by the Left that were the specific target.

The media onslaught on the 'loony Left', and the 'loony London Left' in particular, contributed to the timing of the general election. The Labour loss at the Greenwich by-election in March 1987 was widely attributed to the success of the Tories' propaganda campaign against left-wing councils. There was, as the Goldsmiths' Media Research Group (1987) pointed out, an 'almost symbiotic relationship, at least as far as local government in London is concerned, between the Conservative Party and Fleet Street'. In 1986, Conservative Central Office, had spotted the potential of targeting the 'loony Left' not merely to gain local votes but as a national propaganda tool. The idea was to discredit Kinnock's 'moderate' image by focusing on the activities of Left councils. With a compliant press ready to give extensive coverage to the half-baked tales about left-wing councils, irrespective of their veracity, the 'loony Left' onslaught contributed to the election campaign and the result, particularly in London where Labour lost three seats and gained none. Indeed, it is significant that in the capital, Labour came closest to winning a seat in Westminster North, an area where the local council, Westminster, has always been in Tory hands.

The radical nature of the Tories' proposals on local government, many of which were specifically tailored to meet the supposed threat of the Left councils, will change the face of local government more fundamentally than any other package of measures this century. However, the Tory victory had a more immediate impact on the Left councils, who were forced into a rapid about-turn on their spending plans.

The U-turn

It was only after Labour's election defeat on 11 June that the extent of the Left councils' reliance on a Labour victory became clear. The strategy of creative accounting that had enabled them to survive the first three rounds of ratecapping came to an end that night. The strategy had been based on the premise that a Labour government would bail them out by scrapping ratecapping, increasing rate support grant and relaxing borrowing controls on capital spending. The various schemes and devices had taken the councils successfully through to mid-1987 without any significant cuts, but the defeat spelt an immediate change in climate. As Dave Sullivan, leader of Lewisham, put it in a paper issued to his Labour group a month later, 'There is absolutely no possibility that we can survive the current year and immediate budget making process, let alone the next five years, without the penalty of surcharge unless spending is reduced and income increased' (Sullivan, 1987).

Even before the election defeat, there had been some reappraisal of the way that the Left councils were being run. The failure of the miners' strike and the defeat over ratecapping had led to a clearer separation between the hard and soft Left. Early in 1987, the executive of the London Labour Party, concerned at the 'loony' image, drew up plans to improve the party's poor image in the capital, but any concrete results from this new thinking emerged too late to have an effect on the general election result. At a local level, some leaders had begun to show a growing concern for value for money and efficiency as surveys indicated a lukewarm public response to services in contrast to the widespread support for the NHS. It was the election defeat, however, which really forced a rethink.

Almost before the ballot papers had been counted, Margaret Hodge, leader of the Association of London Authorities and of Islington, was working on a strategy for the councils to survive another Tory term. Hodge wanted to ensure that the soft Left retained the initiative by pre-empting any moves by her opponents within the London Labour Party. To cope with the new crisis, she set out three options: outright defiance by refusing to set a rate; abdication through mass resignation; or remaining in power and 'using all the resources and imagination at our disposal to further the interests of local people'.

Hodge discounted the first two options. Defiance, she said, 'had been tried, failed and discredited' during the ratecapping campaign. Mass resignation would leave the Tories or the Alliance in power, thereby betraying the electorate who had voted in a Labour administration. The only option, therefore, was to remain in power even though this would mean 'unpleasant choices'. In essence, Hodge was accepting Kinnock's rejected call during the ratecapping campaign for a 'dented shield'. The justification, however, was that Labour would retain control of local authority resources and could maintain high-profile campaigning.

The Hodge strategy went beyond a mere defensive action in the face of cuts. She argued that the rationalisation of services forced on the councils by the government could be turned to their advantage (Wolmar, 1987). She suggested a policy of 'base budgetting', a term that was later picked up by other financially stricken authorities, starting with a blank sheet of paper when drawing up the budget rather than merely adding increments to the council's budget each year. Secondly, the key to her approach was to make council services popular, 'so valued, like the National Health Service, that people will help us to defend them'. To bring this about, the unions would have to be won over as services were rationalised. 'Changes in working practices that mean people will have to be more flexible, such as two people doing the job that three did previously,' she suggested. Her strategy, therefore, was that council services could still be improved, even though there might have to be cuts and 'hard choices'.

Two weeks after the election, Hodge presented these arguments to the ALA and her policy was overwhelmingly accepted. The only dissent came from Linda Bellos, Lambeth's leader. Yet, eight months later, Bellos was to push through a budget in Lambeth involving cuts of around £40 million.

The councils had little choice. They had begun to exhaust the potential of creative accounting and even if Labour had won, there would have been painful decisions to make. Many of the schemes were one-off transfers of funds which could not be repeated. Furthermore, the 'deferred purchase' schemes which involved getting projects such as construction done now and paying for them later, had already been outlawed by Nicholas Ridley, the Environment Secretary, in the summer of 1986. During the following spring Ridley twice issued statements to the banks warning them that the government would not back local authority loans. This sent a shiver through the markets and the ratecapped councils found it increasingly difficult to obtain funds even for their routine borrowing, let alone creative accounting deals. This was, according to Islington's finance director, because 'the banks have been scared off. They just will not do deals with us at this time, even though they know we are a blue chip investment. The Japanese, who set up many of the earlier deals, have dropped out entirely' (interview).

Because these councils had been running budgets that were way above the government-set limits, thanks to creative accounting, once these sources of funds were exhausted huge gaps opened up between what the ratecapped councils were spending and what they could raise through the rates. This time the gaps could only be closed by spending cuts.

The crisis forced a new series of spending battles. In Camden, the collapse of an attempt to lease and leaseback several properties including the town hall forced the council into making £1 million worth of cuts from its official budget of £138 million at its July council meeting – these were to be met by a £7 million cut in overtime, a recruiting freeze and a 'budget scrutiny' exercise. The Labour Group was divided; eleven Labour rebels, using the same *Briefing* label which had brought the Left to power and who voted against the cuts, were expelled from the Labour group, an echo of the type of internal battles that had taken place over spending cuts following the Crosland 'the Party's over' speech, especially in Manchester. But this time they represented the rump of a movement whose time had come and gone. Now the soft Left was in the ascendant.

Over the next few months, the vocabulary of left-wing leaders changed from 'campaigning' and 'confrontation' to 'savings' and 'freezes' as other authorities made similar decisions. Those in the worst financial position were, like Camden, forced to make cuts for the immediate financial year, 1987/8, while all were forced to reduce spending substantially for 1988/9.

Bitter battles also took place in several other London boroughs. Haringey's hard Left leader, Steve King, who had succeeded Bernie Grant just before the general election, was ousted in early September 1987 following a vote of no confidence as he attempted to push a spending plan which would have led to an illegal budget deficit and surcharge for the councillors who supported it. Instead, within two weeks, his replacement Toby Harris implemented cuts of £15 million against the opposition of 14 Labour councillors. There was no doubting the harsh reality of the cuts – £2.5 million from education, £3.3 million from housing, £880 000 from social services, a freeze on most vacant posts, and a £4 per week council rent increase. To survive through to 1988/9, several other councils imposed similar measures, saving money through rent increases, often the first for two or three years, and the freezing of job vacancies. Hardly any of the left councils were unaffected – Brent and Hackney both put up rents by £2, Lambeth froze 75 per cent of vacancies and put rents up by £2.50, and Southwark decided to work to an 18 per cent vacancy rate for white-collar workers and 10 per cent for manual workers.

Outside London, Liverpool, Sheffield and Manchester were all preparing cuts programmes for 1988/9, but they were largely able to survive 1987/8 unscathed. Graham Stringer, Manchester's leader, who had come to power in 1984 following a lengthy and bloody battle with the Right over spending cuts, followed Margaret Hodge in winning people over to the new realism. The Labour group sounded out the local district party on reversing the basic policy on job losses and cuts, and gained support from both unions and constituency parties. With this backing, the councillors drew up a cuts package emphasising that the council's commitments to decentralisation, equal opportunities and channelling services to those most in need would be maintained. Stringer promised, for example, that the number of home helps and meals on wheels would not be reduced, although the number of social workers would be cut; and that the plans to restructure the council's services through 'mini-town halls' would not be affected. There was, briefly, a successful right-wing backlash. Right-wing Labour councillors combined with the Tories to push through a policy of scrapping the council's police monitoring unit, its commitment to decentralisation and the *Manchester Magazine* in December but this was reversed at the next council meeting. In the event, although it had to lose 4000 of its 40 000 jobs, the Labour group's budget for 1988/9 was passed with, amazingly, no dissent. According to Stringer, 'it was the first time that the Labour group had voted all together since the cuts battles of the mid-seventies' (interview).

In Sheffield, the council cut £27 million from its 1988/9 budget, shedding around 2000 jobs, but like the other councils managed to avoid compulsory redundancies. Every council committee was forced to cut its budget by 10 per cent, and faced three years of frozen cash limits, irrespective of inflation. The council was less able than Manchester to protect direct services, cutting 500 teaching posts, one from each primary school and ten from each comprehensive. However, housing was left virtually intact, six libraries scheduled for closure were reprieved and social services lost only around 5 per cent of its £50 million budget.

While there was some opposition in Manchester and Sheffield, it was muted in comparison with the response in London where the battles echoed the vicious and at times physical infighting of the ratecapping campaign. In Haringey, Camden, and Lambeth there was a series of chaotic and angry council meetings, played out to public galleries full of local Labour party and union activists. However, the protests, though vociferous, were not as well supported or as extensive as the demonstrations during the rate-capping struggles of 1985.

Creative accounting was not entirely dead and a deal by Brent to raise £30 million through the sale and leaseback of council property prompted Nicholas Ridley to take immediate action with a statement in the House of Commons on 9 March 1988 banning such schemes. Islington and a couple of other councils managed to sign deals later that night before the midnight deadline. These deals enabled Islington in particular to escape the cuts process more lightly than the other authorities.

It was in Brent that there was the greatest turmoil over cuts, partly because the Labour group was more divided than else-where, and partly because the council did not act swiftly enough. Following the resignation of Merle Amory, a moderate black councillor, Dorman Long was elected leader in late 1987, defeating his hard Left opponent Ron Anderson by one vote. Brent had persistently delayed taking crucial decisions over the budget and following a legal warning of the risk of surcharge in July 1988, councillors were forced into desperate cuts well into the financial year in order to balance the books. They came up with a deeply damaging cuts package of £17 million, in effect, entailing twice that amount of cuts since they were being implemented halfway through the financial year. The package included ending school meals, closing all council-run day nurseries for under 5s, the closure of voluntary-run centres for the handicapped and the elderly which were supported by council grants, the redundancy of 233 teachers and a £7 per week average rent increase.

The backlash against this politically inept package was swift and effective. Ken Livingstone, Brent East's MP, described the coun-cil, with an eye for the headlines, as the 'most incompetently and insensitively managed' in his experience, and likened it to the Pol Pot regime in Cambodia. Thousands of residents demonstrated vociferously against the proposals and some of the worst cuts, such as cutting the school meals service, were overturned. Despite this partial reversal, education was particularly badly hit and Brent's reputation, already reeling from the Beckford and McGoldrick affairs, was such that observers predicted that an immediate local election would have wiped Labour off the map.

Margaret Hodge had argued that the cuts offered an opportun-ity to restructure services, enabling councils to provide at least the same level of service, if not a higher one, at the same cost (Wolmar, 1987). Other soft Left leaders such as Lewisham's David Sullivan and Haringey's Toby Harris also suggested absorbing the cuts through efficiency savings. In fact, there was little evidence of the councils being able to achieve this aim. The cuts had to be made so fast, and were so deep, that there was little opportunity to cushion their effect or make rational decisions.

Although every council managed to stick to the policy of no compulsory redundancies, the cuts nevertheless had a serious impact on basic services. For example, in Camden there were 78 fewer social workers, over a quarter of the complement, while in

Haringey one in five teaching posts was lost. In Hackney three out
of 17 libraries closed and ILEA had to cut £93 million from its
projected £1100 million budget, losing 6000 jobs, of which 2000
were teaching staff, in the process.

Those cuts which had the most obvious public impact such as
library, youth club and nursery closures, cutbacks on teachers and
social workers, the closing of arts facilities and grant losses for
voluntary organisations frequently led to well-supported local
campaigns against the council. As many of these decisions, such as
the closure of Camden's Shaw Theatre and various libraries in
Hackney and Camden, affected articulate and well-organised
middle-class people, these campaigns gained considerable publicity and support. Ironically, the protests attracted a far wider
spread of people than had ever turned out to demonstrate against
ratecappping three years previously – working-class tenants protesting about rent rises joined middle-class library users and the
Trotskyists on the steps of the town halls.

The Left councils' new initiatives, such as the race and women's
units, suffered in the same proportion as other services from job
freezes and deletion of posts. Their budgets were an easy target for
cuts and several units were left without a lot to do. However, by
keeping the units functioning, the councils showed their continuing commitment to this area of work. A few of the initiatives
did bite the dust – for example, Brent and Hackney scrapped plans
for nuclear-free zone officers – but the more mainstream work
such as equal opportunities monitoring of employment policies
survived. The work of voluntary groups was also accorded high
priority and, with the exception of Lambeth, Lewisham, Brent and
Camden, grants were cut by proportionately less than the councils'
own spending. Elsewhere, nearly all voluntary organisations
escaped with little worse than loss of inflation increases.

The Tory plans

During the first ten years of Thatcher's premiership, Left Labour
councillors faced 50 new acts concerned with local government, 12
major changes to the local government finance system and dis-
proportionate cuts in government grant.

Yet, hard as the task of coping with this stream of attacks was,

the next phase of Tory legislation brought in by the 1987 government appeared to create even greater obstacles for progressive
Labour councils. As Mrs Thatcher made clear in her 1987 Conservative Party conference speech, largely devoted to local government, the intention was to banish 'municipal socialism' from the
land. Piers Merchant, a defeated Tory candidate in Newcastle,
rather gave the game away in a post-election interview in *The
Times*, whose reporter asked him what needed to be done to
revive Tory fortunes in the inner city. He replied: 'The government has to break up the monopoly of power in the Labour party,
perceived as the voice of the region. It must not allow Labour
nominees to keep on in public positions where the government has
the gift of appointment. Housing must be taken out of the control
of the Labour-controlled authorities.'

The language of Tory ministers has been rather more circumspect but the task for Thatcher's third term was clear: to break up
the power bases of the Labour Party in the inner cities; to remove
sources of alternative political ideas and practices; and to dismantle centres of public provision. The aim was also to go further
than this. The Left was the fall guy for the new right agenda which
was nothing short of a revolution in local government.

Poll tax

The transformation of local government finance, of which the poll
tax is the dominant feature, is by far the most significant of the
unpheavals. The much maligned rates, which Mrs Thatcher had so
rashly promised to abolish, have played a noble – and under-rated
– role in the financing of local services. Cheap to collect, and
almost impossible to avoid, they have formed a rough and ready
property tax, since those in larger, more expensive property have
had to pay more. The fairness of rate assessments has been
hampered by the failure of any government to carry out the
recommended five-yearly revaluations which would have ensured
a closer link between property values and rate payments. The rates
have, furthermore, been arbitrary between households and have
penalised single people in large housing. Nevertheless, rates are
still broadly egalitarian. By and large, richer people pay higher
rates, and local businesses are forced to contribute towards local
services. While before the war, rates provided by far the major

part of local authority finances, as the demands on councils increased, central government became more willing to fund the expansion through the subsidies and grants. Through the rate support grant mechanism, resources were channelled from affluent to poor areas.

All this will end with the poll tax, and its necessary corollary, the unified business rate. The government has claimed that the tax will be fairer and, that as more people will pay it, local councils will become more accountable to their electorate. In fact, the poll tax, by introducing a flat rate payment per adult head of population, is glaringly regressive as there is no relationship between ability to pay and level of payment. The millionaire living alone in a mansion pays the same as the woman in a tiny bedsit down the road.

The accountability argument is equally flawed. The government's reasoning is that of 35 million electors in England, 18 million are liable to pay rates, of whom a third receive a full or partial rebate, leaving just 12 million full ratepayers. As many more people will pay the poll tax, they will have 'earned' the right to vote for local council policies. This argument ignores the fact that a similar number of poll tax payers will receive rebates. It also assumes that simply because one person is considered to be 'the ratepayer' in the household, the other adults do not contribute towards the rates. Viewing the family as a series of discrete individuals who do not contribute to the collective household is a cynical vision coming from a party which cherishes 'family values'. The Green Paper, *Paying for Local Government* (HMSO, 1986), admits that the majority of the new payers will be 'non-householder tax units', i.e. wives, grown-up children and parents of existing ratepayers. Those who currently don't contribute would normally be those who cannot afford to do so. Moreover, the unified business rate is to be paid into a central pool and then reallocated on the basis of population. If the rate support grant continues at just under the 50 per cent level, this will mean that only a quarter of local authority funds will be raised through the poll tax and the rest will be distributed from a central source. This will make it much more difficult for councils to raise money from the local population since a one per cent real rise in spending will require a four per cent rise in the poll tax level. The final nail in the government's accountability argument is that it has retained the right to cap the poll tax. Local accountability will only be allowed to operate in one way – to push the poll tax level down, not to all councils to raise more money by increasing it sharply.

The government's third criterion for any new system was that it should be 'technically adequate'. Yet, by increasing sixfold – as more people will pay the tax and they will be entitled to pay it in instalments – the number of bills to be sent out, the poll tax will saddle local authorities with vastly increased collection costs. Because there will be two stages at which people will avoid payment – the compilation of the register and the time of payment – there will also be much higher levels of evasion and failure to collect. Experts predict that in some urban areas up to a fifth of the tax will not be collected. Compiling accurate registers – electoral registers only cover 93 per cent of the adult population – will involve curtailing civil rights. While it is argued that the right to vote will not depend on payment of the tax since the two registers will be different, the registration officer for the poll tax will have the right to consult the electoral register. In addition, local authorities will be expected to build up banks of computerised information to ensure payment, gained from housing benefit records, libraries, leisure centres, solicitors and estate agents.

It is not surprising, therefore, that Labour councils are but a tiny part of the very broad-based opposition to the tax. It has been opposed not just by all the local authority associations, but by the CBI, the British Council of Churches, the Chartered Institute for Public Finance and Accounting, the National Council for Civil Liberties and substantial sections of the Tory party. As Ian Aitken put it, 'I very much doubt if Mrs Thatcher can count on the wholehearted endorsement of more than one or two (Cabinet) colleagues besides her secretary of State for the Environment' (*Guardian*, 21 December 1987).

So why, given this staggering breadth of opposition, are the Tories introducing this controversial tax? First, they dislike the concept of a property tax, and rates remain the only tax still based, loosely, on the value of property. This reflects their hostility to progressive taxes, as the budget of March 1988, which reduced the top tax rate to 40 per cent, showed. As Nicholas Ridley proudly put it during the bill's parliamentary passage: 'Why should a duke pay more than a dustman?' Ridley's position is summed up in a statement made during the 1987 election campaign: 'I think in terms of local authority services, people should be paying for what they get. It has nothing to do with how rich you are. In this country, we are too sold on the idea that the rich should pay for other people's services.'

The second philosophic thread behind the tax is the corollary of the accountability argument. It is what nineteenth-century protagonists called the 'disenfranchisement of the paupers'. The argument then, as now, was that there is a large underclass of very poor people who rely on benefits from the state to survive. As they all have the vote, there is nothing to stop them electing politicians who promise them high benefits. This constitutes a heavy burden on the pockets of the affluent. The poll tax, by increasing the number of people who contribute towards local taxation, ensures that fewer people benefit in this 'irresponsible' way. If poor people are forced to finance local services out of their own pockets, they will be less likely to support high spending. Moreover, many poor people will try to evade the tax by not registering, neither for the tax nor on the electoral register, thereby losing their vote.

There is, finally, an element of political misjudgement about the introduction of the poll tax. When Mrs Thatcher blurted out her commitment to abolish the rates in 1974, she had not done her homework. It was a politician's promise, made off the cuff. If the poll tax had been seriously put forward in her first term of office when her power was kept more in check by her political colleagues, it would have been quietly buried. As Michael Heseltine, then Environment Secretary, has said, he could not remember a discussion about the poll tax in which 'it was not rejected as expensive, inefficient and unfair'. By 1986, Mrs Thatcher was virtually unchallengeable. Her 1974 promise had to be realised. The other option, local income tax, was dismissed out of hand because it would be somewhat progressive. Mrs Thatcher had no alternative.

Other legislation

The poll tax dovetails with the rest of the Tories' legislative programme to reduce local government's power and scope. Yet the programme is presented as increasing local authority accountability and giving people more direct say over local services. The 1987/8 Parliamentary session brought in three acts which form part of this overall pattern, covering housing, competitive tendering (and, *inter alia*, local government publicity), and education. Furthermore, new plans for the inner city entirely sidestep local authorities, most notably by increasing the number of urban development corporations, but also by simply ignoring the potential of councils to play a positive role in urban regeneration.

The housing plans probably best demonstrate this attempt to squeeze local authorities between the aspirations of local people and increased central government control. For the first two terms of Mrs Thatcher's government, there was no housing policy, only a housing tenure policy – a drive to increase the number of owner occupiers. The growing realisation that a significant proportion of council homes were unsaleable and, equally, that many people do not want, or cannot afford, to buy, has forced the Tories into initiatives on rented accommodation. The overall strategy is to do away with council housing. Where there is to be new housebuilding, it will be done by housing associations, at the new 'market rents'. Council housing is to be marginalised and, the government hopes, reduced still further after the potential of the 'right to buy' is exhausted. In the Housing Act 1988, tenants were to be given the right to choose to transfer to other landlords, including private developers. On estates, they have to do so collectively, but tenants of houses can choose a new landlord alone. This 'pick a landlord' scheme is a further attempt to reduce the role of local authorities and it is based on the assumption that tenants are likely to choose any alternative to local councils when offered the choice. In fact, a Gallup poll in April 1988 showed that 51 per cent of council tenants wanted to keep the local authority as landlord, 21 per cent preferred a building society, housing association or tenants' co-op, and only one per cent would consider a private landlord.

The creation of Housing Action Trusts which take housing in a particular area away from local authority control and rehabilitate it is another demonstration of this antipathy. Because of the high investment cost involved only a handful of such trusts are envisaged, although there seems to be no clear evidence that the estates chosen are the worst estates. Their promotion as a solution to local authority housing problems fits into the government's strategy of marginalising local councils, particularly in urban areas controlled by Labour.

These housing measures must be viewed in the context of a 75 per cent cut in spending on housing investment in Mrs Thatcher's first two terms, and of plans to forbid councils from subsidising rents with money from the general rate fund. The latter will eventually push rents up threefold in some areas of London and limit their ability to offer rented housing at a price ordinary people can afford. All these will effectively spell the end of any major local authority housing programmes.

The Local Government Act 1988 covers competitive tendering, contract compliance and local authority publicity. Competitive tendering applies to refuse collection, cleaning of buildings, catering, street cleaning, ground maintenance and vehicle maintenance, and leisure and sports centre management. Moreover, the government has given itself powers to add services to the list without recourse to primary legislation. Although a number of authorities had contracted out services since 1979, the number of new services being offered to private companies was dwindling. According to a *Local Government Chronicle* survey (3 July 1987), only 36 council services had been put out to tender in the previous financial year and these included such tiny contracts as golf club catering in Dacorum and floral decorations in Gravesham. Overall, privatised services accounted for just £120 million or less than 0.3 per cent of local government expenditure. This poor response to privatisation initiatives forced the Tories to turn to compulsory tendering. As with the poll tax, this was not welcomed by the majority of the Tories' local government colleagues who were opposed to compulsion. On the other hand, a few Tory-controlled authorities in the forefront of the privatisation initiatives, such as Wandsworth and Merton, were instrumental in encouraging the party to support such legislation.

The aim of compulsory competitive tendering is, according to *The Economist* (2 September 1983), 'as much to weaken the unions' monopoly as to save money'. Local authorities have prided themselves on providing good conditions for their workforces, and setting an example of good employer practices. As a result, in some areas, council employees enjoy terms and conditions that they could not obtain in the private sector. If the councils are to win the contracts against competition from private companies, they will have to do so at the expense of job security and working conditions for their staff. While in some cases this may force councils into a long overdue examination of work practices, resulting in a reduction in over-staffing and improved service delivery and efficiency, the overall effect will be to worsen the conditions for council employees, with those at the bottom end of the salary scales often being worst hit.

Information collected by the Services to Community Action Team (published in *Public Service Action*, no. 30, August 1987) revealed that 21 contractors had been sacked or had abandoned contracts in local government over the previous three years, the majority of which concerned school cleaning. The main complaint which led to these contractors' failures was poor standards. Although some of the contracts listed were small, the survey was not exhaustive and there were some notable failures by big companies such as Initial (BET) and Pritchard Services (part of the Hawley Group). Even Wandsworth, held up as the model Tory council by the government, had been forced to sack Pritchard Services from its grass cutting service. The most notorious failed privatisation was the sale by Westminster City Council of three of its cemeteries for £1 in 1987 to developers who allowed them to fall into neglect, forcing the council to buy them back for several million pounds.

The Act also ends 'non-commercial' contract conditions, in an attempt to outlaw the 'contract compliance' policies of many Labour authorities. Contract compliance has been used widely to ensure that contractors have, for example, good health and safety conditions, provide training, and employ local people. They have also tried to prevent the use of labour-only ('lump') sub-contractors who evade tax provisions. More controversially, many of the Left's councils have refused to let out contracts to firms who invest in South Africa, who are involved in industrial disputes or who produce military equipment.

Environment Secretary Nicholas Ridley, in introducing the legislation, said that people 'did not want the council's views and posturing on national policy issues to be a surcharge on the rates, through the imposition of conditions in contracts for the provision of services'. In fact, the new provisions will prevent the enforcement of existing legal obligations on health and safety, equal opportunities and employment of people with disabilities, and will allow the use of labour-only sub-contractors who avoid paying tax.

On race, the government was forced to accept an amendment allowing local authorities to fulfil their statutory duty under the

Race Relations Act 1976, which is to 'secure that their various functions are carried out with due regard to the need to promote equality of opportunity and good relations between persons of different racial groups'. Race was not the only embarrassing issue for the government over the abolition of contract compliance. During the Bill's passage through Parliament, the then industry minister Kenneth Clarke was proposing the use of contract compliance to encourage public contractors to take on local labour, while the government's own policy document on Northern Ireland was setting out ways in which employers could be forced to take on more Catholics. Indeed, in Mrs Thatcher's role model, the US, contract compliance laws cover 80 per cent of jobs in manufacturing, and 83 per cent in transport, public utilities and communications.

The third part of the Local Government Act 1988 was an attempt to strengthen the restrictions on local authority publicity brought in two years previously in the 1986 Local Government Act. Designed to prevent 'political publicity' by left-wing councils, these had been so weakened, following the necessity to appease a Lords revolt, that they had virtually no effect. Angered, the government tried again, this time outlawing material which 'promotes or opposes a point of view on a question of political controversy which is identifiable as the view of one political party and not of another'. This tortuous and tautologous definition appears to hit Tory councils – say, trying to boost council house sales – as hard as Labour ones. Until the matter is tested in the courts, it remains to be seen whether the new law is a major constraint on local government publicity, especially over campaigns by local councils to prevent motorways or nuclear waste dumps being built in their areas.

Finally, there is the Education Reform Act. At its centre is the educational equivalent of the 'pick a landlord' scheme, the right of parents to vote to take their children's school out of the control of the local education authority. In addition, education authorities will no longer be able to restrict the number of pupils entering each school on administrative or management grounds. Each school will have to take any number up to its physical limit. Schools are also to have greater control over their budgets through 'local financial management' under which the education authority will allocate a certain amount to each school to spend as it sees fit.

Taken with other recent changes increasing the number of parent governors at the expense of those appointed by the authority, these effects follow a consistent pattern – the weakening of the control of the local education authority over its schools. Ostensibly, the idea is to give more power to parents and governors. In fact, while many of the changes appear to give some parents greater freedom over their children in the short term, their actions could well lead to the restriction of the rights of future parents. For example, if a local school is shunned, perhaps not for the best of motives – such as a high proportion of ethnic minorities – it may have to shut down, leaving future generations with less, not more choice. Equally, once parents at a school have voted to make the school leave the control of the local education authority and become a grant maintained school funded directly by the Department of Education, future parents will not be able to reverse that decision.

Thatcher's vision

Throughout the introduction of this unprecedented legislative programme, the government has attempted to hold up Left councils as bogeys. The justification for draconian new powers against local government was constantly made in terms of protecting the public against 'socialism'. In fact, some of the new measures – such as those designed to stop political campaigning – affect ideologically motivated Tory councils as well as Labour ones. Others are crude measures to reduce local government power. The government is continuing this centralising trend even though it is clear that Left councils are retreating on all fronts. Those with the greatest internal problems have made swingeing reductions in core services. Many are already funding fewer voluntary groups, cutting back on spending in controversial areas, and ending token gestures of international solidarity. Councils are keeping a low profile, beginning to look inwards, and to tackle industrial relations and management problems. Even the media have begun to tire of the 'loony Left' as a target.

The Left was being used in reality as a stalking horse to mask the Government's own agenda. The intention is to reduce the role of local councils to a minimum, to dismantle public provision and to hand over large sections of the traditional welfare state to the private sector. Right-wing Tory councils like Wandsworth, Westminster and Bradford, taken over by the Tories in the summer of 1988, are enthusiastically promoting a vision of lean, low-spending and minimalist councils, providing fewer services with a shift from collective to private and charitable forms of welfare. The new legislative programme is designed to force similar changes, not only in Tory areas, but in Labour's heart-lands. With Mrs Thatcher determined to stamp her mark on the future of local government, and Labour in retreat, the ascendant 'new realists' have a hard task if they are to challenge the steady march of the Thatcherite vision.

11 Into the 1990s

It was inevitable that the new Left councils should find themselves locked into conflict with a radical Conservative government. Councils determined to redistribute local resources, to experiment with new approaches to collective provision and local planning and to act as a platform for socialist alternatives were bound to draw Tory fire. Left councils were seen as a direct challenge by a centralising government intent on reducing local power and public spending.

Indeed it is surprising that despite round after round of cuts and constraints, Left councils found so many creative ways to spend money, and develop new campaigns. Most Labour councils of the 1970s with far fewer constraints, had been dull and unimaginative. Left councils expanded spending on key services, developed new economic strategies, and changed the way services were provided. They forged new links with the voluntary sector, attempting to open up town halls and to involve the wider community in local decision-making. Many of the new initiatives have since been adopted by a wide range of more moderate Labour councils, and even some Tory ones. Some, such as equal opportunities and decentralisation, have moved into the mainstream of local government thinking. Perhaps the most lasting contribution of the new Left was its recognition of the flaws in traditional service delivery and its impetus for modernisation.

Despite these achievements, however, the Left's record remains patchy. The new councils spent more money than ever before, but did not succeed in radically improving the nature and delivery of local services. Some councils did achieve popular changes, while remaining well and effectively run. In others, despite a real increase in spending, services deteriorated. Management structures failed, and decision-making processes ground to a halt. Industrial relations became increasingly fraught, and Left councils were caught between the conflicting interests of trade unionists, consumers and local party activists. Services too often remained uniformly designed, and hierarchically organised and delivered. The gap between the decision makers and the clients was narrowed, but not closed.

Finding solutions to the crisis of welfare at a local level was a hard task even in the best of circumstances. Yet the new Left faced formidable odds. The councils where the Labour Left took control predominantly covered rundown urban areas, with some of the highest levels of unemployment in the country. They had high proportions of poor quality council housing, and faced heavy cuts in social benefits, health provision and public transport. Communities were fragmenting, and social problems multiplying. It was increasingly difficult to meet social needs successfully at a local level, while they were being systematically ignored by policy at national level. On top of this the councils were locked in permanent conflict with Whitehall, faced persistent cuts in their own funding and a gradual reduction of their powers.

The new councillors were young and inexperienced. They had fistfuls of manifesto commitments but little idea about policy implementation. They also inherited unwieldy and stubborn bureaucracies resistant to radical change.

However, the Left must take some of the responsibility for the problems they encountered. Far from being a uniform group with a clear and single vision, the new Left was a fragile alliance of activists with no common plan or set of priorities. Some members of the new Left saw the priority as changing service delivery and devolving power. Others, like the Liverpool Militants and traditional 'workerists', remained wedded to old orthodoxies: the importance of 'class struggle', and the paternalistic model of local government with power restricted to a few leading councillors and party activists. Other hardliners saw reform as a hopeless compromise with Thatcherism, and wanted to use local government as a vehicle for building a movement of opposition with the aim of political confrontation with central government.

As a result, much of the time and energy that should have been devoted to reform was spent in internal wrangles about how to defeat Thatcherism. At first, the Left united around attempts to defeat Government policies of cuts, ratecapping and abolition. By the end of the ratecapping campaign, the alliance shattered, and a clearer rift opened up between the hard Left determined to use the tactic of illegality to escalate the conflict, and the soft Left who accepted the role of Labour councils as a 'dented shield'. Until this point, it was the political style of the hard Left and its use of rhetoric and gestures as a substitute for taking hard political decisions that usually won the day. But the soft Left, too, frequently evaded hard choices, delayed decisions and failed to get to grips with the problems of service delivery. The soft Left, too, at least initially, seemed more concerned with the level of spending than the quality of services.

The Left was too preoccupied with campaigning initiatives to pay sufficient attention to industrial relations, good management or monitoring systems. Public support for local services was taken for granted – yet the day-to-day experience of them made consumers ambivalent and the government was setting out to capitalise on that public dissatisfaction. The Tories had moved the battle onto the terrain of public perceptions – attempting to demonstrate that private services were more flexible and responsive than council services. By failing to demonstrate that collective provision could be innovative, efficient and successful, Left councils failed to win the public support that was needed to hold back the Thatcherite revolution.

The aftermath of defeat

The role of the Left in local government is increasingly precarious in the aftermath of a third Tory victory. Damaging legislation, on the poll tax, competitive tendering, and on housing is already on the statute book. More is to come. The Left cannot respond through renewed confrontation since the surcharged councillors in Lambeth and Liverpool are a reminder of the wastefulness of courage against ridiculous odds. Many councillors have recognised the damage done by neglecting service delivery to stage set-piece battles. They are concentrating on the more mundane task of increasing efficiency, in order to compete successfully with the private sector. Real cuts and redundancies have been made. The influence of Trotskyist groups and the hard Left has so dwindled

that the element of intimidation which pushed many Left councillors into confrontation is no longer present. The hard Left
throughout London launched campaigns against the Labour council leaderships for making cuts, but was unable to muster enough
support for a realistic challenge. Only over the issue of the poll tax
was the possibility of direct action and illegality on the agenda,
principally in Scotland.

Faced with having to make cuts, many on the Left have argued
that there is no longer any future for Labour in local government.
They felt that the prospect of further cuts and the combined threats of
competitive tendering, opting out in education and housing, and the
poll tax, meant that there was no longer any point in controlling
a local council since it would involve merely administering Conservative party policies under central government diktat.

In reality, the idea of Labour withdrawing from local government is a non-starter. A major political party opting out of an
important part of the democratic process would lose credibility.
The result of withdrawal would be to hand local government over
to the opposition parties at a time when the number of people
voting Labour in local elections outnumbers those willing to do so
in general elections. In 1987, Labour was the controlling party
in 155 local councils, and a dominant influence in a few more. In
May 1988 Labour councils were elected in several of the Tory
southern heartlands, such as Brighton, Southampton and Cam-
bridge. For millions of people, Labour councils are the only
protection against an increasingly eccentric *laissez-faire* government strategy.

'A dented shield'

Labour councils will still have an important job to do, attempting
to protect existing services, and trying to minimise service loss
through privatisation. Despite the new legislation, an apocalyptic
vision of the future for Labour councils is unjustified. The Left is
often too willing to believe the Tories' own rhetoric. The government seldom achieves all its objectives smoothly, and local councils have displayed considerable invention in the past. Even
Nicholas Ridley does not expect his vision of the council which
meets annually for the allocation of contracts to materialise. As we

have pointed out, the government failed for several years to control local government spending. Thatcher's third government was forced into embarrassing climbdowns on a number of its housing proposals and may have to move more slowly than it wishes, since many of its policies are proving unpopular even amongst its own councillors. The quality of newly privatised services is so poor that it is possible for councils to compete successfully with the private sector for contracts. And the opt-out procedures for schools and council estates involve so much uncertainty that the vast majority of parents and tenants will probably remain with 'the devil they know'.

The problems created by the introduction of the poll tax are more fundamental. Inevitably, the poll tax will reduce the scope for high-spending, redistributive policies. From 1990 in England and Wales, it will prevent councils raising money from business and the wealthier sections of the community, to provide services for low income households who mostly receive rebates. In future councils pursuing a 'high taxation, high service' provision policy will hit the pockets of the poorest residents.

It will be far harder to expand services to meet local needs, particularly since the government has retained the power to limit overall spending, through poll tax capping. Inner city areas will be hit hardest, since the replacement of commercial and industrial rates with the unified business rate will slash their income.

However, the new subsidy system introduced with the poll tax will still be more generous than the system of the 1920s and 1930s when Labour councils began to spend ratepayers' money on a large scale on health and housing. In those days there was only minimal rate equalisation and government grant – and no rebates. Labour councils in poor areas had to ask working people to pay high rates to sustain high-spending policies. They did so because the services provided were popular and essential. Expanding and improving services in the 1990s will not be impossible.

The problem is that while poll tax payers will recognise the need to provide street lighting, refuse collection and parks, the ability of a council to continue to redistribute resources from better-off residents to the lowest income households will depend on its success in winning democratic consent to do so.

Even where councils manage to protect services, however, they may be forced to do so at the expense of the terms and conditions of council employees. The reference to jobs was quickly dropped from the traditional slogan of 'saving jobs and services' once cuts were being made. Competitive tendering will bring council departments into direct competition with private companies employing fewer workers and paying lower wages. Councils will have a difficult task balancing the need to protect minimum standards and equal opportunities policies, while ensuring that whole sections of the workforce are not made redundant because they are less productive than their competitors.

Commentators are already beginning to say that 'town hall leftism has itself now failed' (Corrigan, Jones, Lloyd and Young, 1988, p. 11) as Left councils begin to reverse some of their earlier decisions, take a tougher line with the unions, and pay attention to strong management and implementation systems. The failures, muddles and defeats of the past few years mean that the experimental phase of the 1980s is being seen as merely a temporary product of the affluence of high spending councils.

There is, indeed, a sense that the fire has gone out of local government, and that, in particular, the scope for initiatives has vanished. While Labour will continue to control councils and fight elections, more individuals will drop out as councillors again begin to find local government unexciting, unrewarding and even intolerable within the new constraints. It has already become increasingly hard to find good candidates. The new legislation in the Local Government and Housing Act 1989 will exclude many of those working for local authorities from holding office, and this will further deplete the ranks of good candidates with relevant skills and knowledge of local government.

Innovation – under fire

Yet local government still offers a big challenge for the Left. Some councils such as Sheffield, Brighton and Southampton have begun the process of restructuring collective provision, in ways which involve consumers and extend choices, and as a first step towards reflecting the changing pattern of modern wants in their communities. Left Labour councils have started to recognise that public services are no longer to be provided in a uniform way – that the communities they serve are heterogeneous, with a range of lifestyles. There is an important third option for the Left – that of continuing the process of innovation in local government, despite being 'under fire' from the centre.

There are a number of initiatives and new thinking in local government which could build on the positive aspects of the Left's experience of control but which recognises the mistakes. In the present climate they involve making difficult choices. The objective of the 'dented shield' approach has been to protect as much existing provision as possible. An innovative approach might involve deciding to develop new initiatives or better services in some areas – and to withdraw from certain other sorts of provision in order to do so. It may not be possible, within the new constraints, for local councils to do everything themselves. The choice may be between doing some things well, or doing everything badly.

Over the next few years, the private and voluntary sectors will have access to resources – including government funding – which will be denied to local authorities. Left councils are having to recognise that if local communities are to win a share of these resources, then partnerships will have to be developed with other agencies. This is not new, since some services have always been provided in co-operation with housing associations, co-operatives, charities and voluntary organisations. The European Left has developed a far more substantial co-operative movement, and far more joint public–private initiatives. In Bologna, a social services co-operative was established in 1974, and socialist local authorities in Italy operate in partnership with more than 300 workers co-operatives to provide a range of social services (Stewart and Stoker, 1988, p. 15).

Left local authorities in Britain have already set up partnership deals, particularly in relation to economic development and inner city regeneration. Sheffield developed a partnership project in the Lower Don Valley to rebuild a deserted and derelict industrial area. Southampton has developed joint initiatives with the private sector to regenerate the docks and to create local jobs and housing. As spending restrictions increase, councils have to create independent bodies such as enterprise boards and development companies which can undertake capital investment. The government has been trying to exclude local authorities from the development process, for example by absorbing Sheffield's Lower Don

Valley projects into an Urban Development Corporation, but the private sector still prefers to co-operate with local authorities rather than work in an atmosphere of confrontation, even if the government prefers to by-pass councils. Despite the outlawing of contract compliance on a formal level, local authorities can still exercise considerable informal influence over the decisions of private agencies. The role of the local authority in local development should be a central strategic one, planning future strategies in consultation with the local community, and acting as a local entrepreneur by identifying gaps in provision and attempting to pool resources across sectors. The test is the extent to which new partnership arrangements can be harnessed to community needs and controlled democratically.

A strategic approach will involve sharpening the role of the local authority in regulating service provision in the private and voluntary sectors. There is, too, a need for continuing direct provision – to set standards, to make provision for people ignored by other sectors, to provide variety of provision, to extend the boundaries of what is considered adequate and constantly to improve quality and experiment with new approaches. Collective provision is under attack. The Tories are attempting to persuade consumers that private provision is necessarily higher quality and creates greater choices than public provision, capitalising on the failures of public services to match aspirations. Labour council workforces have not only to win contracts in competition with the private sector, but to show that collective provision is capable of generating choices and opportunities not available in the private sector. That requires not simply that public services are made to be efficient but that they are innovative and dynamic, capable of responding to changing needs and demands. There is no point in simply borrowing private sector management techniques, since these are solely concerned with cost efficiency. There is a need to develop new sorts of management, capable of meshing the requirements of democratic accountability with those of swift response and efficient service delivery, and capable of meeting a range of social objectives without abandoning a concern with value for money. New initiatives have emerged, many of them based on the work of Professor John Stewart of the Institute of Local Government Studies, in developing the concept of 'public service orientation', which 'recognises that services are provided by the public, that they must be judged by the quality of service and that those for whom the service is provided should have a key role in assessing them' (Stewart and Stoker, 1988, p. 16).

In the context of shrinking resources, it becomes even more important for councils to set objectives and identify priorities. While the scope for increasing the volume of provision may be vanishing, councils can still improve the quality of provision. That includes increasing access to services by overcoming geographical and organisational barriers, and ensuring that no one is excluded through direct or indirect discrimination. Equal opportunities policies are essential to ensure that, for example, meals on wheels services cater for Asian pensioners, or that single parents have the same range of housing choices as two-parent households. It means extending choices – by offering a range of provision, rather than a uniform service, which can be adjusted to take account of consumer demand. That may mean making difficult choices between competing groups of consumers. It means finding out from the public what they want, through surveys, questionnaires and complaints procedures, as well as providing information about what is provided, and how to comment or complain. Finally it means involving consumers in the difficult choices about how and where to spend scarce resources. Such an approach sets far greater store on the communication and contact between service providers and consumers.

In Sweden, the Social Democratic government pioneered a novel approach to public provision using large-scale public surveys to assess services through the eyes of consumers and using these to tailor objectives to the quality or to the extent of provision rather than to the convenience of bureaucracies. Throughout government departments, all staff from cleaners to senior managers have been involved in retraining aimed at replacing narrow professional consciousness with a new collective and client-centred approach. In a number of local authority areas, councils have been freed from some government constraints in an experiment to see whether an overall relaxation of controls would have a positive effect on local authorities. In others, management tiers have been reduced and greater responsibility transferred to the frontline staff such as home helps and nursery school staff. The aim of such self-management has been both to raise the status of the workers and to make the services more responsive and flexible.

In Britain, similar initiatives are being taken in some areas. In Lewisham, the council has attempted to set out core objectives and to develop training programmes for staff based on them. Sheffield has carried out consumer surveys, and begun a major process of consultation, identifying objectives and retraining needs. A number of Left councils, notably Sheffield, are developing targets against which to measure the performance – and the pay – of senior staff. At the same time there are moves to accelerate organisational restructuring and decentralisation, this time not bolting new local offices onto existing hierarchies – but radically changing line management structures, flattening hierarchies, removing levels of middle management and moving towards project self management. Lewisham plans to decentralise housing services to neighbourhood offices with multi-skilled staff – with only three levels in the hierarchy between the housing officers and the director. The example of Islington in creating 24 neighbourhood forums in association with its decentralised offices is being followed by Lewisham and others. This sort of decentralisation may create a genuine change in the relationship between councils and their consumers – since decision making will move down to local areas. Organisational restructuring and the use of new technology means that a far greater proportion of town hall workers can be directly involved in providing a service to the public, rather than in middle management or administrative tasks.

Nevertheless, these changes will encounter the same industrial relations problems as in the past unless there is a clear change of attitude from both managers and trade unions. New approaches to service delivery would involve major changes in working arrangements. Smaller teams mean that more responsibility is exercised by individual staff members. Career structures could depend on the ability to get results, or to innovate, rather than a steady progression up the ranks by 'keeping you head down'. There might be far greater job satisfaction, through more flexible working arrangements and better opportunities to develop skills and take up new opportunities. Barriers between blue- and white-collar staff could fade (with, for example, self-managing teams of home helps) and vigorous equal opportunities policies could provide real opportunities for many women and black workers who at present do not get promoted.

Inevitably, however, the uncertainty caused by cuts in spending intensifies the defensiveness and anxiety of staff, and makes it harder to introduce innovation. We have argued in Chapter 7 that bad management, the failure of politicians to take clear decisions, and poor communications were important factors in the industrial relations problems faced by Left Labour councils. But even the consequences of the industrial disputes have been less serious than the absenteeism, sickness and poor productivity caused by low morale. Unless these problems are addressed, attempts to change service delivery will probably remain isolated gimmicks. One of the key factors in any successful change is good training for all staff but the record of many authorities on training has been abysmal. Unless staff are actively involved in decisions about service delivery, and their views and experiences taken into account, real changes in service delivery are unlikely to take effect.

Nevertheless, public sector trade unions have traditionally been over-defensive about radical change. As we have seen staff, especially white-collar workers, have often proved unwilling to adapt to change or even to co-operate in measures to improve service delivery. Unions have at times looked simply at the terms and conditions for staff, without recognising that any improvements in terms and conditions of work, without improved efficiency, are bought at the expense of consumers. Trade unions must recognise that the future of the public sector, and with it the jobs, terms and conditions of their members – depends on a very different relationship between management and staff, and between providers and consumers of services. A new balance of power must be based on the primacy of service delivery.

Extending local democracy

Finally, Left Labour councils need to expand their attempts at extending local democracy and to explore alternatives to the growingly authoritarian and centralised British state. Because the north–south divide is widening, with the Tory government increasingly responsive only to the prosperous south, the role of local councils speaking on behalf of their communities is becoming more important.

Such an approach requires new democratic forms, and far greater local accountability. To date, the changes such as the

establishment of neighbourhood forums, and increasing the involvement of local people outside the Town Hall in decision
making, have only had a limited impact. The policies of the Left
aimed at extending equal opportunities, involving local people in
decision making and increasing accountability to local Labour
parties uncovered a diversity of interests in the community that
could not easily be reconciled. Conflicts of interests emerged
between service users and council staff, between black communities and the traditional white working class, and between the
Labour parties and their constituents. Furthermore, moves to
extend access to the black community, women, or lesbians and gay
men created a backlash. The experiments of Left councils demonstrated that 'representing' or 'being accountable to' a fragmented
and heterogeneous electorate is not easy. It became clear that
inner city areas were more a series of local communities rather
than a single one.

Attempts to extend local democracy have tended to involve only
a narrow group of activists. This was partly because many Left
councillors had already made up their minds what they wanted to
hear, and listened selectively, but also because it proved difficult –
by definition – to involve the non-activists. There is no culture of
public access to information and involvement in decision making.
The process of developing active citizenship, particularly against
the grain of central government policy, will be a slow one.

The need is for a wide variety of means of representation
enabling citizens to express views in a number of different forums
– as individuals, as members of community and voluntary groups,
as residents in a neighbourhood, as workers and as consumers.
This sort of approach would involve a very different role for local
councils. Labour councillors would no longer simply be able to
assume a mandate for a lengthy manifesto. They would be
expected to develop policies in consultation with all local people,
not just party members, and to adapt to changes in local demands.

More importantly, it would change the relationship between the
council, the party and the electorate. Labour parties should play a
key role in supporting their councillors, providing ideas, and
monitoring their work. But they should not substitute for the local
community. The problem has not been the increasing accountability of councillors to their parties, but the growing gap between
Labour parties and their electorate. A more democratically

accountable local authority would require a different type of local Labour party. If power were devolved to neighbourhood forums, for example, local Labour parties would need to be active in those neighbourhoods, in tenants associations and voluntary groups. Labour could only direct policy at local level by developing a mass membership, with a wide cross-section of people, and by becoming closely involved in local activities and concerns. Such a shift would, in any case, be a first step towards developing a party capable of winning majority popular support at a general election.

The final question concerns the campaigning role of Left Labour councils. In the climate of 'new realism', is campaigning a thing of the past? Since the 1987 general election, the Left has been concentrating on service delivery and on internal changes, rather than on challenging or opposing the new government measures. Furthermore, the Local Government Act 1988 limits the powers of a council to intervene in issues of 'political controversy'. However, it does not prevent councils from telling the truth, and, in some cases information campaigns on the poll tax and the new housing legislation have proved far more successful than a more overtly political intervention might have been. The campaigning initiative seems to have shifted somewhat to organisations of service consumers. A new tenants movement emerged to lobby against parts of the Housing Act 1988, drawing on resources and support from Labour councils. Fierce campaigns were waged by tenants against Housing Action Trusts resulting in a concession allowing them to vote on the establishment of a HAT, and thousands of tenants organised against the transfer of their estates into the private sector. Parents quickly began to organise against what they saw as the damaging consequences of the Education Reform Act 1988. Labour councils, for a change, were supporting and working with campaigns which had their roots in the local community, rather than trying to lead a motley band of local activists into set-piece battles with government.

There is still a key role for the Left in local government. It involves an understanding of the problems Labour councils face, not simply in terms of government constraints, but in terms of the attitudes and perceptions of local people. Perhaps the lessons from the failures of the past decade could not have been learnt in any other way but this has left precious little time for change. Left councils remain the only arena in which alternatives to the 'values' of Thatcherism can be developed and where these ideas can be translated into action. The Labour Party is still perceived by many as old-fashioned, statist, and authoritarian. The Left's control of many key authorities offers an opportunity to demonstrate a very different set of values based on democratic accountability, consumer choice, and equal opportunities, and in tune with the diverse needs of local communities.

Bibliography

Arden, A (1987) *Final Report* (Hackney Borough Council)

Association of London Authorities (1987) *Response to Audit Commission* (ALA).

Audit Commission (1987) *The Management of London Authorities*, Occasional Paper No. 2 (Audit Commission).

Benton, S. (1988) 'What are they afraid of?', *New Statesman*, 11 March.

Best, M. (1988), 'Sector Strategies and Industrial Policy' in P. Hirst and J. Zeitlin (eds) *Reversing Industrial Decline? Industrial Structure and Policy in Britain and her Competitors* (Berg).

Bianchini, F. (1987) 'GLC/RIP – cultural policies in London', in *New Innovation*, 1 (Methuen).

Blunkett, D. and Green, G. (1983) *Building From the Bottom up: The Sheffield Experience*, 491 (Fabian Society).

Blunkett, D. and Jackson, K. (1987) *Democracy in Crisis* (Hogarth).

Boddy, M. and Fudge C. (1984) *Local Socialism?* (Macmillan).

Brusco, S. (1985) 'Local Government, Industrial Policy and Social Consensus: The Experience of Modena (Italy)', paper given to Venice OECD conference, June.

Campbell, B. and Jacques, M. (1986) 'Goodbye to the GLC', *Marxism Today*, April.

Carvel, J. (1984) *Citizen Ken* (Chatto Windus).

Cockburn, C. (1977) *The Local State* (Pluto).

Corrigan, P. Jones, T., Lloyd, J. and J. Young, J. (1988) *Socialism, Merit and Efficiency*, Pamphlet 530 (Fabian Society).

Crossman, R. *The Diaries of a Cabinet Minister, Vol.I* (Hamish Hamilton/Cape).

Department of the Environment (1983), *Local Authorities and Racial Disadvantage: Report of a Joint Government/Local Authority Association Working Party* (HMSO).

Department of the Environment (1986) *Paying for Local Government*, Green Paper (HMSO).

Forrester, A., Lansley, S. and Pauley, R. (1985) *Beyond Our Ken* (Fourth Estate).

Gibbs, J. (1987) *Report of the Enquiry into Nye Bevan Lodge* (Southwark Borough Council).

Greater London Council, *Changing the World, A London Charter for Lesbian and Gay Rights* (GLC).

Greater London Council, *Tackling Heterosexism* (GLC).

Goss S. (1989) *Local Labour and Local Government* (Edinburgh University Press).

Gyford, J. (1985) *The Politics of Local Socialism* (Allen and Unwin).

Hackney Labour Co-ordinating Committee (1987) *Labour Strategy and the Local State* (LCC).

Hain, P. and Hebditch, S. (1978) *Radicals and Socialism* (Institute for Workers Control).

Hambleton, R. and Hoggett, P. (1987) *Decentralisation and Democracy* OP28 (University of Bristol: School for Advanced Urban Studies).

Haringey Council Policy Co-ordination Unit (1987) *Report on Corporate Implications of INLOGOV Report* (Haringey Borough Council).

Hatton, D. (1988) *Inside Left* (Bloomsbury).

Hebbert, M. and Travers, T. (ed.) (1988) *The London Government Handbook* (Casell).

Hoggett, P. (1987) 'Waste disposal – making municipal socialism work', *New Socialist*, March.

Jackman, R. and Sellars, M. (1978) 'Local expenditure and Local discretion', *CES Review*, May.

Labour Party (1981) *The Rights of Gay Men and Women* (Labour Party).

Labour Co-ordinating Committee (1984) *Go Local to Survive* (LCC).

Labour Co-ordinating Committee (1988) *Labour Councils in the Cold, a Blueprint for Survival* (LCC).

Livingstone, K. (1987) *If voting Changed Anything, They'd Abolish It* (Collins).

London–Edinburgh Weekend Return Group (1979) *In and Against the State*, London Conference of Socialist Economists (rev. ed. publ. by Pluto in 1980).

London Strategic Policy Unit (1987) *Women in London* (LSPU).

Mackintosh, M. and Wainwright, H. (1987) *A Taste of Power* (Verso).

Massey, D., Segal, L. and Wainwright, H. (1984) 'And now for the good news' in Cuman J. (ed). *The future of the Left* (Polity Press).

Miller, D. and Mauson, J. (1985) 'Learning from council enterprise', *The Chartist*, 106.

Murray, R. (1988) 'Life after Henry (Ford)', *Marxism Today*, October.

National Council for Civil Liberties, (1981) *Gay Workers, Trades Unionists and the Law* (NCCL).

Ouseley, H. (1983) *The System* (The Runnymede Trust).

Ouseley, H. (1984), 'Local Authority Race Initiatives' in M. Boddy and C. Fudge, C. (eds) Local Socialism (Macmillan).

Ouseley, H. (1988) 'Equal Opportunities Lost: the Case of Education', *Race and Class*, vol. 29 no. 4. Spring.

Parkinson, M. (1985) *Liverpool on the Brink* (Policy Journals).

Seyd, P. (1987). *The Rise and Fall of the Labour Left* (Macmillan).

Sharron, H. (1982) 'Walsall, out of the civic centre into the field', *New Statesman*, 19 March.

Sharron, H. (1985) 'Overcoming TU resistance to local change', *Public Money*, March.

Sivanandan, A. (1987) 'Race, Class and Brent', *Race and Class*, vol. 29, no. 1.

Sivanandan, A. (1988) 'Left, Right and Burnage', *Race and Class*, vol. 30, no. 1.

Stewart, J. (1988) *Understanding the Management of Local Government* (London: Longman).

Stewart, J. and Stoker, G. (1988) *From Local Administration to Community Government*, Research Series 351 (Lesbian Society).

Stoker, G. (1988) *The Politics of Local Government* (Macmillan).

Sullivan, D. (1987) *Picking up the Pieces* (Lewisham Labour Party).

Tatchell, P. (1983) *The Battle for Bermondsey* (Heretic).

Travers, T. (1986) *The Politics of Local Government Finance* (Allen and Unwin).

Wainwright, H. (1986) 'Bye-bye GLC', *New Statesman*, 21 March.

Wainwright, H. (1987) *Labour, A Tale of Two Parties* (Hogarth).

Waller, R. (1988) *Moulding Political Opinion* (Croom Helm).

Ward, M. (1987) *Municipal Monetarism* (Greater London Labour Party).

Widdicombe, D. (1986) *The Conduct of Local Authority Business* (HMSO).

Wolmar, C. (1987) 'The Fresh Face of the Capital's Politics', *New Statesman*, 18 October.

Index